MENTAL RETARDATION DOESN'T MEAN "STUPID"!

A Guide for Parents and Teachers

ROBERT EVERT CIMERA

Rowman & Littlefield Education
Lanham, Maryland • Toronto • Oxford
2006

Published in the United States of America
by Rowman & Littlefield Education
A Division of Rowman & Littlefield Publishers, Inc.
A wholly owned subsidiary of The Rowman & Littlefield Publishing Group, Inc.
4501 Forbes Boulevard, Suite 200, Lanham, Maryland 20706
www.rowmaneducation.com

PO Box 317
Oxford
OX2 9RU, UK

British Library Cataloguing in Publication Information Available

Library of Congress Cataloging-in-Publication Data

Cimera, Robert Evert.
Mental retardation doesn't mean "stupid"! : a guide for parents and teachers / Robert Evert Cimera.
p. cm.
Includes bibliographical references and index.
ISBN-13: 978-1-57886-352-5 (hardcover : alk. paper)
ISBN-10: 1-57886-352-X (hardcover : alk. paper)
ISBN-13: 978-1-57886-353-2 (pbk. : alk. paper)
ISBN-10: 1-57886-353-8 (pbk. : alk. paper)
1. Children with mental disabilities–Education. I. Title.
LC4661.C48 2006
371.92'8–dc22 2005026957

™ The paper used in this publication meets the minimum requirements of American National Standard for Information Sciences—Permanence of Paper for Printed Library Materials, ANSI/NISO Z39.48-1992.
Manufactured in the United States of America.

I would like to dedicate this book to my wonderful wife, my late father, and all of my livestock.

The royalties from this and all of my books are donated to the Humane Society. Please support your local shelters. Adopt homeless animals and have your pets spayed or neutered.

Special thanks to Chris Burke for his inspiration and the foreword to this book.

CONTENTS

FOREWORD

Chris Burke

When I was born, I didn't know that I was born with Down syndrome. I look at my abilities and don't look at my "disabilities." In my opinion, I'm just like an everyday normal person. In most ways, being a handicapped person is no big deal. I am like everybody else who has a regular, normal life.

When I have to put up with obstacles and people who make fun of or doubt me, I just focus on my careers in acting and music or my work for the NDSS (National Down Syndrome Society). I am their Goodwill Ambassador and editor of *Upbeat*, a magazine for and by people with Down syndrome. People write inspirational stories about how they are role models to encourage others to face things in real life. I'm also pursuing a music career along with Joe and John Demasi. We do songs of inspiration and about inclusion.

When I was born thirty-nine years ago, the doctors told my parents I would never be able to walk or talk and should be placed in an institution and forgotten about. Thank goodness my parents ignored the doctors' advice.

I am the youngest of four children. My older sisters, Ellen and Anne, and my brother, J.R., along with my parents, filled my early days with what is now called "early intervention." They played with me and worked with me

to help me learn to walk and talk . . . and, boy, can I talk! My friends tease me that they wish that my parents hadn't done such a good job because sometimes I never shut up!

My parents also made sure that I received the medical care that I needed. But most importantly, they treated me just as they treated my brother and sisters, with discipline and plenty of love!

Growing up with Down syndrome really doesn't stop what I can do. Life isn't about my "disability." It is my ability that is what counts. Obstacles are what you see when you take your eyes off of your goals. Never take your eyes off your goals and make your dreams come true! That is my motto.

—Chris Burke (AKA "Corky" from TV's *Life Goes On*)

Information about Chris, his amazing career, and Down syndrome, can be found at his official website, www.arcark.org/chrisburkeweb.htm. His latest CD, *Singer with the Band*, is available at www.amazon.com.

1

DEFINING MENTAL RETARDATION

GUIDED COMPREHENSION QUESTIONS

By the time you finish reading this chapter, you should be able to

1. List the three defining characteristics of mental retardation
2. Identify the highest IQ that somebody with mental retardation can have, according to currently accepted definitions
3. Explain, in very general terms, what IQ and intelligence are
4. Define and give several examples of "adaptive behavior skills"
5. Explain when the "developmental period" occurs

INTRODUCTION

If you are reading this book, you are probably either a teacher or parent of a child who has been labeled "mentally retarded." Let me first begin by saying that, despite what you might hear on television or what people may tell you, mental retardation does not mean "stupid." Nor are individuals with mental retardation "eternal children" who "stop learning" or "reach their potential earlier than do normal people." All of these are fallacies, so just put them out of your head.

The truth is, mental retardation is a human-created condition that is partly characterized by subaverage intelligence. However, this does not mean that people with mental retardation can't learn or that they stop learning after a certain point in their lives. People with mental retardation *can* learn but, as we will talk about later in greater detail, they may require more time or specific teaching strategies in order to process information effectively.

Further, people with mental retardation aren't always going to be like children. As they get older, they will face many of the same challenges as you and I have. People with mental retardation can continue their education past high school, fall in and out of love, get married, have children, successfully maintain jobs, battle drug addictions, become rich and famous, and do just about everything that people without mental retardation can do. They can even write books and become renowned actors! Just ask Chris Burke, the star of the television show *Life Goes On*. He was kind enough to write the foreword to this book and has been the subject of other books, including *A Special Kind of Hero*.

I decided to write this book because, as a special education teacher, I found that most of my students with mental retardation were limited more by how they were treated by other people (or how they perceived themselves) than their actual ability or "disability." Think about it. When was the last time you have heard somebody ask a child with mental retardation, "What do you want to do when you grow up?" Probably never.

Yet children without disabilities are asked questions like this all the time! It is part of their indoctrination into the adult world. It is how we begin to prepare them for their future. Moreover, we encourage them to play "make believe" where they pretend to be doctors or astronauts or accountants. At school, we even have nondisabled children write essays about their future occupation and make them go to "career days" or visit colleges that they might want to attend.

Because people erroneously believe that mental retardation means "stupid" or "can't learn," kids with mental retardation are never asked what they want to do when they grow up. They never pretend that they are lawyers or bankers or superstar athletes or professors. They aren't given the opportunity to write essays about being a farmer or a construction worker. They aren't invited to career day or encouraged to visit colleges.

And vocational development isn't the only area in which kids with mental retardation get the short end of the stick! We frequently fail to prepare them for *any* aspects of adult life. We don't talk to them about sex or adult relationships. We don't teach them about investing their money or saving for retirement. We don't help them cultivate interests so that they can live rich and rewarding lives. We don't even prepare them for death and dying!

Because we do not prepare children with mental retardation for their lives as adults, their adult lives tend to be very different from our own. Consider the following statistics for a moment.

- 30 percent of students with mental retardation drop out before they complete high school
- 5.7 percent of students with mental retardation participate in any vocational or academic postsecondary education programs.
- 61 percent of adults with mental retardation are unemployed.
- Of those who have jobs, roughly 85 percent work part-time and receive no health insurance benefits.
- The average annual income of adults with mental retardation is $3,078.
- Individuals with mental retardation comprise roughly 2 percent of the general population but over 10 percent of the prison population.
- 25 percent of adults with mental retardation report going to the movies, out to eat, and participating in other community activities more than once a month. Nearly 50 percent report that they do not participate in community activities at all.
- 15 percent of adults with mental retardation live in their own homes or apartments.
- More than half of adults with mental retardation older than fifty years live with their elderly parents or biological relatives.
- Individuals with mental retardation can expect to live roughly sixty-three years, compared to seventy-seven years for the general, nondisabled population.

Generally speaking, adults with mental retardation are unemployed. If they do have jobs, they tend to work in menial positions, such as janitors, or work at fast food restaurants or hotels. Moreover, they rarely receive health insurance, vacation time, or retirement benefits.

Adults with mental retardation tend to live with their parents. When their parents die, they are often shuttled back and forth between their siblings. Or they are put in "elderly living environments," such as nursing homes, at a very early age. They rarely have homes to call their own.

People with mental retardation rarely interact with their communities or utilize recreational programs. They don't play in co-ed softball leagues, join book clubs, or hang out at coffee shops with friends. The average adult with mental retardation basically sits alone, watching television, slowly getting older.

Finally, because of poor nutrition, sedentary life styles, and infrequent access to health care, people with mental retardation tend to live very short lives. The average individual with mental retardation can expect to live until he or she is only sixty-three years old. That's almost fifteen years less than everybody else! Unfortunately, children who have profound mental retardation and multiple disabilities can expect to live even shorter lives. In fact, several conditions linked to mental retardation, such as Aicardi syndrome and Fabry's disease, often result in death by age thirty!

Is this the kind of life that *you* would want to have? Is that the kind of life that you want your child with mental retardation to have? Or any child, for that matter?

My main goal for writing this book is to get people to understand that individuals with mental retardation are more like everybody else than they are different. They *can* live long, rich, enjoyable, productive lives. But they have to be taught and prepared for adulthood, just as any other person.

Yes, people with mental retardation may have difficulty learning, but so does everybody else. That doesn't mean that they can't get good jobs, have their own homes, and do the things that they want to do. Heck, in college, it took me *seven* tries to pass three semesters of Spanish! I "*no hablo Español.*" And I have a house, a wonderful wife, and a great job!

Think about that for a moment. I have a PhD. I have written numerous books and articles. I have presented all over the country. I have even been interviewed for *Time* magazine and cowritten reports for Congress! But I still have a really hard time learning Spanish. No matter how hard I try, I simply can't seem to master the language!

What is funny to me is that there are literally tens of thousands of children with mental retardation who live in Spain, Mexico, and other places who *can* speak Spanish. In fact, they can speak Spanish much better than I ever will! And people consider them stupid? I wonder what that makes me!

The point is, we all have problems learning from time to time or in various areas. I am "mentally retarded" when it comes to learning foreign languages. I also can't seem to learn how to play the guitar. You might be a horrible cook or terrible at balancing your checkbook. But this doesn't stop us from living great lives! Learning difficulties shouldn't stop people with mental retardation from having great lives, too.

Another goal of this book is to provide you with practical information about mental retardation so that you can prepare your child for life. We will be talking about various teaching strategies as well as how to set up trust funds and powers of attorney and many other things. Moreover, at the very end of this book, you will find lists of hundreds of valuable resources. I will provide you with information on other books you might want to read, websites you might want to access, and organizations that you might consider joining. I am sure that you will find everything that you need to prepare your child for his or her future!

I want to point out that some of the topics that we are going to be discussing might make you feel a bit uncomfortable. For example, whether you believe it or not, kids with mental retardation will develop the same sex drives and urges as people with average or above-average intelligence. They will also have monthly periods and wet dreams. They might even be gay or bisexual!

Although these topics might make you feel ill at ease, it is of profound importance that you know how to teach children with mental retardation about these issues. Closing your eyes and denying reality will not make adolescents with mental retardation asexual or prevent them from getting pregnant. Nor will it help them comprehend what is happening to them when they ejaculate in their sleep or when they menstruate.

We must talk about these sensitive subjects if you are going to help your child. Still, I will try to cover these topics as delicately as possible without trying to sugarcoat them. This is important stuff. I don't want you to think otherwise.

I also want to point out that we will be talking in gross generalities. Just as no two "normal" people are alike, the same is true for people with mental retardation. However, in order to talk about mental retardation, we have to make some overgeneralizations. For example, when we just talked about adults with mental retardation a moment ago, I didn't mean to imply to that *all* adults with mental retardation live with their parents and don't do anything fun. Clearly, some do. Statistically speaking, though, people with mental retardation are unemployed, living with family members, and participate in very few social or recreational activities.

The same is true when we talk about specific teaching strategies in upcoming chapters. I don't mean to suggest that such-and-such strategy will work for everybody with mental retardation. It won't.

I could try to qualify myself at every turn and say things like "this strategy may or may not work for you" or "your child may or may not be like this." But that would make reading this rather tedious. So, please, take everything that we discuss with a small grain of salt. If I say that "people with mental retardation tend to do *X*, *Y*, and *Z*" or that "special education emphasizes remediation," remember that your situation might be completely different.

Again, I want to provide you with practical information. But I don't want you to walk away thinking that all kids with mental retardation are alike. They aren't. They are people, and all people have their own peculiarities. We are all different and we are all the same. Please keep that in mind when we are discussing people with mental retardation.

Throughout this book, I will tell you several stories about some of my students and friends. Some will probably make you laugh, and that is okay. Others will probably make you cry, and that is okay, too. Hopefully, all of them will make you think. And when you are all though with our explorations, you will be better prepared and more knowledgeable than you were before! I promise! So let the learning begin!

DEFINING MENTAL RETARDATION

I suppose that the best place to begin our journey is with the definition of mental retardation. That seems logical, right? So, how would you define mental retardation? And don't say, "being stupid" or "dumb"!

At the very beginning of this chapter, I mentioned that mental retardation was a human-constructed condition. Remember? What do you think that I meant by that? Well, I meant that mental retardation exists only because humans have defined it. It doesn't exist naturally or in and of itself. Confused? Let me explain.

When you look outside, you might see a tree. The tree exists whether humans call it a tree or not. In fact, if humans never saw a tree, the tree would still be there. Make sense so far?

Now consider pregnancy for a moment. A woman is either pregnant or she isn't. There is no subjectivity or wiggle room. There is no "sort of pregnant" or "borderline pregnant" or "partly pregnant." It is a yes or no proposition. She is or she is not. Further, even if she doesn't know that she is pregnant, she still is.

Mental retardation is different from a tree or being pregnant. It is defined by humans and, without that definition—it would not exist. Further, you can be "slightly" mentally retarded, "severely" mentally retarded, or not mentally retarded at all. So, it is a continuum, not an exact thing. That is a lot to swallow. So let me give you another example.

Think about the concept of "beauty." What is beautiful is dependent solely upon what humans consider beautiful. Further, what people consider beautiful changes over time and geography, much like the definition of mental retardation has, which we will talk about momentarily.

Mental retardation isn't like being pregnant. Or like a tree. It isn't a natural law, like gravity. It hasn't always existed, like light and dark. It is something very abstract and subjective. It is a concept that is used to describe a perceived condition. But the condition doesn't actually exist without the concept. Still confused?

How about this: Try thinking of mental retardation as if it is a philosophy. Without somebody coming up with the philosophy, the philosophy doesn't exist. Further, the philosophy is exactly what people decided it should be at that given time. Does that make things a little clearer?

I wish that I could just state verbatim what the accepted definition of mental retardation is, but unfortunately, there isn't any. Everybody has a different perspective about what mental retardation is and isn't. Even the federal government has different and conflicting definitions, which probably doesn't surprise you. But, maybe if I throw out several different definitions, we can pick them apart to see what they have in common.

The Individuals with Disabilities Education Act (IDEA)

Probably the most important federal definition of mental retardation is in IDEA, which stands for the "Individuals with Disabilities Education Act." It is an *extremely* important piece of legislation that governs special education and the services that many students with disabilities receive when they are in school. We will talk about IDEA in great detail in chapter 8, so don't worry if you don't know much about it right now. By the time you finish reading this book, you will be an expert on IDEA and mental retardation!

At any rate, IDEA defines mental retardation as "Significantly subaverage general intellectual functioning existing concurrently with deficits in adaptive behavior. And manifested during the developmental period that adversely affects a child's educational performance."

You are probably thinking to yourself, "Well, that really doesn't help me very much. After all, what does *significantly subaverage* mean? And what is *adaptive behavior* and the *developmental period*?"

Those are all *excellent* questions, and don't worry, we will answer them very soon. But let's first look at a couple more definitions.

The American Association on Mental Retardation (AAMR)

Perhaps one of the best-known definitions of mental retardation comes from the American Association on Mental Retardation, or AAMR. They are one of the leading organizations in the field. If you need further information about cognitive disabilities, go to them. Their website is listed in the resource section of this book. If you go there, you will see that they define mental retardation as

> substantial limitations in present functioning. It is characterized by significant subaverage intellectual functioning, existing concurrently with related limitations in two or more of the following applicable adaptive skill areas: communication, self-care, home living, social skills, community use, self-direction, health and safety, functional academics, leisure, and work. Mental retardation manifests before age 18." (www.aamr.org)

So, there's the phrase *subaverage intelligence* again! As you probably already guessed, it is going to be a major component of what mental retardation is. Still, neither the AAMR nor IDEA indicates how "subaverage" somebody's intelligence has to be in order to be considered mentally retarded. But at least the definition from AAMR elaborates on what "adaptive behaviors" are and when the "developmental period" is over. Let's look at one more definition and then start clarifying everything.

The American Psychiatric Association (APA)

The last definition that we will look at comes from the *Diagnostic and Statistical Manual of Mental Disorders*, fourth edition, text revision, or the DSM-IV-TR, which is published by the American Psychiatric Association (APA). This text is utilized by psychologists and psychiatrists to diagnose people with various conditions and is updated regularly. According to APA, mental retardation is

> a condition characterized by significant subaverage general intellectual functioning that is accompanied by significant limitations in adaptive functioning in at least two of the following skill areas: communication resources, self-direction, functional academic skills, work, leisure, health, and safety. The onset must occur before age 18 years. (p. 41)

So, there you have it—three definitions of mental retardation. Notice that they have several things in common. Specifically, they each mention

- subaverage intelligence,
- poor adaptive skills or functioning, and
- onset within the developmental period.

Let's look at each of these features in turn and try to figure out exactly what mental retardation is!

SUBAVERAGE INTELLIGENCE

Although one of the defining characteristics of mental retardation is below average intelligence, this still doesn't mean that people with mental retardation cannot learn. In order to truly appreciate this, you need to know what intelligence is. So, let's first examine what "intelligence" is and then come back and apply it to mental retardation.

What Is Intelligence?

At first thought, the question "what is intelligence?" may appear like an easy one. After all, intelligence is a measure of how smart we are or how much we know, right? Not really.

The notion of "intelligence" is a very, very, *very* complicated one. Entire libraries of books have been written on this topic and even they do not adequately discuss it. Unfortunately, we don't have that kind of time, so we will have to discuss intelligence in an incredibly broad and overly simplistic manner. Hopefully, you will get the gist of what it is.

There are many diverse perspectives on intelligence. You probably are already aware of the whole "nature versus nurture" debate. That is, some people think that intelligence is dominated by our genetics (or nature) and others think that intelligence is mostly affected by our environment (or nurture). But there is more to the controversy surrounding intelligence than those two factors.

For instance, there are those who believe that intelligence is something that can't actually be measured in a quantifiable sense. Moreover, a growing number of people believe in several different "types" of intelligences, such as "social intelligence" (how well you interrelate with people) and "practical intelligence" (which relates to how you can solve daily problems, such as budgeting your time). No matter what school of thought that you adhere to, you have to understand what intelligence is supposed to be in order to appreciate the definition of mental retardation.

First and foremost, intelligence isn't just about what you know. It is supposed to be an indication on how well you learn. So, theoretically, somebody who knows a lot, but has to really study and work hard to learn what she knows, may not be as "intelligent" as somebody who knows less, but understands everything right away.

So, it isn't that people with mental retardation don't know anything. It is just that they have difficulty learning new things. Note that I said *difficulty*; I didn't say *couldn't*. People with mental retardation may simply need more time and concrete examples in order to acquire new skills. In other words, whereas you and I might understand a concept after the first or second try, they might require three or four tries to get it. Or, they might need to see an object before really comprehending what it is. But they *can* learn!

Please don't think that anybody who has difficulty learning has mental retardation. That isn't the case at all. As we will discuss, relatively few people in the general population have mental retardation, but everybody has problems learning once in a while.

Usually, when people have trouble learning new tasks, it isn't because they have mental retardation or anything else. They just lack the prerequisite knowledge. For example, you couldn't learn how to read before you learned what letters were and what sounds went with them, right?

Sometimes, people have difficulty learning because of environmental distracters. For instance, I had difficulty learning math when I was in fourth grade. It wasn't because I couldn't learn math or that I didn't like the subject. It was because the younger students had recess right outside our classroom window during our math period. I couldn't concentrate on what the teacher was saying while they were jumping around, yelling and carrying on. I wanted to do well in class, but the distraction impaired my abilities to learn. I am sure that you have had similar experiences.

It is important to keep in mind that mental retardation isn't the only disability that could prevent a child from learning effectively. For example, students might have difficulty learning to read because they have dyslexia, which is a learning disability that involves seeing letters moving around. Or they might have problems concentrating because they have attention deficit hyperactivity disorder (ADHD). They could even have minor vision problems or sensory impairments, not to mention depression, anxiety problems, or a whole host of other conditions that can adversely affect their learning.

Again, the point is this: Just because somebody doesn't learn as quickly as her peers doesn't mean that she has mental retardation! Some people just aren't very good at certain things. For example, I have problems learning foreign languages, whereas you might be able to speak fluent Spanish after visiting Mexico for only a few weeks. That doesn't mean that you are super smart and that I have mental retardation. It just indicates that foreign languages aren't as easy for me to learn as they are for you. After all, we are all different, and not everybody is exceptional at everything.

Okay, so hopefully, you understand that intelligence is a complex topic, but that, in very general terms, it measures how effectively people learn. Hopefully, you also understand that just because people have problems learning something that does not mean that they have mental retardation. So, how do mental retardation and intelligence come together? Let's see!

Mental Retardation and Intelligence

Intelligence is traditionally measured by standardized tests, which produce an IQ or an "intelligence quotient." How well you score on the test is supposed to indicate how well you learn, which further indicates how "intelligent" you are. So, according to the definitions we looked at, people with mental retardation have to score low on IQ tests.

"How badly do people need to score in order to have mental retardation?" you are probably wondering. Well, it depends on your definition of mental retardation, the intelligence test that you are going to utilize, and your point in time.

"Why point in time?" Because the cutoff for what is considered mental retardation has changed substantially over the years. For instance, if you had an IQ of 85 in 1950, you would have been considered mentally retarded. But now you would be within the "normal" range.

Nowadays, the generally accepted IQ cutoff for mental retardation is 70 to 75. In and of itself, that probably doesn't tell you much. After all, it is like saying that a car costs "1 billion øre." Without knowing what an øre is, you can't really judge if the car is cheap or expensive. So, let's see if I can put that score in perspective.

Look at the bell-shaped bar graph pictured in figure 1.1. It represents the theoretical distribution of IQs throughout a normal population. The area within each bar represents the number of people who have the IQ scores listed along the bottom of the figure.

See how the distribution bulges up in the middle? That basically means that most people fall within the middle of the range. In other words, there are more people of average intelligence than there are people who are at either extreme. Also notice that there are the same numbers of people who do really well on IQ tests (i.e., to the right of the continuum) as there are people who do really poorly on IQ tests (i.e., to the left of the continuum). This is a

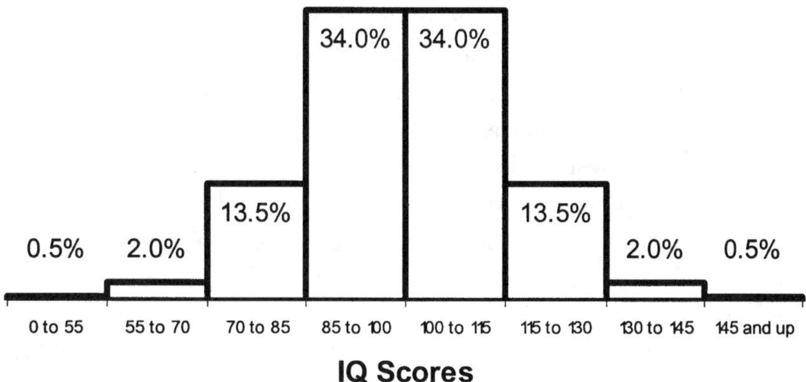

Figure 1.1. The Distribution of IQ Scores

very important point. We will be discussing it in greater detail later on, so keep it tucked away in the back of your mind for now.

The exact middle of the total range of scores is 100. That is supposed to represent the midway point between the uppermost IQ scores and the lowermost IQ scores. In other words, half of people have IQs above 100 and half are below 100. So, if you place everybody in order according to how well they did on an IQ test, that line would hit the middle person. Moreover, that middle person would have an IQ of 100, which is theoretically considered exactly "average."

I say "theoretically" because nobody has measured everybody's intelligence with the same test, so it is impossible to figure out what the average score really is. An IQ score of 100 is just said to be average based upon research on relatively small groups of individuals. Again, this is all theory. So take it with a sizable grain of salt.

Okay, so if you scored a 100 on an IQ test, you would be perfectly average. Half of the people in the world would have higher IQs than you and half would have lower IQs. Right? But does that mean if you get a score of 99 that you are "below average"? Would that mean that you were mentally retarded? No!

What is considered "normal" isn't an exact score, but a range of scores. In most cases, the range for normalcy is between 85 and 115. These scores are denoted on the bottom middle two bars. Roughly 68 percent of the population is thought to fall within this spread.

Now look at the bar that is just to the right of the middle bulge, the one representing IQs between 115 and 130. Roughly 13.6 percent of the population is thought to fall within this range. These people are considered to have "above-average" intelligence.

Look at the corresponding bar on the other side of the curve. Roughly 13.6 percent of the population has IQs between 85 and 70. These individuals are considered to have "below-average" intelligence. Sometimes they are called "dull normal," but that term is often seen as derogatory, so it is rarely used anymore.

Are you starting to see a bit of a pattern? Because the hypothetical bell-shaped curve is symmetrical, the number of people above and below the median IQ (i.e., 100) will be identical. Further, there is the same number of people considered to be "above average" as "below average."

Now look at the extremes of the continuum. To the far right, the last two bars where the arc of the curve goes way down. That indicates that very few people, or about 2.27 percent of the general population, have IQs above 130. These people are often referred to as "gifted."

Do you see the same trend on the other side of the continuum? Just as to the far right, the last two bars on the left side of the arc dip very low. These include IQs below 70. This is where mental retardation begins. Oddly, there are exactly the same number of people who are gifted as there are mentally retarded (i.e., 2.27 percent of the general population).

You might be asking yourself, "Why is 70 the cutoff for mental retardation? Why not 73.5 or 98 or 102?"

Well, this is the strange part. Remember when I compared mental retardation to beauty and said that it is a "human-created condition"? The cutoff that denotes mental retardation (i.e., an IQ of 70) is completely arbitrary. There is nothing special about having a 70 IQ. It isn't like having an IQ of 71 makes you so much smarter than somebody who has a 69 IQ. It is a more or less random boundary assigned to help define this very subjective condition that we call "mental retardation."

As I mentioned before, the cutoff for mental retardation has changed substantially throughout the past fifty years. At one point it was 85. Later it was 80. Now it is generally assumed to be at 70, sometimes 75 depending upon whom you talk to and what test is used. (For our purposes, we will just stick with an IQ of 70 since that is probably the most widely accepted uppermost limit of mental retardation.)

In the future, if scientists and politicians want to decrease the number of people with mental retardation, all they have to do is lower the cutoff point! For example, if the uppermost IQ for mental retardation were 55, less than 1 percent of the population would have the condition. On the other hand, if the cutoff were still at 85, about 16 percent of the population would have mental retardation. See how I am getting that? I am just adding the percent of people who fall within each IQ range presented in figure 1.1.

There are several other important issues to realize here. First, intelligence is measured in relation to the general population as a whole. It is impossible to say that one person is intelligent without comparing him or her to somebody else. Don't believe me?

Okay, imagine that a Martian comes down and visits with you. How would you be able to tell if he or she or it was a smart Martian when you have never seen another one before? You couldn't! All that you could say was that the Martian was smarter or dumber than you or the average person that you know. But you couldn't say that it was smart or dumb for a Martian. Maybe every single other Martian is far smarter than the one you met, in which case he would be considered mentally retarded. Or, maybe your Martian was the smartest of them all, in which case he would be considered gifted for his species.

So, in other words, IQ scores are what we call "norm-referenced." That is, they are compared to the norm, or average, of a population. In isolation, an IQ of 70 or 100 or 1,000 doesn't mean a thing. You have to have something to which you can compare it.

A second important issue to realize is that the cut off for mental retardation was not selected because an IQ of 70 represented a particular level of intelligence or ability. It isn't like people said, "Well, children with a 70 IQ can't do this and that, so that is where we will say mental retardation begins." The cutoff of 70 was selected because pointy-headed academics, such as myself, thought that roughly 2.5 percent was the "appropriate" proportion of the population who should have mental retardation.

Think about it this way. If they had the cutoff at 100, half of us would be considered mentally retarded! That would offend a lot of people! On the other hand, if they had the cut off at an IQ of 5, practically nobody would be mentally retarded. In effect, 70 was selected not because it means anything in particular, but because of how it relates to the population as a whole. As I said before, the people who defined mental retardation just happened to feel that approximately 2.5 percent of the population had mental retardation, so they selected the uppermost IQ of 70. It is a very arbitrary line with no actual significance.

A third important concept to comprehend is that there will always be people who do better on IQ tests than other people. So, there will always be a spread of IQ scores. There will always be people with average IQs and there will always be people who will have above- or below-average IQs. We will never be "equally" intelligent. At least, not with regard to how we currently view intelligence.

Since there will always be people at the bottom of the bell-shaped curve, there will always be people who are mentally retarded *in relation to* the rest of the population. Make sense? Let's see.

Imagine that you have everybody in the entire world in a line according to how intelligent they are—or more precisely, how well they did on a standardized intelligence test. You put everybody in order so that the smartest person is way at the head of the line, followed by the next smartest, and so on until you come to the unfortunate person who scored the lowest. The person in the exact middle of the line will always have an IQ of 100.

"Okay, I got it," you are probably thinking. "Move on!"

Okay, I will. But first, you have to see an extremely important point that will change your world and how you see people with mental retardation! Ready? Here we go!

You know that an IQ score of 100 is average. Hopefully, that makes sense. You also know that an IQ score of about 70 and below is considered "mentally retarded," right? In other words, people with mental retardation have IQ scores that are significantly below average, which is one of the defining characteristics of mental retardation.

Now, let's suppose that scientists discover the "smart gene"! Through genetic engineering, everybody is able to have children who are *twice* as smart as themselves! So, if you have an IQ of 100, which is right in the middle of the range of normalcy (i.e., between 85 and 115), your kid would have an IQ of 200! Now go back and look at the bell-shaped curve. Can you see where your child would be? Actually, you can't because an IQ of 200 is off the charts! That means your kid would be more than gifted! She would be *super-gifted*! She would be right at the front of the line! Or would she? Think about it for a second.

If your daughter had an IQ of 200, she would be really, really smart compared to you, me, and our generation. After all, we have an average IQ of 100. However, she would *not* be super intelligent compared to her own generation. Remember, everybody else has doubled their kid's IQ as well. So, the average IQ for her generation would be 200. In other words, compared to her friends, she would be completely average!

Now here comes the tricky part! Think about your daughter's generation. Everybody is *twice* as smart as we are today, right? The person in the middle of their line would have an IQ of 200. So who would be considered mentally retarded in their generation?

If everybody's IQ doubled, the cutoff for mental retardation would be 140! That is to say, somebody in the future with an IQ of 140 would be at the bottom 2.5 percent of the population and would be considered mentally retarded *compared to their peers*, even though an IQ of 140 now is considered highly gifted! See the irony?

Again, keep in mind that what is considered mentally retarded is in relation to the population as a whole. So, if you are an average person now, you can learn as well as half of the people. However, if I were to pick you up and put you on another plant with super-smart life-forms, they might consider *you* mentally retarded even though your abilities haven't changed! Kind of interesting, eh? There is one more piece of the puzzle that you need to understand.

Whether it is because of better nutrition or more effective schools or whatever, we as a species have gotten smarter over time (or at least, we do better on standardized IQ tests than we ever have before). Approximately every ten years the average IQ score goes up about three points. So, technically, the average IQ score should be increasing. For example, if the average IQ in the early 1900s was 100, the average IQ now should be approximately 130. Which, as we discussed, is very good!

However, through statistical procedures, test makers have forced the average IQ to always be 100. So, a century from now, the average IQ of people will still be 100, even though they might be much smarter than we are today.

In other words, an IQ score at the beginning of the last century does not equal the same IQ score obtained today. Nor is the score earned today going to mean the same when this century is over.

It is really easy to think of mental retardation as something intrinsic about the person who has it. You might think of mental retardation as some sort of genetic defect or something wrong with their brain. You either have mental retardation, or you don't—much like being pregnant. But that isn't the case.

As I said before, the cutoff for mental retardation is completely arbitrary. Further, what is considered mentally retarded is the result of comparing the person to the rest of the population. Increase the average intelligence of the population and you or I could be considered mentally retarded! How does that make you feel?

A Final Word about IQs

There is one last issue that I want to address and then we will be done and we can move on to the next topic.

Whenever I give presentations on intelligence, people always seem to ask me the same question, "Is intelligence permanent?" That is, "Do IQs change over time or do you have the same IQ throughout your entire life?"

My answer to them is, "No, your intelligence is *not* permanent." In fact, our IQ scores can fluctuate wildly. For example, recently I took three IQ tests over the course of two consecutive days. The first test indicated that I had an IQ of 122. The second was 107. And the third was 116. So, clearly, IQ scores are highly influenced by numerous factors, such as how well you are feeling that particular day, the room you are in when you take the test, and so on.

After I say that, people usually reply, "Yes, well . . . but that isn't what I meant to ask. That is just how well you did on the test. I want to know whether our actual intelligence changes over time. In other words, can an 'average' person become 'gifted' and can a child with mental retardation become 'normal'?"

This question is a little trickier to answer. I don't want to just come out and say "yes" because that might give a lot of people false hope. So please read what I am about to say very carefully.

Yes, our intelligence can change over time, but just how much is still being hotly debated. Most experts seem to think that we can improve our intelligence five to ten points by studying, utilizing more effective ways of learning, and exposing ourselves to educational experiences.

Conversely, we can drop our IQ scores to next to nothing if our brains are damaged by drugs or alcohol, or by having been struck by heavy, blunt objects. The smartest person in the world could get into a car accident and end up mentally retarded!

In the case of people who are mentally retarded becoming "normal," this is difficult to answer completely accurately. But, in short, my answer is "it depends on who you are talking about." Yes, people with mild mental retardation have been known to raise their IQs so that they are no longer considered "significantly subaverage." Actually, the phenomenon is not uncommon. After all, good teachers and effective educational programs, especially early education programs, can do wonders for everybody—especially kids who are already behind.

However, I do not want people to expect to "cure" all children with mental retardation by showing them endless flash cards or by buying them educational computer games. Such activities could obviously help some kids, but not all. In other words, a five- or ten-point increase in intelligence is probably not enough to make a child with profound mental retardation appear "normal."

But this is not to say that we should not try to educate children with severe mental retardation! Please understand that appropriate education is paramount to the success of all children, with and without mental retardation. Just because some children with mental retardation cannot be "cured" does not mean that they can't be taught things that will improve their lives.

Okay, that is enough about intelligence and IQ. If you have any more questions about these topics, I suggest that you review some of the resources provided at the end of this book. Let's move on!

ADAPTIVE BEHAVIOR

Remember way back when we started talking about the definition of mental retardation and I said that there were three main components to most of these definitions? I mentioned the primary component was "subaverage intelligence," which we have discussed at length. The second component is poor adaptive skills, which we will talk about in this section. The third involves age of onset, which we will discuss a little later on.

So, what are "adaptive behaviors"? How do they tie into mental retardation? Is it possible to have mental retardation and have perfectly good adaptive behaviors? How poor do your adaptive behaviors have to be to be considered "retarded"? We have loads of questions to answer, so let's get started!

What Are Adaptive Behaviors?

First of all, "adaptive behavior" is a very broad and subjective term, yet it is one of the three critical components of how mental retardation is defined. Consequently, it needs some explanation, especially with respect to how it applies to young children.

Usually, adaptive behavior refers to the ability to cope and function in a changing environment. Basically, it involves skills needed to live as independently as societal norms dictate. Being able to cook, cross the street safely, work, and participate in recreational skills are all general examples of adaptive behavior skills.

How Bad Do Adaptive Skills Have to Be to Be Considered "Poor"?

You are probably thinking, "Now wait a minute! I can't boil water without burning it! I ruin cereal! Does that mean I have poor adaptive skills?" Well, yes and no.

Nobody has perfect adaptive behaviors. I personally get lost with alarming regularity. I frequently forget where I park my car, and I sometimes spend an hour combing mall parking lots trying to find my vehicle. You probably have had similar experiences from time to time. Everybody has.

So, how bad do your adaptive behaviors have to be in order for them to be considered poor? There is no exact answer. However, there are a couple things that might put this question into perspective.

Frequency of Poor Adaptive Behavior

First, just because somebody has problems with various adaptive behaviors once in a while, doesn't mean that they have poor adaptive skills. For instance, if you burn your food once every few months, or if I forget where I park on occasion, that doesn't mean that we have a problem.

When we talk about poor adaptive skills and mental retardation, we are talking about skills that are much worse than would be considered normal. We all have good and bad days. People with poor adaptive skills have problems with specific behaviors on a more or less routine basis. So, if you burn food nearly every day and if I can *never* find my car, then, yes, we both probably have poor adaptive skills.

Severity of Poor Adaptive Behavior

Secondly, in order to qualify for mental retardation, the person's poor behaviors have to significantly affect his life. That is to say, your destructive cooking skills and my inability to find my car have to hamper our ability to live independently. So, if you have a hard time getting a good meal because you burn things and I get fired from work because I am always late, then, yes, we probably have poor adaptive skills.

Just to recap, adaptive skills help us live independently. They allow us to do things for ourselves. While we all have problems with adaptive skills now and then, people with mental retardation have difficulties frequently and to such a degree that their lives are adversely affected. Got it?

Now you are probably thinking, "Wait a minute! Nobody lives independently, at least not completely! So why are you expecting people with mental retardation to live independently?" Good observation and question. Let's discuss this a little more.

It is true that nobody lives completely independently. For example, I am willing to bet that you don't fix your own teeth. You probably go to a dentist for that. You might work on your own car, but other people probably make the parts that you install. And so forth. So, true, you are not completely independent. Neither am I, nor is anybody else for that matter. So, don't get too hung up on the idea that because nobody lives independently, kids with mental retardation therefore shouldn't be expected to either.

The difference between people with mental retardation and "average" people is that average people can usually adjust to unexpected changes, anticipate various outcomes in given situations, and cope with the demands of day-to-day life. Notice that I said "usually" and not "always." This is not to say that those of us with IQs above 70 are perfect. We aren't. But, generally speaking, if the roof is leaking, our car needs to be fixed, or the fire alarm is going off, we can manage fairly well.

People with mental retardation often have difficulty dealing with unexpected challenges that require changes in their traditional behavior. Again, note that I said that they have *difficulty*. I didn't say that they *can't* cope with daily challenges or changes. They certainly can. However, such behavior generally is harder for them than it is for the general population. Average people might have some trouble performing a few skills requiring adaptive behaviors once in a while. People with mental retardation will have problems with more skills than do average people and the problems that they will have tend to significantly impair their lives. Let's discuss some examples and then go on.

I am sure that you will agree that social skills are very important in almost every facet of our daily lives. It affects how we work, learn, and play with our peers. Just imagine how different your life would be if you were always rude and obnoxious and wiped your nose on your sleeve and always told people *exactly* what you thought of them! You probably would have great difficulty getting and keeping a job, let alone friends! Keep in mind that nobody "lacks" social skills. Some people might have horrid social skills, but everybody has social skills to one degree or another.

Having good or appropriate social skills involves many adaptive behaviors. For instance, suppose that you walk into a room and see somebody to whom you want to talk. Do you walk right up to her and start talking? Is she already talking to somebody else? Does it look like she wants to talk to you? Is what you want to say appropriate for the situation? These are all questions people have to process before they begin to socialize appropriately.

People with mental retardation have difficulty answering these questions. It isn't that they can't socialize appropriately. It is just they often exercise poor judgment. For example, a person might walk up to somebody at a funeral who is crying and ask, "Is there any food around here?" While asking if there is food nearby isn't necessarily inappropriate when you are at a social gathering, it probably is when you are asking a grieving widower who is watching his dead wife be buried.

Let me give you another example. Suppose that you are at a party and somebody comes up to you and interrupts your conversation. He butts right in and starts talking about something completely unrelated to what you and your friends were discussing. Further, he touches you inappropriately and makes crude comments. Maybe he even grabs and clings to you. Are these poor adaptive skills?

Well, it depends! What if the person at the party was only four years old? Well, then, no. He is just acting like a normal four-year-old would.

My point is this. Having poor adaptive skills is very subjective, even more so than having subaverage intelligence. What is an example of poor adaptive skills in one situation might not be poor adaptive skills in another situation, or to another person.

Culture can play a huge role in regard to what is considered appropriate or inappropriate behavior. For instance, my mother's family lives in New York, and they are first-generation Italian-Americans. They stand very close to people and will touch them when they are talking. Further, they tend to be very emotional and loud. I am not saying that is bad—it is just who they are.

My father's family, however, is Swedish. They are very proper and reserved. They might shake somebody's hands, but that is as far as touching goes. Further, they tend to stand a few feet away from people, and they talk in very calming tones. I never see them waving their hands or gesture when they are in the middle of the conversation. Again, this isn't good or bad, it is just how they are.

When the two families get together, there is always some degree of tension. My paternal grandfather freezes in terror whenever my Italian cousins give him a big bear hug or slap him on the back. Further, he tends to back away ever so slightly whenever they stand too close to him. Of course, the Italian side of the family doesn't understand why the Swedes don't talk more and often call them "standoffish."

They aren't standoffish at all. Actually, my Scandinavian relatives are very funny and love telling stories and will sing at a drop of a hat. But they just don't interact in the same way as do my Italian family members.

Can you see the point that I am trying to make? Both sides of my family view the behaviors of the other side as being odd. From their respective perspectives, I am sure that they each think that the other has poor social skills—but that doesn't mean that either family actually does.

You see, in order to consider adaptive skills to be poor, you have to take into account many factors. As we discussed earlier, age is one of them. You can't expect a four-year-old to have the adaptive behavior skills of an adult. Culture is another. The situation is a third. I am sure there are a near infinite number more.

What if Somebody Has a Low IQ, but Fine Adaptive Behaviors?

At this point, you might be saying to yourself, "Okay, I understand that mental retardation involves having a low IQ and poor adaptive skills. But aren't those two things redundant? I mean, if somebody has a really low IQ, don't they also have to have poor adaptive skills just as a result of their intelligence?" This is an excellent question. The short answer is "no," but let me explain in greater detail.

I have a friend who has a foster son. Let's call him Tommy. Tommy has had a very rough life, as most foster children have had. In addition to many other adversities, Tommy's biological mother keeps getting kicked out of apartments and moves around frequently. She moves around so much, in fact, that Tommy has been in fourteen different schools in four years! That's about a new school every ten weeks or so. Actually, he misses a great deal of class time in between schools. So, he really only averages about six to eight weeks per school. Needless to say, his learning has suffered tremendously.

Tommy is in fourth grade, but he reads and writes worse than an average kindergartener would. He can recognize and write most of his letters, but he can't read words beyond "cat" or "the." He can count to twenty or so, but has a very hard time with basic addition and subtraction. He doesn't even know many colors.

On an IQ test, I am sure that Tommy would appear to have mental retardation. First of all, he hates taking tests because they make him feel stupid. He usually doesn't even try, or he throws a big fit and gets kicked out of class so he doesn't have to take them. Secondly, even if he did try, Tommy simply cannot read well enough to understand the directions, let alone the questions. Consequently, I am sure that his test score would indicate that he has an IQ below 70.

Despite what his test scores might indicate, Tommy is certainly not mentally retarded. In reality, he is very sharp intellectually and is very good at figuring things out. In fact, he is great at reading situations and manipulating people so that he gets what he wants. In other words, he has exceptional adaptive behavior skills, thus—he can't have mental retardation.

So, to answer your original question directly, yes, it is very possible to have a low IQ and fine adaptive behaviors. It is also very likely to have an average IQ or above, but have poor adaptive skills. Albert Einstein is a wonderful example of this.

Albert Einstein was obviously an exceedingly intelligent person. Some people say that he was the smartest person of the twentieth century. But he was also noted for his rather peculiar behaviors. For example, he had horrible social skills. He would forget people's names, interrupt them when they were talking, and just walk away in the middle of conversations. He couldn't match his socks and frequently would forget to put both of them on. He would wander around for hours looking for the glasses that he was wearing. He twice forgot about food that he was cooking and nearly burnt down his house. He even was stranded for the better part of the day on a lake because he lost the oars to his rowboat! While brilliant, Einstein clearly had poor adaptive skills. So, IQ and adaptive skills don't have to go hand in hand.

DEVELOPMENTAL PERIOD

In this chapter, we have been attempting to define mental retardation. Thus far, we have talked about how individuals with mental retardation must have significantly subaverage intelligence. Specifically, people with mental retardation have IQ scores below 70 or 75, depending upon the particular test that is used. We also discussed how people with mental retardation must also have adaptive skills that are so poor that their lives are adversely affected. Think that we are done? Not yet. There is one final component to defining mental retardation—age of onset.

Mental retardation is considered a "developmental disability." That is, it is thought to be present "within" an individual before birth or shortly there-after.

At the very least, its principal symptoms (e.g., subaverage intelligence and poor adaptive skills) must be present by age eighteen.

At first thought, this probably sounds like an easy concept, right? Well, it gets more complicated. Just wait!

Imagine that you are perfectly average person in every way. When you were born, you had ten little fingers and ten little toes. You learned to walk and crawl and talk all at the appropriate times. When grades came out, you were always exactly in the middle of your class. Your IQ was 100 and your adaptive skills were typical for your age and cultural background. And so forth.

But then one day you got into a car crash and your head hit the dashboard. Because of this accident, your brain became damaged. You forget much of what you have learned, and it takes much longer for you to process new information. In fact, tests reveal that your IQ is now 69. Further, you have substantial difficulties dealing with changes in your environment and have other poor adaptive behaviors. Do you now have mental retardation?

Well, it sort of depends. If you are under age eighteen years old, then yes, some people might consider you to be mental retarded. If you were older, say forty-eight, then no, that would not be considered mental retardation since it began after the "developmental period." You would probably be labeled with "traumatic brain injury" (TBI).

Now, I should point out that some people would consider the eighteen-year-old in the above situation as being TBI too, since the cause of the mental retardation was known to be the result of a head injury. You see, as we will discuss in chapter 3, the cause of mental retardation is usually not known. So, when the cause is known, such as in the case of a traumatic brain injury, people are often labeled with the cause rather than mental retardation. The idea is that having TBI is more acceptable and less stigmatizing than is mental retardation.

The main point is this—age of onset matters. People cannot "develop" or "acquire" mental retardation after the developmental period is over (i.e., after the age of eighteen). Whether the result of a car accident, high fever, drug use, Alzheimer's, old age, or any other circumstances, people who end up developing poor adaptive behavior and a subaverage intelligence after age eighteen do not technically have mental retardation.

SUMMARY

In this chapter, we discussed several very important topics. First of all, we talked about how there is really no single, completely accepted definition of mental retardation. However, several of the prominent definitions have three things in common.

The first defining characteristic of mental retardation is "subaverage intelligence." We discussed how intelligence isn't really about how much you know, but about how well you learn. We also talked about how intelligence is allegedly measured by standardized tests that produce an IQ (intelligence quotient). People with mental retardation do very poorly on these tests and have IQs below about 70. Keep in mind that 100 is the median score for the "average" population.

The second factor that was common in most definitions of mental retardation is "poor adaptive skills" or "poor adaptive abilities." Adaptive skills are those skills that help us live as independently as we are expected for our age and cultural background. However, nobody has perfect adaptive skills. We all have problems adjusting to changes once in a while. But people with mental retardation have problems more frequently than do other people. Further, the problems that they experience adversely affect their lives.

Finally, we talked about age of onset, which is the third common characteristic found in the popular definitions of mental retardation. We talked about how people don't develop mental retardation later in life, but they can suffer injuries that can cause mental retardation, as long as the injury occurs before the end of the "developmental period," which is thought to be at age eighteen.

The thing to keep in mind is that all three of these characteristics must be in place before somebody can have mental retardation. You can't have mental retardation and just have a low IQ. You would also have to have poor adaptive skills and display these symptoms before you reached age eighteen.

The question then becomes, "How do you determine whether somebody has a "subaverage IQ" and "poor adaptive skills"? This will be the focus of our next chapter! So take a break and then read on!

2

DIAGNOSING MENTAL RETARDATION

GUIDED COMPREHENSION QUESTIONS

By the time you complete this chapter, you should be able to

1. Explain who can diagnosis a child with mental retardation
2. Explain the difference between "reliability" and "validity"
3. Identify ways of measuring intelligence
4. Identify ways of measuring adaptive behavior
5. Determine whether your child has been assessed appropriately
6. Identify different "levels" of mental retardation

INTRODUCTION

In chapter 1, we talked about what mental retardation is and isn't. We discussed several prominent definitions of mental retardation and found three factors that are common among them. Specifically, we determined that mental retardation is characterized by subaverage intelligence, poor adaptive skills, and an age of onset occurring within the developmental period (i.e., by age eighteen).

In this chapter, we are going to discuss how mental retardation is diagnosed. We won't go into enough detail so that you will be able to assess your own children or students. That would require several textbooks and many years of training. However, by the end of this chapter, you should be able to figure out where to go to see if your child has mental retardation as well as determine whether your child was diagnosed correctly (that is, if he or she has already been diagnosed). I will also help you understand the assorted "types" or "levels" of mental retardation and clear up any misconceptions that you may have about them.

WHO CAN DIAGNOSE MENTAL RETARDATION?

Before we begin discussing how children are diagnosed with mental retardation, let's first answer the question, "*Who* can diagnose children with mental retardation?" The answer might surprise you.

Not too long ago, a mother of a child with Down syndrome came up to me after I finished presenting at a conference and started asking questions. During our conversation, she mentioned that that her son was diagnosed with mental retardation "shortly after birth." Out of curiosity, I asked, "by whom?" What she told me made me sick!

Apparently, immediately after her son was born, even before she could see him, the obstetrician had the nurse take the baby away. He then told this woman that her son was mentally retarded! The story is very sad, and I can't tell you it in full right here, but the point is, this doctor didn't perform any kind of assessments to establish whether the child was actually mentally retarded. He just looked at him and made his diagnosis!

I should point out that just because people have Down syndrome, it doesn't mean they also have mental retardation. That's a misconception. People with Down's can have average IQs, but we will talk about such things in the next chapter.

At any rate, this obstetrician had no business making a diagnosis right then and there. Actually, he had no business making a diagnosis of mental retardation at any time. You see, just because he is a medical doctor, doesn't mean that he is qualified to assess somebody's intelligence or adaptive skills. And he certainly was not qualified to diagnose people with mental retardation simply by looking at them!

"So who is qualified to diagnose a child with mental retardation?" you are probably wondering. As you might anticipate, the answer is a bit tricky.

First of all, any diagnosis that would enable a child to be eligible for special education is officially made by the M-Team (or Multidisciplinary Team). It might be called something different in your state, such as a D-Team (i.e., Diagnostic Team), or an E-Team (i.e., Evaluation Team), or PPT (Pupil Personnel Team). But basically, in all schools, there is a more or less permanent group that is responsible for determining whether children qualify for special education.

Regardless of what they are called, these teams consist of school personnel who assess children, interpret the results, and then determine whether kids are eligible for services. The teams usually include a school psychologist (or school counselor) and several special education teachers. Sometimes the principal or some other school administrator is also involved.

Please don't get me wrong. In many circumstances, medical doctors *can* diagnose children with disabling conditions. For instance, medical doctors can diagnose children with a traumatic brain injury or with seizures or cerebral palsy or tons of other medical diagnoses. However, *in order for a child to be enrolled in special education*, the M-Team has to make the official determination of whether there is a disability that adversely affects the child's education. So, in the end, it is the M-Team's call, not the doctor's.

Probably, more often than not, the M-Team will just accept a doctor's diagnosis—but not always. For instance, I have worked on several cases where a pediatrician has diagnosed a child with ADHD (i.e., attention deficit hyperactivity disorder) or Tourette's syndrome and the M-Team has disagreed.

Again, the bottom line is that the official diagnosis is usually a team decision. That way, there is less of a chance that one person's biases or interpretations will result in a misdiagnosis. Further, if there is a misdiagnosis, the blame and legal ramifications can be spread around the entire team. In fact, it has become a rarity to find individual professionals, such as pediatricians or psychologists, who are willing to make diagnoses of disabilities independently. They don't want be sued if they are wrong. Instead, they will refer their patients to various specialists for comprehensive evaluations. Or, they will make "recommendations" that the parents are supposed to take back to the child's school. As you will later learn, the fear of lawsuits hangs perpetually over both the medical and educational communities.

Perhaps because of this fear of lawsuits and litigation, diagnostic teams must include people who are specially trained to give and interpret standardized tests. When mental retardation is suspected, standardized tests must be given to assess the child's intelligence and adaptive behaviors. Medical doctors, such as obstetricians and pediatricians, don't have this kind of training. I am not saying that they aren't skilled practitioners; I am merely pointing out that they usually do not know much about intelligence or adaptive behavior, let alone how to measure these constructs accurately.

Not everybody can give a standardized IQ test correctly. So, if you have a child who is being diagnosed with mental retardation, make sure that you ask about the qualifications of the person administering the test. In most cases, they should have at least a master's degree in educational psychology, such as a school psychologist. Sometimes evaluators can have graduate degrees in special education, but even so, they are not qualified to give all standardized tests.

If a team of school officials is trying to diagnose your child with mental retardation and you don't feel comfortable with their qualifications, it is within your rights to have a third party perform an independent evaluation at the school's expense. But, again, we will talk about such legal issues in a later chapter. For now, the main point of this section is this: Only trained people with the appropriate education and experience should give and interpret standardized tests. We will talk about who needs to have what qualifications for which tests later. So, let's move on.

THE BASICS OF ANY ASSESSMENT

Whether you are trying to ascertain if a child has mental retardation or a learning disability or is gifted or completely "normal" in every possible way, the fundamentals for assessing children are basically the same. That is, you want to accurately assess the child's ability. But this isn't as easy as it sounds. There is a lot you need to know, including two very crucial concepts.

Validity

The first concept is validity. An assessment is valid when it measures what it is supposed to measure. For example, using a ruler to measure somebody's height is completely appropriate. After all, rulers measure distance. Therefore, you are using the correct instrument for the task. Using a ruler to measure somebody's intelligence would not be a valid assessment because you are using something that doesn't actually measure intelligence.

This sounds like common sense, right? It should be, but there are a lot of invalid assessment procedures out there. The story I told you about the doctor gauging a child's intelligence by looking at his facial characteristics is a good example of how professionals often use invalid techniques.

Actually, that kind of thing happens all the time. When teachers think that a kid has mental retardation or a learning disability or whatever, they will often justify their beliefs by selectively observing the child. I'll give you an example.

One of my current research projects investigates the perceptions that teachers have about kids with ADHD (attention deficit hyperactivity disorder). I show teachers a video of a child in a classroom who is looking around, talking to his peers, and playing with his pencil. To some teachers I say, "Here is a student whom we believe has ADHD. What do you think?"

Thus far, roughly 83 percent of these teachers have agreed with me. They nod their heads enthusiastically and say things like, "Of course, he has ADHD! Look at that behavior! He is *so* hyperactive, he should be on medication or something!"

I then show the same video to other teachers and say, "Do you think that this student has ADHD?" A little less than half (44 percent) of them say "yes." A good many tend to be on the fence and will say things like, "I can't tell." Or, "I need more information to be sure."

When I show the video to the final group of teachers, I say, "Here is a child that we selected at random. Do you think that he has ADHD?" Fewer than 5 percent of the teachers have said "yes." Moreover, very few of them are undecided. In fact, most of them (78 percent) think that the child in the video is just an average kid!

The implications are pretty clear. If teachers think that a child has a disability, they will be able to "see" the disability in the child. They will interpret the data in such a way as to justify their beliefs. Of course, the student in the video doesn't have any disabilities at all. He is a completely normal kid, if such a beast exists. But, when I suggest that he has ADHD, almost all of the teachers will believe that he does. Further, they will point to his behavior to justify their beliefs—the same behavior that other teachers will point to and say, "No! That is not ADHD. That is just an ordinary boy!"

It isn't just teachers who do this. We all do. The power of suggestion is extremely potent. It is much like taking a drink of water when you think that you are drinking milk. For a split second, the water actually tastes like milk—just like how normal kids can look like they have ADHD or a learning disability or mental retardation when teachers already think that they have one of those conditions.

Okay, so in order to conduct an appropriate assessment, you have to use valid techniques. You can't let your preconceived notions cloud your subjectivity. Otherwise, you won't actually really be measuring the child; you will be measuring your own biases. This is why it is *very* important to have multiple people assessing your child. The more people, the less likely any one bias will be dominant. Make sense? Let's continue.

Reliability

The second concept that you need to understand about assessment is reliability. Something is reliable when it measures something consistently. For example, if you measure your child's height with a ruler two or three times and you get the same results, your assessment of her height is reliable. That is, you got the same results over and over again.

The challenging thing about reliability is that sometimes we measure variables that change over time. For example, your child might grow a couple inches over the course of the year. Or, she might learn to read better after an intensive reading class. Or, she might become smarter as she gets older. In other words, things change. Still, if I were to give you a reliable test twice in a relatively short period of time, say one month, I should get roughly the same results. Notice that I say *roughly*.

Let's suppose that you have a valid test that measures math ability. You give it to your daughter in the morning and she scores at the 50th percentile;

that is exactly in the middle of all her class, so 50 percent of her peers score better than she does and 50 percent score worse than she does. Then you give the same test to her at lunch and she scores at the 52nd percentile. Then again at the end of the day and she scores at the 49th percentile. Is this test reliable? Probably. All of the scores were fairly close to each other, so it is okay if they vary a few points in either direction. Now, if the score varied tremendously, such as the 50th, 90th, and 10th percentiles, then the test is probably unreliable, assuming that your daughter tried equally as hard on all of the tests and nothing was distracting her.

Reliable but Not Valid

"Can something be reliable but not valid?" my students often ask me.

Yes. A classic example is how people used to think that storks brought babies. You see, long ago, storks would pass though towns in the springtime as they migrated to their summer homes. Right as they were passing through, people would tend to have babies. Keep in mind that there isn't much to do in the wintertime, so people tend to have babies nine months later, or in early summer.

At any rate, people put these two events together even though they were completely unrelated. In other words, they thought that the coming of the storks somehow involved people having babies. It sounds funny to us. But if you think about it, it is an honest mistake. After all, babies did tend to be born while the storks were passing through—that is, their assessment was reliable (i.e., consistent). However, since the storks had nothing to do with babies, their assessment wasn't valid. Make sense?

Valid but Not Reliable

Okay, can you give an example of something that is valid but not reliable? This is a bit tricky. Whatever you come up with has to measure what it claims to measure, but not consistently.

My favorite example of something that is valid but not reliable is the rain gauge that I have outside my kitchen window. It is a long, plastic tube that measures how much rain that we get by collecting raindrops. Hopefully, you know what I am talking about.

Clearly, it is a valid way of measuring how much rain has fallen. After all, it collects raindrops. But it is horribly inaccurate. Why? Well, my window faces east, so if the wind is coming from the west, the rain gauge is sheltered by the house, and it doesn't collect any rain even in a downpour. I have looked at it after a daylong thunderstorm, thinking that it would be overflowing, only to find that it was almost totally dry!

Applying This to Mental Retardation

Okay, so hopefully you understand a little bit about validity and reliability. There is a great deal more to it than what we covered, but you should have the general gist. Specifically, in order for assessments to be worth anything, they must be valid; that is, they have to measure what they are supposed to measure. And they also have to be reliable; that is, they measure things consistently. But you are probably wondering how all of this ties into your life and mental retardation.

Let's suppose that you have a daughter whom you think might have mental retardation. Perhaps her teachers have complained that she isn't making "satisfactory progress." Or, maybe you have noticed that she just doesn't learn as fast as her older brothers and sisters. How do you confirm or refute your suspicions?

First of all, you want to contact several people who know something about giving and interpreting tests. As we discussed earlier, you want to make sure that there is more than one person involved in the diagnostic process so that individual biases are minimized. Calling a child psychologist might be a good place to start, but you also want to get people who know the child involved. That includes her teachers, her peers, and even you and your daughter! Then your whole team gathers information about your daughter's intelligence and adaptive skills. Both of these are discussed in the sections below.

ASSESSING INTELLIGENCE

Intelligence can be assessed in a number of ways. Certainly there are IQ tests, which tend to be used far more frequently than any other method. But there are also other methods, such as observing the person performing challenging tasks. In this section, I will give you a very general overview of how intelligence is assessed. But more importantly, I want to give you questions to ask yourself and your child's evaluators.

Standardized Tests

Assessing a child's intellectual abilities is paramount when diagnosing the child with mental retardation. You simply cannot determine if somebody has mental retardation without measuring his or her intelligence. While this book will not make you skilled enough to actually give standardized tests, I want to give you some questions to ask so that you know that your child is in good hands. They involve

- Qualifications of the examiner
- Age of the tests
- Readiness of the child
- Effects of the testing environment
- Effects of the evaluators
- Interpretation of the results

What Are the Qualifications of the Examiner?

One of the first questions that you should ask when having your child assessed for mental retardation is, "Is the examiner qualified to give the standardized tests?" As we discussed earlier, not everybody is trained to give tests correctly.

Generally speaking, only psychologists or psychiatrists can give assessment devices that measure intelligence. However, there are a few that can be administered by classroom teachers or school counselors. To find out who can give what, look at the list below. If the tests used on your child are not indicated, ask the evaluator if you can look at the scoring manuals. The scoring manual will explain what qualifications are needed to give that particular test. You can also search the Internet. Just type in the name of the assessment into any search engine and you should be able to find out the qualifications required for its administration.

The following tests can only be given by psychologists:

- Columbia Mental Maturity Scale (CMMS)
- Comprehensive Test of Nonverbal Intelligence
- Kaufman Brief Intelligence Test (K-BIT)
- Slosson Intelligence Test-Revised (SIT-R)
- Stanford Binet Intelligence Test
- Test of Nonverbal Intelligence-Third Edition
- Wechsler Scales of Intelligence

These tests that can be given by teachers:

- Brigance Diagnostic Inventory of Basic Skills
- Kaufman Test of Educational Achievement (KTEA)
- McCarthy Scales of Children's Ability Test (MSCA)
- Norris Educational Achievement Test (NEAT)
- Peabody Individual Achievement Test-Revised (PIAT-R)
- Test of Academic Achievement Skills-Reading, Arithmetic, Spelling, and Listening
- Wechsler Individual Achievement Test (WIAT)
- Wide Range Achievement Test-3 (WRAT-3)

So, ask the examiner what his or her background is! Don't be shy. Ask if he or she has a master's degree and, if so, in what. I am sure that you look into the qualifications of your child's medical doctors. Why not your child's evaluators?

You also want to ask how many times the examiner has administered each particular test. Tests take a great deal of skill to give. Even people with PhDs, such as myself, need practice giving tests in order to give them correctly. I have literally evaluated hundreds of children; however, when a new test or a new edition of a test comes out, I still need to practice giving it. Just because I have a PhD and many years of experience doesn't mean that I am proficient with *every* assessment device ever published! So, make sure that the people who assess your child are not only educated but also have recent experience. I would hope that they have given the test at least ten times before they test your child, if not more.

How Old Are the Tests?

Another very important question to ask is, "How old are the tests that you are giving to my child?" You see, publishers like to update tests frequently. They do this for two reasons.

First, publishers want to make money. If they come out with a new edition every couple of years, then everybody has to throw out their old editions and buy the current one. And each test can cost several hundred dollars, so there is *a lot* of money to be made!

But, more importantly, tests are constantly being improved. No test is perfect. They all have questions that are biased against one population or another. So, test makers are constantly updating questions and performing research to see if they can enhance the reliability and validity of their instruments.

Generally speaking, if a test is more than seven or eight years old, it is probably out of date. That is not to say that it is completely worthless; it just means that I wouldn't base my findings exclusively on it. (Actually, you should *never* base a diagnosis on any *one* test.) The examiner should give your child several different IQ tests. Hopefully, the others are more current.

If a test is more than ten or fifteen years old, I definitely would *not* use it! Further, I would probably look for another examiner. If an examiner isn't going to keep up-to-date instruments, he or she probably isn't going to update his or her skills either. Again, being trained and keeping your skills sharp is very important when assessing children. I don't know how many times I have been in meetings where the psychologist used tests that had stopped being published over twenty years earlier or had diagnosed a child with a condition that no longer exists! Ugh!

Again, just because somebody says that she is qualified doesn't mean that she is good at what she does! Remember, this is your child. His future is on the line. So, make sure that the evaluator is trained, but also that he or she is using the newest assessment devices possible!

Is Your Child Ready?

Was your child up for taking the test? Tests are only useful if the children taking them did their best. If they were distracted, uneasy, not feeling well, or otherwise not at the top of their game, then you might as well throw the test results out! They are meaningless.

Think about it this way. Your child is taking a test that she probably doesn't want to take with a person whom she probably doesn't really know. Now throw in the fact that she is hungry or tired or bored or upset, and the test will not accurately measure her intelligence. Remember, a difference of five or ten points on an IQ test will often mean the difference between a normal child and a child with mental retardation. To ensure that the results are as accurate as possible, consider the following questions:

- How was your child feeling the day of the test? Was he happy? Was she preoccupied?
- Did she have a good meal before hand? Was she tired after eating too much? Did he forget to have breakfast?
- When was the test given? Was it too early in the day? Too late? After a physically or mentally challenging activity or a long day?
- Was your child nervous about taking the test? Defiant? Anxious?
- Did your child appear to want to do well on the test? Did she not care in the slightest?

Basically, what you need to determine is whether or not the tests were given at a time when your child would be at his or her best. You know your child better than any evaluator. So, if the evaluator wants to give the test at a time that isn't appropriate for your child, such as right after a long day of school, tell the evaluator to reschedule. Ethical evaluators should be willing to accommodate your child's schedule in order to get the most accurate picture of your child's abilities as possible. If the evaluator doesn't want to reschedule the assessments, then get a different evaluator!

Making sure that your child is up to taking the test is very important. If she isn't up to taking the test, the evaluator won't be able to accurately assess her actual ability. If you believe that a test was given on a bad day, then have the test be regiven at a better time. Again, it is *very* important that multiple tests are implemented at various times and locations. This will help minimize the chances of one bad day affecting the results. I have a funny story that illustrates this point wonderfully.

One of my friends has a cute little nine-year-old girl named Samantha. My friend and her husband go on and on about how brilliant Samantha is. They think that she is a genius and say so with great regularity. It is actually kind of annoying. You probably know the type.

At any rate, my friend finally decided to have Samantha tested for a gifted and talented program offered at a prestigious private school. However, when they got the results back, my friend was completely floored! Not only was her daughter not gifted, the results indicated that she had below-average intelligence! I think that her score was 82 or something like that. They couldn't understand it! After all, their daughter had already skipped a grade and was taking accelerated classes. What happened?!?

As it turned out, the school counselor gave the test right before recess, and Samantha didn't want to miss out on the fun. Further, the counselor said something to the effect of "You can go outside when you are done here." As you might have guessed, Samantha gave wrong answers on purpose so that the test would be over sooner! Talk about a smart kid!

Well, anyway, after realizing this, the parents had Samantha retested when she was more willing to actually try her best. She ended up scoring a very respectable 126—good, but not brilliant. Her mother still claims that the test undervalued Samantha's intelligence by twenty points. So it goes.

Had everybody relied on only the first test, Samantha probably would have grown up thinking that she was "dull normal." Could you imagine how that would have affected her development?! Again, the main point is, make sure that your child takes multiple tests!

Were the Test Results Biased by the Environment?

In addition to your child's state of mind, you should also ask yourself, "Was the test given in a suitable environment?" Think about it this way. Imagine that you were given a test right at this very moment. You feel good and rested and want to perform your best. But there is noise in the background, maybe people are talking or wiggling in their chairs, or maybe the ticking of the clock on the wall is distracting you. No matter how well you want to do, no matter how hard you try, could you do your best? I have two stories that should drive this point home.

I wasn't a particularly good student when I was a kid. I got Cs and Ds throughout high school, so my grades weren't going to get me into college. Nor could I play sports, so I wasn't going to get an athletic scholarship. If I was going to get into a decent university, or *any* university for that matter, I had to do well on my SATs. As a result, I was very motivated to do well. I studied, took the pre-SAT study class, made sure that I had a good night sleep, and so on and so forth. I did everything that I could to be at the top of my game.

When it was time to take the SAT, I ate a good meal, showed up early, and brought not the suggested three number-two pencils, but four! I even wore my lucky sweatshirt! I was all set.

Unfortunately, I took the test at a community college that was across the street from a church. What makes this unfortunate was that it was Sunday and the church was playing John Denver tunes on their steeple bells. Throughout the entire test, I had to listen to "Leaving on a Jet Plane," "Rocky Mountain High," and "Annie's Song" over and over and over again. It was quite maddening. As you can imagine, I didn't do especially well. Another example involves one of my students.

Donald has autism and, like most people who have autism, gets very upset when his daily routines are changed. So, when his teachers took him out of his normal class and brought him to a room (in which he had never been) with the school psychologist (whom he had never met), Donald got very upset. He started rocking back and forth, screaming his lungs out. He beat his head against the table, nearly breaking his own nose in the process, and repeatedly tried to bite the psychologist. The psychologist, who was understandably extremely flustered, ran out of the room and declared in his final report that Donald's IQ was "unmeasurable."

Donald's reaction to the testing environment is certainly extreme, but the fact that the testing environment affected him is not untypical. We are all influenced by our surroundings. Sometimes our surroundings distract us and adversely affect our abilities. Other times, our surroundings enhance our ability to concentrate and perform at our utmost.

When your child's intelligence is being assessed, you need to pay careful attention to where the test is going to be given. The environment should be familiar, but not so familiar that it is distracting. It should be quiet, comfortable, and relaxing, with a good light source. I usually recommend that testing occur in a place where the student has taken tests before, such as in his classroom—but only after the other kids have gone, and not during recess! Otherwise your student could do what Samantha did!

Some people advocate that tests should be administered at the student's home. I don't disagree with this. After all, your child would probably be most comfortable at your house. However, I would strongly recommend that tests not be given in the child's bedroom or in the living room, especially if the child is still pretty young. There are just too many distractions. Basically, you don't want to administer tests to child wherever there are other people, toys, or television sets.

In the final analysis, you know your child better than anybody. You probably have a pretty good idea regarding where your child works best and what is distracting to him or her. Before any testing is done, pass your insights along to the rest of the examination team. Make sure that they assess your child in an environment that is going to be appropriate for the task at hand.

Were the Results of the Evaluation Biased by the Evaluator?

Much like how the student is feeling or distractions within the environment, the evaluator could also be detrimental to the evaluation's reliability and validity. I'll give you an example from my own experiences.

When I first started giving standardized tests, I thought that I was pretty good at it. I took numerous classes on assessment and practiced for hours whenever a new edition came out. I even videotaped myself giving the assessments just so I could evaluate my own skills.

One day, I was watching a tape of myself giving a test to a student when one of my colleagues walked into the room. He watched for less than a minute and said, "You realize that you are cuing the student, don't you?"

I had no idea what he was talking about. So, he pointed out that whenever my student gave a correct answer, I would smile and nod my head. When the student answered incorrectly, I wouldn't smile or nod. Plus, I paused ever so slightly. The student picked up on this and would then change her answer. As I watched the tape, I was horrified to see that my colleague was right. I was cluing my student in whenever she said a wrong answer!

In effect, I invalidated the tests that I was giving. I was no longer measuring my student's ability to answer the questions, I was measuring her ability to read my expression!

Now, when I train my college students to give assessments, I make them videotape themselves. I believe that this is not only a good way for evaluators to check their own skills but the tapes can also be very valuable in assessing the child's behavior. You can go back and see how many times the student fidgeted or looked away or sighed.

Further, having a videotape of the child during her testing sessions enables other professionals to give their opinions as well. Again, much of assessing children is personal interpretation. Having a videotape that several people can watch is a nice alternative to having a dozen people sitting with the child while the tests are being administered.

I would recommend that you ask evaluators to videotape any assessments that they conduct on your child. Moreover, make sure that you get copies of all tapes, answer keys, and assessment reports. Over the years, you will accumulate a large amount of information, so you should probably get a file cabinet in which you can store and organize what your gather.

If the evaluator is unwilling to videotape his work with your child or if he refuses to give you copies of the answer keys, get another evaluator. The evaluator is supposed to work for you and, legally, you should have access to all information that is gathered on your child. I would question the ethics of any evaluator who is unwilling to share his results with parents or other professionals.

Another way that evaluators can unknowingly affect your child's test results is by just being in the room. Many children, especially those who are young or extremely shy, get nervous around strangers. Consequently, they are paying more attention to the evaluator than to the questions on the test. If this sounds like your child, you should have your son or daughter meet the evaluator several times before the actual assessment. Some psychologists will actually sit down and play games with children before the test, just to get them relaxed.

Were the Results Interpreted Correctly?

Okay, so your child was feeling fine when the tests were given. The tests were up to date and administered by a skilled and qualified professional in an appropriate setting. Everything seems to indicate that the results of the tests are valid and reliable. Now comes the hard part! The evaluation team, which should include you, has to interpret the scores.

When trying to determine whether a child has mental retardation, a lot of people just go right to the IQ score and check to see if it is above or below 70. If it is below 70, the child has mental retardation. If it is above 70, the child doesn't have mental retardation. Right? No!

Standardized tests give much more information than just an IQ score. There are numerous subtests that measure everything from reading comprehension to mathematical reasoning to attention to detail. Don't ignore these subtests! They can provide you with crucial information about your child.

Let's use the Wechsler Scale of Intelligence as an example. It is one of the main assessments used to evaluate intelligence, so you will probably come across it at some point in your child's life.

The Wechsler Scale of Intelligence is comprised of several subtests that fall into two groups, verbal and performance. Verbal subtests involve language skills, such as verbal expression and comprehension. Performance subtests involve nonverbal areas, such as fine motor control and visual discrimination. The subtests for the Wechsler Scale of Intelligence are listed below. Don't worry about what each measures. Just understand that each assesses a different area of learning.

Verbal Subtests	*Performance Subtests*
Information	Picture Completion
Similarities	Picture Arrangement
Comprehension	Block Design
Digit Span	Object Assembly
Sentences	Coding
Vocabulary	Digit Symbol
	Symbol Search
	Mazes
	Animal House
	Geometric Designs

Each of the verbal and performance subtests is scored on a scale of 1 to 19. Scores from 15 to 19 are considered superior, and scores from 6 to 14 are considered in the average range, with 13 and 14 being high average and 6 and 7 being low average. Scores below 4 could, but not always, indicate mental retardation.

Once each subtest is scored, three IQs can be calculated. Scores from the verbal subtests result in a Verbal IQ. Verbal IQs indicate how well individuals learn verbally as well as how proficiently they can perform verbal-related tasks. Scores from the performance subtests result in a Performance IQ, which indicates how well individuals learn via nonverbal means (e.g., visually) and can perform nonverbal tasks.

The third, and probably most important, measure of intelligence is the Full Scale IQ. This is what is used to determine eligibility for mental retardation. As we noted in the first chapter, in order for somebody to have mental retardation, their Full Scale IQ must be below 70 or 75, depending upon the test and definition that is utilized. Full Scale IQs are calculated based upon the combine scores from both verbal and performance subtests. So, in essence, the Full Scale IQ is a mixture of both verbal and nonverbal abilities. Make sense so far? Let me give you an example; then we can discuss how all of this applies to diagnosing mental retardation.

Suppose that we have two students, Norah and Richard. Both students have taken the Wechsler Scale of Intelligence under ideal circumstances. That is, they were well rested, had a good evaluator, and they did their very best on the test. Additionally, they both had Full Scale IQ scores of 70. Do they both have mental retardation? If you just look at their IQs, then yes, they do. But look at how they each scored on the subtests (see table 2.1) and then try to decide.

Notice anything strange? Now keep in mind that they both tried their hardest and were not distracted or had a poor evaluator. Do they both have mental retardation? They both have Full Scale IQs of 70. Therefore, they must both have mental retardation, right? Let's see.

Look at Norah's scores. All of her scores were within a couple points of each other. So, she was pretty consistent in her abilities. Unfortunately, she was consistently way below average. Remember, a score of 8–12 is considered average and her highest score was 5, which is considered "borderline developmentally delayed."

Now look at Richard's scores. What do you notice with his results? First, his scores are all over the place! His low score is 1 and his high score is 12.

Table 2.1. Sample Test Results for Norah and Richard

	Norah's Scores	Richard's Scores
Verbal Subtest		
Information	4	1
Similarities	4	1
Vocabulary	4	2
Comprehension	5	3
Sentences	5	2
VERBAL IQ	72	50
Performance Subtests		
Picture Completion	4	12
Picture Arrangement	5	5
Block Design	4	10
Object Assembly	4	4
Coding	2	11
Digit Symbol	4	10
Symbol Search	4	3
Mazes	3	9
Animal House	4	9
Geometric Designs	4	8
PERFORMANCE IQ	68	92
FULL SCALE IQ	70	70

That is a pretty big range! Typically, average people will score within 3–4 points from high to low. Second, Richard's Performance IQ is 92, which is respectably average. So, does he have mental retardation? No. Why?

If somebody has mental retardation, they have "subaverage intelligence" across the board. That is, they score consistently far below their peers on all of the subtests, such as how Norah did. Richard did extremely poorly on the verbal portion of the test but did more or less average on the performance sections. If anything, he probably has a learning disability that affects his ability to process verbal information. Maybe he has a communication disorder. We don't know. However, we do know that he does *not* have mental retardation. Kids with mental retardation usually wouldn't score within the average range on any of these subtests. And they certainly wouldn't have a performance or verbal IQ in the 90s!

So, in other words, although Full-Scale IQs are used to diagnose mental retardation, you really have to go deeper. You have to look at the subtests to see if there is any information that could help you rule in or out mental retardation.

You also have to look at the individual answers that the student gave. Imagine if you looked at Norah's answer key and found that she circled "C" for all of her answers! What would that indicate to you? Well, among other things, it probably indicates that she didn't really try. It also indicates that 70 probably isn't her actual IQ! Again, the main point here is that you can't just look at the IQ score to determine whether somebody has mental retardation. You have to look at the areas in which the student did well and the areas the student did poorly. You also have to figure out why!

Observations

Although standardized tests are certainly the mainstay when it comes to assessing intelligence, you shouldn't forget the value of good old-fashioned observations. After all, a lot of people just do not perform well on tests. Let me give you an example.

I am working with a teenage girl named Tiffany. Tiffany's teachers and parents are concerned that she might have mental retardation. Her performance on schoolwork is well beneath her peers, she seems to have a general lack of understanding of very basic concepts, and her behavior is rather immature. However, every time somebody tries to give her a standardized test, Tiffany shuts down. She simply refuses to participate. She sits there and either gives answers that are clearly sarcastic or she doesn't give any answers at all. So, there is no way to assess her IQ via the traditional methods. What would you do?

Well, it isn't very scientific, but several of us observed Tiffany. We watched how she learned, how she solved problems, and had her explain her reasoning. We also looked at past reports, schoolwork, and notes from previous teachers to determine whether she reached developmental markers, such as when she was able to read and write, on schedule.

We found that Tiffany actually developed slightly ahead of typical peers and was able to tackle very complicated problems, especially figuring out complex computer games without being told how to play them. She was also able to explain the reasoning behind her problem-solving strategies with remarkable precision. Moreover, she was very self-aware of her cognitive processes (e.g., how she learns), something that is untypical of most teenagers, let alone those with cognitive disabilities.

Through our observations, we were able to feel fairly confident that Tiffany *did not* have mental retardation. We deduced that her poor academic performance and troubling behavior was probably more along the lines of an emotional disorder. I personally believe that she suffers from depression, and that her often bizarre behaviors are the result of unreported drug use. But these topics are for another book.

The bottom line is that sometimes you can't use standardized tests to measure a student's intelligence. Maybe they refuse to take the exam, or maybe they have a learning disability, such as dyslexia, and can't read the test very well. Or, maybe they have difficulty focusing their attention so that, even if they tried their best, a standardized test would not accurately reflect their abilities. Or, maybe they just have test anxiety and freeze whenever a paper-and-pencil test is placed in front of them.

In any of these cases, I would suggest that you observe your child and try to determine how he or she learns. Try to compare his learning to that of "average" peers. Look at developmental milestones and see if they were on target. Children who have mental retardation will most likely learn to read, write, and count after their classmates. Further, as we will talk about in chapter 5, people with mental retardation have very poor abstract reasoning skills. When we gave Tiffany riddles and word problems, she was not only able to solve them, but she was also able to explain her logic with appropriate clarity.

So, while giving standardized IQ tests is probably the preferred method of assessing somebody's intelligence, there are other ways. Talk to your child and ask her how she figures things out. Give her riddles or challenging tasks and see how she goes about accomplishing them. Look at past reports from teachers and see if they ever noticed anything. Actually, you should do all of this in addition to giving her standardized IQ tests. That way, you gather more information on your child and the more information, the better!

ASSESSING POOR ADAPTIVE SKILLS

As we discussed earlier, intelligence is only one defining characteristic of mental retardation. Individuals with mental retardation must also have poor adaptive skills in multiple areas. So, how do you assess your child's adaptive skills? Let's find out.

Standardized Tests

As with assessing intelligence, there are many standardized test that evaluate adaptive behavior. A few of them are listed below. Generally speaking, anybody who knows the child can complete these tests, not just psychologists.

- AAMR Adaptive Behavior Scale- School Version (ABS-S:2)
- AAMR Adaptive Behavior Scale- Residential and Community Version (ABS-RC-2)
- Bayley Scales of Infant Development-Second Edition (BSID-II)
- Child Behavior Checklist (CBCL)
- Developmental Assessment for the Severely Handicapped (DASH)
- Kindergarten Readiness Test (KRT)
- Light's Retention Scale (LRS)
- The Adaptive Behavior Evaluation Scale-Revised (ABES-R)
- The Denver Developmental Screening Test-Revised (Denver II)
- The Preschool Evaluation Scales (PES)
- Vineland Adaptive Behavior Scale (VABS)

However, before you go out and give some of these tests, we first need to review several very important points. First, I want to remind you that what is considered "poor" adaptive behavior is very subjective. Furthermore, it can involve many variables, such as culture, age of the student, and the situation. Therefore, we must take great care when saying that somebody has "good" or "bad" adaptive skills. What is inappropriate in one culture or situation may be perfectly normal in another.

As with intelligence tests, I *strongly* recommend that you make sure that the evaluator gives multiple tests. This will help minimize bias. You see, tests that measure adaptive behavior are much different than tests that measure intelligence. Tests that measure intelligence are answered by the student, and questions tend to focus on knowledge and reasoning ability. For example, an intelligence test question might ask the student to solve a math problem or point to a certain picture.

Tests that measure adaptive behavior are far more subjective. They ask questions about your child's behaviors and how "appropriate" they are. For example, they might ask "Does the student act safely in public?" or "Does the student communicate effectively?" What is considered "safe" or "effective" is left up to the person completing the test to determine.

Further, unlike intelligence tests, students typically don't answer tests measuring adaptive behavior. Yes, the student can fill out the questionnaires too, but these assessments are normally completed by people who know the student, such as his or her classroom teachers, the school psychologist, and especially you!

Because there is a large degree of subjectivity to these assessments, the more people completing them the better. So, make sure that you answer the questions. Also make sure that each of your child's past and present teachers (if possible) are asked to complete the test. The more people who are involved, the more accurate the information will be.

Additionally, it is really important for people who know your child in different environments to rate his behaviors. After all, you know how your child behaves at home, but not at school. Your child's teachers know how he acts in the classroom, but not on the school bus or during lunch or recess. In order for somebody to have mental retardation, he or she has to exhibit poor adaptive skills in several different environments. Without multiple people completing the adaptive behavior scales, the assessment team will not be able to see if your child's adaptive behaviors are poor across the board.

If you aren't asked to participate in the assessment of your child's adaptive behavior skills, volunteer! If the evaluator says something like, "You don't need to worry about it," "We'll take care of it," or "You need to be specially trained to complete the tests," then get a different evaluator. Again, you know your child better than anybody. In many respects, you are the more qualified to assess her behavior than anybody else!

Observations

It is difficult to measure a student's adaptive behavior without actually observing the student. Regrettably, that is exactly what many people do. They get a whole bunch of standardized tests and then answer the questions based upon their memories. Don't do this!

No matter how objective you think you are, you have certain biases—especially when it comes to your child. So, when you get to a question that asks something like, "Is the child a danger to himself or others?" and you answer it off the top of your head, you are likely to remember what you want to remember, rather than an accurate representation of your child's behavior. I'll give you an example.

I am in my mid-thirties. Yet, for whatever reason, my mother still pictures me as her eight-year-old son. She insists that I sleep until noon and that I don't like any vegetables. When I tell her that I am a vegetarian and that I workout every morning at 5:30, she doesn't seem to believe me. To her, I am still the snotty little kid who would go to bed at 3:00 in the morning, wake up at noon, and refuse to eat anything that was green. If she had to complete an assessment on me, I am sure she would indicate that I wet the bed (which I haven't done in over thirty years!).

My point is, if you actually watch your child, I mean *really* watch with an open mind, you will probably be surprised. You might find out that your child is more independent and better mannered than you originally had thought. Or, that she is further behind her peers developmentally than you were at first willing to admit.

So, before you complete any behavioral checklists or rating forms, observe your child. Observe him in different environments and at varying times. Watch him when he is playing with other kids and when he is by himself. Try to study his behavior in a number of different contexts and over an extended period of time. Make sure that the other evaluators (e.g., whomever is assessing him) do the same. It is the only way to get an accurate picture of his adaptive behaviors.

HOW MENTAL RETARDATION IS DIAGNOSED

Okay, thus far we have talked about who can diagnose mental retardation. We have talked about how intelligence and adaptive behaviors are assessed. Now we need to put everything together. Let's talk about how mental retardation is actually diagnosed.

Once the assessment team has observed your child multiple times in various environments and given several different types of standardized tests, it is time to make sense of the data. This is when you and everybody else who is involved with your child's life sits down around a table and discusses everybody's findings. Basically you want to ask yourself these questions:

- Do the assessments consistently indicate that your child has a subaverage IQ?
- Do the assessments indicate that your child has poor adaptive skills in multiple environments?
- Is your child under the age of eighteen, or did your child exhibit symptoms of mental retardation prior to age eighteen?
- Do you believe that the assessments are valid and reliable?

If you and the rest of the team answer "yes" to these questions, your child probably has mental retardation. If you have trouble answering these questions and need more information, then continue the assessment process until you feel comfortable with the final diagnosis.

Please keep in mind that this is no trivial decision. This is possibly one of the most momentous conclusions that you will ever have to come to. If the team is correct, and your child does have mental retardation, you are taking the first step in making sure that she gets the help and services that she will need to live a long and happy life. If the team is wrong, and your child is mislabeled with mental retardation or is misdiagnosed with some other condition, her future will be confused and chaotic.

Think about that for a moment. Imagine how differently your teachers and parents would have probably treated you if somebody misdiagnosed you with mental retardation back when you were a kid. Imagine what your life would be like right now. Would you be sitting here reading this book? Would you even know how to read? Would you be the person you are today?

I cannot emphasize enough the importance of this decision and the diagnostic procedures that we have been discussing throughout this chapter. Your ability to ask the right questions and make sure that the correct assessments are given by the appropriate people in the perfect environments is crucial for your child to get the education that she needs. If you have any doubts about the data that has been collected about your child, or any doubts about the people who are interpreting the data, start the assessment process over.

Keep having your child assessed until you know for sure whether she has mentally retardation.

TYPES OR LEVELS OF MENTAL RETARDATION

Once an evaluation team has determined that a child has mental retardation, somebody is likely to start talking about different "levels" or "types" or "severity" of mental retardation. It is really important that you understand what they are telling you. It is also important that you recognize when they are telling you things that are wrong!

Mental retardation, as a condition, results in a wide variety of outcomes. Many individuals with mental retardation can live more or less normal lives. They can even go to college! In fact, two of my past undergraduate students were labeled mentally retarded when they were little. Others may require constant supervision and care. As a result, people often ask me to explain the different "types" of mental retardation.

I try to explain that there really aren't different "types" of mental retardation. As we will discuss in chapter 3, there are many different causes of mental retardation. There are also many different disabilities that are associated with mental retardation, such as autism and Down syndrome. But, strictly speaking, mental retardation is one, albeit diverse, condition.

As soon as I say that, somebody is likely to sit up and disagree with me. He or she will say, "That isn't right! I have a nephew who has mental retardation, and he is completely different than a child in my neighborhood who also has mental retardation!"

To which I typically reply, "That is doubtlessly true. You probably also know several 'normal' people who are completely different from each other."

My point, of course, is that you can't say "mental retardation" and then claim to describe the person as a whole. Yes, people with mental retardation share similar characteristics, such as subaverage intelligence and poor adaptive skills, but not all people with mental retardation are the same. Despite how they are portrayed in the media, not all people with mental retardation like bowling, act like happy children, or drool over themselves. As a group, people with mental retardation are extremely diverse.

Although there aren't different "types" of mental retardation, there are different "levels" used to describe the severity of the condition. In fact, there are several different classification systems used to denote the severity of mental retardation. Several are discussed below.

Mild to Profound

Perhaps the most common way to classify the severity of mental retardation is by the "mild to profound" approach. As you can see from table 2.2, each level of mental retardation is defined by a range of IQ scores. Mild mental retardation, the least pronounced, is typically thought to include individuals with IQ scores from 70 to 55. Moderate mental retardation spans from 55 to 40. Severe mental retardation and profound mental retardation range from 40 to 25 and 25 and below, respectively. Because measuring IQs below 40 is very difficult, some people combine severe and profound mental retardation. Moreover, some people even add the category of "borderline mentally retarded," which would include people with IQs between 70 and 75, and sometimes 80.

If you use this classification system, people with mild mental retardation are far more numerous than individuals with moderate or severe mental retardation. Specifically, approximately 93 percent of people with mental retardation would be considered "mild." Another 5.6 percent would have moderate mental retardation. And only 1.4 percent would have either severe or profound mental retardation.

However, many people do not like this method for categorizing mental retardation. They state that the labels are very judgmental, and that the IQ cutoffs are completely arbitrary. Because of this, the American Association on Mental Retardation (AAMR) proposed another classification system, which we will discuss next.

Table 2.2. IQ Ranges for Mild to Severe Mental Retardation

Level of Mental Retardation	*IQ Range*
Mild Mental Retardation (MMR)	70 to 55
Moderate Mental Retardation (MoMR)	55 to 40
Severe Mental Retardation (SMR)	40 to 25
Profound Mental Retardation (PMR)	25 and below

AAMR's Classification System

Unlike the "mild to profound" method of classifying mental retardation, AAMR's system doesn't focus on a person's IQ score or what they can't do, but rather how much support that they need to live as independently as possible. Categories range from intermittent, where support is needed only periodically and usually for short periods of time, to pervasive, which involves near-constant, intensive supports in nearly every environment.

Intermittent. Supports are required on an as-needed basis. Supports might only be provided during transitions, such as when people with mental retardation lose a job or when obtaining their own home, but not on a continual basis.

Limited. Supports are provided regularly, but not constantly. Further, the supports are not intensive. For example, an individual within this category might only require help grocery shopping or paying their bills every week or so.

Extensive. Supports are required regularly and frequently. They typically involve reoccurring tasks, such as cooking or bathing.

Pervasive. Supports are required on a constant, daily basis. Further, the supports needed are intensive, such as providing full assistance when toileting.

The problem with AAMR's classification system is that it is extremely subjective. After all, what is the difference between the support that "normal" people need and the support required by people with "limited" mental retardation? I need help with my taxes each year; does that mean that I have intermittent mental retardation? What if you have somebody who needs lots of support in some areas, such as communication, but only a little support in other areas, such as recreational activities or learning? Would the person have both "extensive" mental retardation and "intermittent" mental retardation? Although AAMR's classification system is theoretically important in that it shifts the focus away from IQ and on to the needs of the person, it is impractical and rarely used.

Educable and Trainable

Another classification system uses the descriptors "educable" and "trainable" to categorize people with mental retardation. Specifically, people who

Table 2.3. IQ Ranges for Educable and Trainable Mental Retardation

Level of Mental Retardation	*IQ Range*
Educable Mental Retardation (EMR)	70 to 50
Trainable Mental Retardation (TMR)	Below 50

have IQs between 70 and 50 are often considered "educable mentally retarded" (EMR). People with IQs below 50 are sometimes considered "trainable mentally retarded" (TMR). See table 2.3. These systems fell out of favor in the late 1970s because it implies that some people can be "taught" while others are "trained" like dogs. Still, it is not uncommon for schools and professionals to still use these terms.

DIAGNOSING THE LEVELS OF MENTAL RETARDATION

Whether somebody has mild or profound, intermittent or pervasive, educable or trainable mental retardation, the assessment process that we discussed earlier remains the same. The only difference between various levels of mental retardation is when the diagnosis tends to take place. Specifically, the more severe the disability, the earlier it tends to be diagnosed.

As a total group, children with mental retardation are identified on average just before they reach their fifth birthday. Children with mild or borderline mental retardation, however, are identified several years later or, more specifically, at approximately ten and a half years old. Conversely, children with severe mental retardation are identified within two months after birth. Some genetic conditions resulting in mental retardation can even be identified before the child is actually born!

The disparity of ages at which mental retardation is diagnosed raises several important points. First of all, it underscores the diversity that exists within the population. There is such a *huge* difference between the functioning ability, and even the physical appearance, of people with mild mental retardation and those with profound mental retardation that it becomes difficult to talk about both extremes in one book.

Secondly, because children with mild mental retardation often appear to be "normal" kids, they often go undiagnosed for several years. Sometimes they never get diagnosed. Because they are identified later, students with mild mental retardation tend to struggle in school for several years prior to being assessed. As a result, when they finally enter special education, they are already well behind their peers.

You are probably sitting there wondering what each level means—or, more precisely, what characteristics individuals with various levels of mental retardation have—so that you will be able to get a general idea how mental retardation will affect your child or student. Don't worry. We will discuss that topic throughout chapter 5! So, keep reading!

SUMMARY

In this chapter, we talked about who can diagnose people with mental retardation, how the diagnosis is made, and what the various classification systems for mental retardation mean. Specifically, we discussed how you should have multiple people involved in the diagnostic process. This will lessen the chance that the results will be affected by personal bias. Further, people who give tests must be trained and experienced. Don't just let anybody administer assessments to your child. Ask about their background and training!

When children are diagnosed with mental retardation, they often are labeled with a "type" or "level" of mental retardation that denotes its severity. One of the most common ways to describe the severity of mental retardation is by the "mild to profound" approach. Using this approach, individuals with mild mental retardation are far more prevalent than individuals with profound mental retardation.

You are probably now wondering, "What causes mental retardation? Is it a genetic thing? Is it caused by lack of educational opportunity? Or by poor nutrition? Can it be prevented?" These are all excellent questions. Fortunately, they are the topics of our next chapter!

3

CAUSES OF MENTAL RETARDATION

GUIDED COMPREHENSION QUESTIONS

By the end of this chapter, you should be able to

1. Identify prenatal causes of mental retardation
2. Identify postnatal causes of mental retardation
3. Discuss issues related to the prevalence of mental retardation

INTRODUCTION

In the first chapter, we discussed what mental retardation is. In the second, we discussed how it is diagnosed and by whom. Now I want to turn our attention to what causes mental retardation as well as its prevalence within the general population.

Let me first begin by saying that I didn't want to write this chapter. In fact I kept going back and forth as to whether or not I should include it. After all, to me, the reason why a child has mental retardation is far less important than how parents and teachers prepare that child for life. However, at nearly every workshop that I hold, somebody always seems to ask me a version of the same question, "Did I cause my child to be mentally retarded?"

It is a gut-wrenching question with staggering ramifications. In the vast majority of the cases, I have to reply, "I don't know." That's because in approximately 80–90 percent of the cases, no specific cause can be identified.

Even in the remaining 10–20 percent of cases, the cause of mental retardation is rarely crystal clear. Yes, there are situations when we know that a child has a chromosomal condition or abnormality, such as with Fragile X and Down syndromes. But, as we will discuss in the next chapter, such instances account for a relatively small percentage of the overall prevalence rate of mental retardation.

Further, even with most chromosomal-related conditions, mental retardation is not guaranteed. Why do some children with Down syndrome, for example, develop severe mental retardation, while others develop only mild mental retardation or no mental retardation at all? In the vast majority of cases, we simply don't know.

What we *do* know is that there are numerous potential causes of mental retardation. Further, the more severe the mental retardation, the more likely that there are several causes interacting, including genetic factors. In fact, approximately 68 percent of children with severe mental retardation have chromosomal or genetic abnormalities, compared to about 11 percent of kids with mild mental retardation. Mild mental retardation is probably caused more by environmental or biohealth variables, such as exposure to toxins, lack of educational stimulation, or poor prenatal care. However, by and large, we rarely know *exactly* why an individual child has mental retardation.

I realize that probably doesn't make you feel any better. If you are like most parents, you probably want some definite answers as to why your child has mental retardation. But, usually, the answers simply aren't out there.

Although we cannot usually say for sure what causes mental retardation, we can often rule things out. For example, if your child was a full-term, normal-weight baby, we can rule out complications as the result of prematurity. And, if you never consumed alcohol or drugs while your were pregnant, we can rule out fetal alcohol syndrome (FAS) and fetal alcohol effects (FAE). So, let's do this. Let's talk about the various potential causes of mental retardation and go from there. Then you can see which ones may or may not apply in your particular situation.

To help us organize the many diverse causes of mental retardation, let's talk about them in relation to periods of human development. Specifically, I am going to categorize the potential causes of mental retardation into two groups. The first will involve prenatal factors, or factors that are present before the child is actually born. As you will see, these include inherited conditions and damage to the fetus's brain due to toxins or restricted blood flow. The second will involve postnatal factors, such as malnutrition, lack of educational opportunities, and severe illnesses.

But, before we begin discussing these two groups, I need to talk about something extremely important. You see, I know that a lot of parents consciously or unconsciously blame themselves for their child's disability. Further, I also know that these feelings of guilt can really devour a person and can cause an immense amount of stress and anxiety on the individual as well as on the family.

So, let me just say that, excluding a few conditions such as shaken baby or fetal alcohol syndromes, the chance of a parent directly causing mental retardation is extremely, *extremely* remote. As I said before, most causes of mental retardation are unknown. Further, most cases of mental retardation are probably caused by a number of interacting factors, not just something that a parent may or may not have done, such as had a cup of coffee or didn't take enough vitamins.

While I can't say with absolutely certainty, I am willing to bet that the average child with mental retardation probably has mental retardation simply because of a random set of events and elements just happened to fall into place. It is like winning the lottery or being struck by lightning. It is more or less just plain chance. So, again with the exceptions of shaken baby and fetal alcohol syndromes or a handful of other situations that we will discuss later, I can say with relative confidence that you did *not* cause your baby to have mental retardation!

Secondly, as I said at the beginning of this chapter, the cause of the mental retardation really isn't important. What is important is how parents and teachers deal with what fate has randomly generated. That is why I wrote this book. I wanted to help people make the most of the situation, not dwell upon the "whys." So, while we will discuss the etiology of mental retardation in this chapter, I want the emphasis of this book to be on how to help children with mental retardation live the best lives possible.

A LOOK AT THE OVERALL PREVALENCE OF MENTAL RETARDATION

It always amazes me how prevalent people perceive mental retardation to be. Earlier this semester, I asked my students to get out a piece a paper and write down what percent of the general population that they though had mental retardation. The highest response was 45%. The lowest was 0.00000001%. It was almost as if some of my students thought that nearly every other person was mentally retarded, whereas others thought that it is so rare that it is almost a myth, much like people getting attacked by Bigfoot or something.

Mental retardation isn't a myth. It exists in every town, in every state, and in every region of the United States. It exits in every country, although different countries call it different things. People with mental retardation can be found in every ethnicity, social strata, socioeconomic status, gender, sexual orientation, religion, political affiliation, and every demographic that you can think of. So how common is it?

While research studies differ in their findings, the generally accepted prevalence rate of mental retardation is between 1.5 to 2.5 percent of the general population. A few people will say it is 3 percent. But the most widely accepted number appears to be right around 2.14 percent.

Why the range? Well, as we discussed in first chapter, there isn't total agreement as to what mental retardation is; further, the definition keeps changing. So, it is difficult to ascertain exactly who has mental retardation and who doesn't. Moreover, each research study uses different methods, which could vary the results significantly.

Of course, we could just stop right there and accept the fact that approximately 2 out of every 100 children have subaverage IQs and poor adaptive skills. Or, I could tell you that approximately 7.1 million Americans have mental retardation. Or, that one in ten American families has a member with mental retardation. But there is a lot more to the story than that!

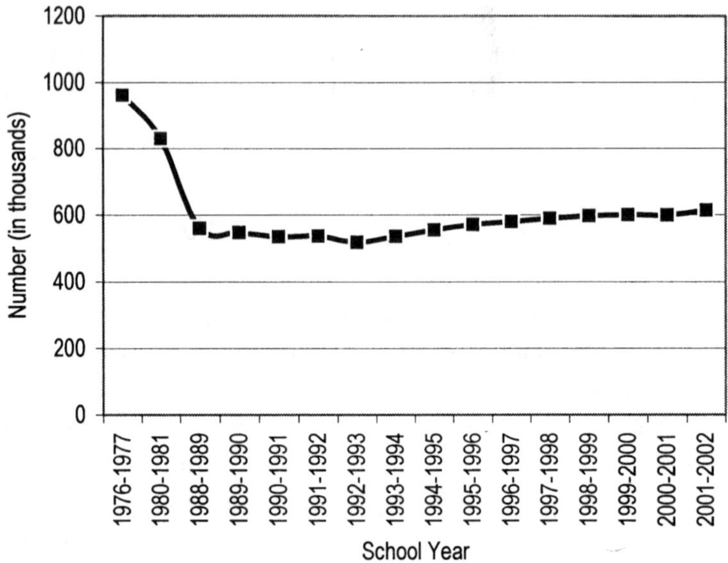

Figure 3.1. Number of Students in Special Education with Mental Retardation (1976–2002)

For instance, look at figure 3.1; it denotes the number of students with mental retardation who were served in special education programs across the United States from 1976 to 2002. Notice anything surprising?

You are probably thinking, "Wow! There were close to 1 million students with mental retardation in special education in 1976–1977! Then there is a huge drop in the 1980s followed by a gradual rise. Why? Did the overall population of children in special education decrease?"

No. Actually the number of children in special education has increased over the years. So, why was there that huge dip? The main reason is because learning disabilities became more popular; or to be more accurate, they became more publicized. You see, prior to the 1980s, learning disabilities, such as dysgraphia and dyslexia, existed. In fact, they probably existed at the same rate as they do today. However, in the 1980s, people became more aware of them.

How does this affect the number of kids with mental retardation? It is very simple. Having a child with a "learning disability" became far more acceptable than having a child with the stigmatizing diagnosis of "mental retardation." So, when children really had mild mental retardation, they were

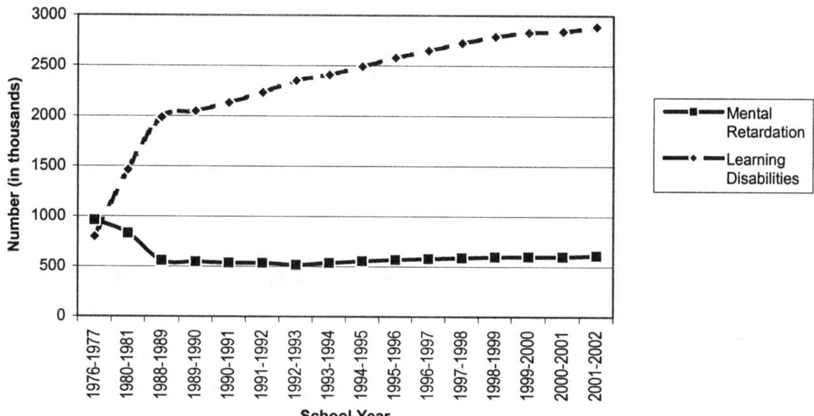

Figure 3.2. Number of Students in Special Education with Mental Retardation and Learning Disabilities (1976–2002)

frequently given the label of learning disabled. Don't believe me? Look at figure 3.2.

Look at the years 1980–1981 and 1988–1989. See where mental retardation takes a dramatic dip and where learning disabilities skyrocket? Kind of an amazing coincidence, eh?

When I was a schoolteacher, telling parents that their child was mentally retarded was probably the hardest thing that I had to do. Most parents took it extremely hard. It was like their perfect little boy or girl had died. Many parents openly broke down and cried.

Several of my colleagues would try to avoid causing this pain by telling parents that their child had a learning disability, rather than mental retardation. They would then say things like, "You know, the actor Tom Cruise has a learning disability. So does Cher and so did Albert Einstein!" The parents would be upset, of course. But they wouldn't feel as devastated as they would when we said "mental retardation," which they often perceive as a death sentence or something worse.

I should point out, just in case you don't know, learning disabilities and mental retardation are *not* related in the slightest. As we already covered, people with mental retardation have subaverage intelligence and poor adaptive skills. People with learning disabilities, however, can have any IQ. They can even be gifted, such as Einstein. Further, their adaptive skills can be superb.

While people think they are being kind by misdiagnosing kids with mental retardation, they are really doing more harm than good. Mental retardation and learning disabilities are completely different. Further, they require radically different types of educational interventions and programming.

Mislabeling a child who has mental retardation with a learning disability is like treating a cancer patient for asthma. Valuable time and energy are lost. And, when it comes to kids' education, time is of the essence. A month or a year or two years wasted means that that child will be that much further behind his or her peers.

I am sorry—I am on a soapbox. I am stepping off now. Still, it is a very important, and all too common, problem. Maybe my next book will be on learning disabilities. Because everybody seems to confuse the two conditions, I should call the book *Learning Disabilities Don't Mean "Mentally Retarded!"*

We will go into greater detail about the stigma of mental retardation later. For now, just understand how dirty a word "retarded" is. It has such a negative connotation, in fact, that the Wisconsin state government has gotten rid of it. Kids here are no longer diagnosed with mental retardation. They are now diagnosed with a "cognitive disabilities" (or "CD"). Unfortunately, because it affects a person's cognitive abilities, learning disabilities are also referred to as "cognitive disabilities" in some states. So, you can see how all of this becomes very confusing and political.

Even though children with mild and borderline mental retardation continue to be misclassified with learning disabilities, there has been a gradual increase of the incidence rate of mental retardation since the 1980s. Why? Well, there are two potential explanations.

First of all, technology and medical advances have saved many infants who would have died thirty, twenty, even ten or five years ago. Many of these children have disabilities, including severe mental retardation. So, in effect, these lifesaving technologies have increased the number of people who have lived long enough to be diagnosed with mental retardation.

Second, as required by law, teachers and school officials now have to actively look for kids with disabilities, so many more children with mild or less obvious conditions are being identified than in the 1970s. We'll talk about the law and mental retardation in chapter 8.

Mental Retardation and Ethnicity

It is difficult to discuss the prevalence of disabilities without taking about ethnicity, especially when the disability is mental retardation. That's because many people have claimed that a person's ethnicity is likely to influence whether somebody is diagnosed with mental retardation. In other words, if a child is a cultural minority, school personnel are far more likely to diagnose that child with mental retardation than if the child happens to be white.

There is a great deal of evidence to support this claim. Look at table 3.1. It lists various groups of disabilities that are served via special education. It also indicates what percent of those special education students are what ethnicity.

As you can see, of all the kids with mental retardation being served in the public schools across the United States, roughly 9.3 percent of them are white. An astounding 18.9 percent are African American! That is more than twice the number of white students!!!

Keep in mind that there are far more white Americans in the general population than African Americans. According to the latest census, whites comprise about 69.2 percent of Americans, while African Americans, Hispanics, Asian Americans, and Native American comprise about 12.1 percent, 12.6 percent, 3.7 percent, and 0.8 percent, respectively. So, one would think that there would be far more white children with mental retardation than African American children or Asian American children just because of there are simply more of them. But this isn't the case.

There are several plausible causes for this inequity. The first is that assessment devises, such as IQ tests, have long been criticized for being biased against nonwhites. These tests are likely to undervalue the intelligence of children from a minority background and thus increase the prevalence of mental retardation in those communities.

Another explanation could reside with the fact that various cultural minorities are more likely to live in poverty. Unfortunately, people living in poverty have children with mental retardation at higher rates than do more affluent people. We will discuss the economic causes of mental retardation later in this chapter.

A third explanation for the disproportioned number of children with mental retardation among cultural minorities is that different cultures have

Table 3.1. Percentage of Special Education Students with Various Disabilities by Ethnicity

Disability	*African American*	*Asian American*	*Caucasian American*	*Hispanic American*	*Native American*	*All Students in Special Education*
Learning Disabilities	45.2	43.2	48.9	60.3	56.3	50.0%
Communication Disorders	15.1	25.2	20.8	17.3	17.1	18.9%
MENTAL RETARDATION	**18.9**	**10.1**	**9.3**	**8.6**	**8.5**	**10.6%**
Emotional Disturbances	10.7	5.3	8.0	4.5	7.5	8.2%
Other Health Impairments	3.7	3.9	5.9	2.8	4.1	5.1%
Multiple Disabilities	1.9	2.3	1.8	1.8	2.5	2.1%
Autism	1.2	3.4	1.4	0.9	0.6	1.4%
Orthopedic Impairments	0.9	2.0	1.4	1.4	0.8	1.3%
Hearing Impairments	1.0	2.9	1.2	1.5	1.1	1.2%
Developmental Delay	0.7	0.6	0.6	0.2	0.7	0.5%
Visual Impairments	0.4	0.8	0.5	0.5	0.4	0.4%
Traumatic Brain Injury	0.2	0.3	0.3	0.2	0.3	0.3%
ALL DISABILITIES SERVED VIA SPECIAL EDUCATION	100%	100%	100%	100%	100%	100%

different perspectives of what disabilities mean. For example, if a culture views a disability as being a sin or a punishment from God or a curse, members of that culture might not be inclined to have their child tested for a disability. They might also disagree with any findings that suggest their child is anything but perfectly normal. Conversely, people from cultures that are more open to receiving help and working with special education programs may be more liable to get their child assessed or agree with diagnoses.

Of course, there are certain conditions associated with mental retardation that occur mainly in specific populations. For example, Tay-Sachs disease is a condition that leads to mental retardation and is predominately found in Ashkenazic Jewish families. Likewise, sickle cell anemia is more common in families of African descent. So, it could be that the variable rates of mental retardation among various cultural minority groups are caused by genetic factors.

Although the ultimate reason for the disproportionate number of African Americans with mental retardation probably involves all of these variables, we must still be aware of the effects from this overidentification. Many families might not completely trust the assessment process or the interpretation of the findings, and rightfully so. It is for this reason that I strongly recommend that all parents, regardless of their ethnicity or socioeconomic status, or whatever, get involved in the assessment process. Ask questions. Ask to have all testing videotaped so that you can watch the proceedings. And, above all, if you have even the slightest doubts about the outcome, get a second opinion!

Mental Retardation and Economic Standing

Just as with ethnicity, there is a great deal of controversy surrounding the association between mental retardation and socioeconomic status. As you can see from table 3.2, the majority of children in special education who have mental retardation come from families making $25,000 or less a year. Only about 18 percent of students with mental retardation come from families making more than $50,000 a year.

As with ethnicity, there are a number of reasons for this disparity. First, poor families often do not have access or partake in pre- or postnatal care. As

Table 3.2. Percentage of Children with Disabilities by Household Income

	Annual Household Income	
Disability	*<$25,000*	*$25,000+*
Learning Disabilities	31.0%	37.9%
Communication Disorders	25.6%	43.2%
MENTAL RETARDATION	**54.4%**	**18.2%**
Emotional Disturbances	42.8%	27.9%
Other Health Impairments	23.7%	45.0%
Multiple Disabilities	34.8%	35.8%
Orthopedic Impairments	30.2%	38.9%
Hearing Impairments	30.7%	40.3%
Visual Impairments	29.6%	35.8%

a result, many of their children suffer from otherwise preventable conditions, such as low birth weight or prematurity. Many of these conditions result in mental retardation.

Secondly, families in lower socioeconomic strata often live in neighborhoods with older homes. These older homes are likely to have lead-based paint or other toxins that can, if ingested, cause mental retardation. Poor neighborhoods also often lack educational resources, such as libraries and museums. Further, the resources that they have, including their public schools, are typically underfunded and inadequate.

Finally, there are legitimate concerns that children of affluent families are treated differently by school districts than are other children. Specifically, critics have indicated that children from wealthy families who have IQs within the mild mental retardation range are more likely to be diagnosed with a learning disability than a child from a poorer family. As we discussed earlier, there is no association between mental retardation and learning disabilities; however, teachers often will mislabel children on purpose because a learning disability has less of a stigma than mental retardation.

I should point out that mental retardation exists across all cultural and socioeconomic classifications. All cultures have children with mental retardation. So too do the richest and poorest families. Still, one cannot over look the strong associations between some groups of people and the prevalence of mental retardation.

"But what actually *causes* mental retardation?" you might be asking yourself. This is a difficult question to answer, but we will attempt to do so in the next few pages!

PRENATAL CAUSE OF MENTAL RETARDATION

Although there are certainly individuals who were born perfectly normal but developed mental retardation later in early childhood, these cases are thought to be a small portion of the total prevalence of mental retardation. Most children have mental retardation as the result of prenatal causes and are thus born with it (although they might not be diagnosed until they get well into childhood or adolescence).

Some experts believe that the first nine weeks of pregnancy is the most crucial. This is when key parts of the brain are forming. It is also when embryos and fetuses are most vulnerable to environmental influences, such as secondhand smoke or the consumption of alcohol.

There are so many prenatal factors that *might* lead to mental retardation that it would be impossible to cover them all. However, I think that we should talk about at least two general types. Specifically, I want to discuss genetic causes of mental retardation and then nongenetic factors that result in damage to a fetus's brain.

Genetic Causes of Mental Retardation

Recent research has identified over 250 genetic causes of mental retardation. The majority of these can be placed into two categories. The first is when the genetic material that the mother and father are passing on to the child becomes damaged. In other words, the child's otherwise normal chromosomes develop abnormally. In such cases, the child may have several disabilities of varying severity, depending upon which chromosome is damaged and to what extent. As we will discuss in later sections, Fragile X syndrome is an example of this type of genetic cause.

The second group of genetic causes of mental retardation involves conditions that are inherited directly from the biological parents. In such cases, the genetic material is passed to the child without incident; that is, the chromosomes are not actually damaged. Rather, they contain DNA that leads to certain conditions, such as Down syndrome, that often result in mental retardation.

Causes of Mental Retardation from Fetal Brain Damage

In addition to genetics, many individuals develop mental retardation as a result to damage to their brain. Most people seem to think brain damage can only occur as the result of a fall or a blow to a head, such as during an automobile accident or taking a tumble down some steep stairs. While those can certainly cause cognitive impairments, there are other, far more common, sources of brain damage that result in mental retardation.

In this section, I want to talk about some ways damage is done to a fetus's developing brain that causes mental retardation. Please keep in mind that the factors that we will be discussing don't *always* result in mental retardation. For instance, although expecting mothers who smoke increase the likelihood that their child will have mental retardation, not every child born to smoking mothers will be mentally retarded. In other words, many of the factors that we are about to discuss are not definitive causes of mental retardation, but contribute to the likelihood that a child will have difficulty learning. The factors that we are going to be discussing include

- Prematurity and low birth weight
- Anoxia
- Illnesses
- Drugs, alcohol, cigarettes, and other toxins
- Age of the mother and number of children

Prematurity and Low Birth Weight

Two of the leading causes of prenatal brain damage and, thus mental retardation, are prematurity and low birth weight. Generally speaking, the average child is in the womb for forty weeks, or 280 days, and will weigh between 3,000 to 4,000 grams at birth. Again, these are estimates. Some children are a little early or late or light or heavy. Not to brag, or anything, but I was actually a little bigger than 4,200 grams! Moreover, my nephew was actually more than two weeks late and was finally "induced" to come out of the womb!

Approximately 10 percent of all live births are either premature or low birth weight. Of these, roughly 30 percent will have mental retardation or some other disability, such as cerebral palsy. In comparison, only 2 percent of full-term and appropriate-weight babies will be mentally retarded.

Birth weight and gestation period typically go hand in hand, but not always. It is very possible to have a full-term baby who has low birth weight. Multiple births, such as twins or triplets, are common examples of this. When twins or triplets are born, they are usually very small—even though they were in the womb for the standard forty weeks.

Further, some children can reach 3,000 grams and are born prior to the fortieth week. My niece was 3,234 grams and was born nearly two weeks early. She is perfectly fine and doesn't have mental retardation.

There are many reasons why a child might be born early or with a low birth weight. For instance, first pregnancies are 23 percent more likely to result in a child who is either premature or has a low birth weight than subsequent births. Moreover, children born to young mothers, that is, mothers under twenty years old, are between ten and fifteen times more likely than older mothers to have a child who is either premature or have low birth weight.

Women who smoke during, or prior to, pregnancy are even *more* prone to having small or premature children. One study found that children born to mothers who smoked while pregnant were twenty times more likely to be underweight than children of nonsmokers. Another study suggested that mothers who smoke while pregnant more than double the chances that their child will have a disability.

Of course, the mother's diet and nutrition is obviously going to be a factor that contributes to the health of the baby. Many people simply assume that mothers need to gain a lot of weight when pregnant. However, they don't realize that there is a "quality" aspect of the weight that they gain. For example, expecting mothers who are obese are far more likely to have children with disabilities than are mothers of an appropriate weight. The same is true for women who are anorexic. Their children are also at risk for developing learning problems, physical abnormalities, and behavioral issues.

Anoxia

In addition to being of low birth weight or premature, fetuses can also develop brain damage from the lack of oxygen. This is called anoxia, and it usually occurs when the umbilical cord gets pinched closed, thus cutting off or reducing the blood flow to the fetus. Sometimes, the cord gets wrapped around the fetus's neck or body, restricting the blood supply that way.

There are now ways of detecting and correcting such problems. Often, if a child is in danger of being harmed, doctors can perform a cesarean section and deliver the baby early. Procedures can also be performed that would untangle the fetus and allow it to remain in uterus.

Illnesses

Another potential cause for fetal brain damage resulting in mental retardation is maternal illness. For example, when pregnant woman contract rubella, or German measles, the prenatal development of their child's brain can be adversely affected. The same is true if the mother contracts various sexually transmitted diseases, such as syphilis and herpes simplex. Even getting the flu or a common cold could adversely affect the development of an unborn child. High fevers are especially dangerous for the unborn. So, the importance of an expecting mother to remain healthy cannot be understated!

Drugs, Alcohol, Cigarettes, and Other Toxins

The most common cause of brain damage to a fetus appears to result from exposure to toxins, including the consumption of drugs or alcohol. A recent press release indicated that as many as 2 out of every 1,000 children who have mental retardation are the result of their mothers consuming drugs and alcohol when they were pregnant. Unfortunately, this number is rising.

But it isn't just an issue involving women. There is growing evidence suggesting that prolonged drug and alcohol use by fathers can damage sperm and, thus, also cause mental retardation. If you don't know much about fetal alcohol syndrome (FAS) and fetal alcohol effects (FAE), don't worry. We will be discussed that topic in the next chapter.

Alcohol and illegal drugs aren't the only toxins that can harm a growing fetus. There are many common chemicals that can be very toxic to the unborn. For example, women shouldn't paint or use certain household cleaners when they are pregnant. When they inhale the fumes, so does their baby. If the baby's room needs to be cleaned and decorated, have somebody other than the expecting mother do it!

Age of the Mother and Number of Children

We already talked about this as it applies to prematurity and low birth weight, but the age of the mother influences the chances of having a child with mental retardation in other ways. For instance, as prospective mothers become older, the prospects of passing on faulty genetic material or abnormalities increase. Down syndrome is a good example of this.

The chance of a mother below the age of thirty having a child with Down syndrome is about 1 out of 1,000, or 0.1 percent. This chance increases to 1 out of 400 once the mother turns thirty-five, or 0.25 percent. And it further increases to 1 out of 105 once the mother is forty years old. See table 3.3.

In addition to age, the chance of having children with mental retardation increases after each child. For example, if a mother below the age of thirty-six

Table 3.3. Chances of Having a Child with Down Syndrome by Maternal Age

Age of Mother (at conception)	*Chance of Having a Child with DownSyndrome*
<30 years old	1 in 1,000
30 years old	1 in 900
35 years old	1 in 400
36 years old	1 in 300
37 years old	1 in 250
38 years old	1 in 180
39 years old	1 in 135
40 years old	1 in 105
42 years old	1 in 60
43 years old	1 in 50
44 years old	1 in 35
46 years old	1 in 20
48 years old	1 in 16
49 years old	1 in 12
50 years old	1 in 10

already has a child with Down syndrome, the chance of her having a second child with Down syndrome is roughly 1 in 100. A woman in her forties who already had a child with Down syndrome increases her chance of having a second to about 1 in 50.

Summary

There are many more factors that increase the risk that a fetus's brain will become damaged or not develop properly. We talked about many of these, but certainly not all. Moreover, as we discussed earlier, these factors aren't a perfect predictor of the future. Not every child born to an anorexic mother who smokes and does illegal drugs will be mentally retarded. However, she is simply *more* prone to having children with mental retardation than the general population.

Now you are probably asking yourself a whole bunch of questions, such as: "How much weight is an appropriate amount to gain while being pregnant?" "I heard that it is actually good to drink a glass of red wine when pregnant. Is that true?" "Will exercising while I am pregnant increase my risks of having a child with mental retardation?" "Can legal drugs, like aspirin or cold medications, cause mental retardation?"

These are all wonderful questions, but the truth is they shouldn't be answered in a book. If you have these questions, ask your doctor. Every situation is different, and your doctor should have a better understanding of your risk factors than any author who has never met you.

Actually, that raises a very good topic for discussion. If you are pregnant, get a doctor whom you trust. Make sure she or he is well informed and is willing to answer all of your questions as fully as you like. Also, if you hear about a new "fad" and want to check it out, ask your doctor for articles or medical studies. In short, be as informed as possible and do what you can to minimize your own personal risks for having a baby with mental retardation.

POSTNATAL CAUSES OF MENTAL RETARDATION

In addition to being born with mental retardation, people can "develop" it later on in life. Although, as we said in the first chapter, in order for poor adaptive skills and subaverage intelligence to be considered mental retardation, it must be apparent by age eighteen—so it isn't likely a ninety-year-old man could become mentally retarded. If he developed subaverage intelligence and poor adaptive skills, he would probably be experiencing senility or Alzheimer's.

Still, it is very possible that an otherwise normal and healthy infant can become mentally retarded. Further, as with fetal alcohol syndrome and fetal alcohol effects, many of the postnatal causes of mental retardation can be prevented through appropriate health care and education.

Shaken Baby Syndrome

Among the preventable postnatal cause of mental retardation is shaken baby syndrome. Shaken baby syndrome is a term describing trauma to a child's brain from vigorous shaking. You see, our brains aren't attached to our heads. They are connected to the spinal column, of course. But they aren't tethered to the skull. There aren't any shock absorbers inside our noggins. So, when our heads suddenly go in one direction, such as when we are in a car accident, our brains rush in that direction and then slam into our skull. This can cause damage to the part of the brain that makes contact.

You and I can wing our heads around without a problem. We can ride in roller coasters where our heads thrash from side to side and will be perfectly fine. Infants, however, are another story. They are very fragile, and their brains can be easily damaged. So too can their necks. In fact, in addition to mental retardation, another symptom of shaken baby syndrome is also paralysis. Hearing difficulties and vision loss are also common.

Please don't think that only child abusers cause shaken baby syndrome. They certainly are a leading cause. But so too are accidental acts, such as playing rough with a child. As a matter of fact, a few years ago, there was a recall of an infant's rocking chair—you know the ones where you put the child in a little seat, crank the handle, and the seat rocks back and forth. Apparently this particular brand rocked too fast and had a jerky motion that caused injury to infants who were placed in it.

Also, please don't think that shaken baby syndrome is a rare phenomenon. A recent article stated that 50,000 cases are reported *each* year in the United States. Further, one in four of these babies dies. Of the survivors, approximately 80 percent will develop pervasive disabilities, including mental retardation, cerebral palsy, and seizure disorders.

I also want to point out that perpetrators of shaken baby syndrome can be found in every cultural group, socioeconomic status, and strata of educational attainment. However, perpetrators tend to be males in their early twenties and are usually the child's father or boyfriend of the mother. Females who injure babies tend to be young babysitters or childcare providers.

Perhaps I am preaching to the choir, but *never* shake or play rough with an infant. Their brains and bodies are very fragile, and even the smallest accident can have lifelong implications. If your baby is crying and you get frustrated—stop, calm down, and try again.

Traumatic Brain Injuries

Not all brain injuries that cause mental retardation are the result of shaking. Kids can fall down and hurt themselves all of the time. I fell on a stick once and nearly poked my eye out; I still have the scar. But I was fortunate.

One of my students was apparently a very normal child, but she fell down, hit her head on the corner of a chair, and developed seizures. A few months later, the parents started to see that she wasn't "quite the same." She was later diagnosed with mental retardation.

Keep in mind that mental retardation must occur before age eighteen. So, an adult who falls down or gets hit in the head will not develop mental retardation. They would be labeled with TBI (traumatic brain injury), which may produce results identical to mental retardation, depending upon the nature of the injury.

Still, it is very possible for mental retardation to be caused by trauma to the brain from an external force. At the very least, hopefully this makes you appreciate how fragile your life is. We are all a slip in the bathtub or a tumble down the stairs away from having cognitive and adaptive problems similar to mental retardation.

Uncontrolled Seizures

Several of my other students probably had mental retardation because of uncontrolled seizures. You see, in overly simple terms, our bodies are big bags of water with a vast network of wires (i.e., nerves) through which electricity shoots from place to place. A seizure is when the wires kind of short-circuit and the electricity goes where it shouldn't.

When you think of seizures, you probably picture somebody flopping around on the floor, foaming at the mouth, and urinating on himself. This is known as a tonic-clonic, or grand mal, seizure. Although it is a very common type of seizure, it is not the only variety.

For example, there's something called absence, or petit mal, seizures. People having absence seizures don't convulse on the floor. They stare off into space for a few seconds, often blinking frequently, and then return to normal. People experiencing absence seizures appear to be daydreaming and will not realize that anything has happened to them.

Regardless of the type of seizure, people's brains can become severely damaged if the seizures go on too long. Again, seizures are like electrical storms. The wayward electricity can "burn out" the surrounding neural pathways. So, if the seizures are occurring in the part of the brain controlling high-order reasoning or speech, that area can be permanently damaged. The person might actually lose previously acquired skills or abilities, such as the ability to smell or recall information. They can even fall into a vegetative-like state.

The scary thing about seizures is that parents frequently do not realize that their child is having them. The child could have seizures for hours in the middle of the night and nobody would know. Or, the child could have less apparent seizures, such as absence or focal-motor seizures. I'll give you an example.

I lived next door to a little eight-year-old girl named Chloe who kept wetting her bed. Her parents were embarrassed about it, so they never told anybody. After several months of hoping that it was just a passing phase, they eventually brought their daughter to the doctor, who recommended some behavior modification strategies. But they didn't help. She kept wetting the bed every few days or so.

The parents then thought that Chloe had some "unresolved" psychological issues, so they brought her to a child psychologist who did "in-depth analysis." But the psychologist couldn't pinpoint anything in particular. Chloe appeared to be healthy and well adjusted, although extremely ashamed over ruining so many sheets and mattresses.

To make a long story short, after nearly a year of therapy and counseling, the parents realized that Chloe was having chronic seizures nearly every night. She would go to sleep, have a seizure, urinate in her bed, and then come to. Neither the parents nor Chloe knew what was happening until the mother noticed that Chloe was lying in her bed, stiff like a board. When they mentioned this to a doctor, the doctor ordered an EEG and determined what was happening.

Thankfully, Chloe seems unaffected. She is a bright, cheerful little girl. However, she is lucky. The seizures are now controlled by medication. She could have easily continued having seizures for many years as her brain slowly damaged itself.

Toxins

In addition to chronic seizures, children can develop mental retardation as the result of being exposed to various toxins and environmental pollutants. Of these, lead and mercury poisoning are probably the most common. Lead is particularly problematic because years of using leaded gasoline have polluted our environment. It is everywhere. It can be found in old toys, pottery, batteries, some paints, contaminated ground water, and many older homes. It is so pervasive, in fact, that approximately 16 percent of children living in cities of over one million inhabitances have elevated lead level in their blood. A list of common symptoms of lead poisoning in children includes:

- Decrease appetite
- Stomachache
- Sleeplessness or restless sleep
- Decreased coordination
- Tremors and/or convulsions
- Weakness
- Difficulty concentrating
- Confusion
- Diminished ability to learn
- Diarrhea and/or constipation
- Fatigue
- Change in behavior
- Joint pain
- Visual impairments
- Failure to grow and gain weight at a normal rate
- Hallucinations
- Agitation

Mercury is another toxin that could produce mental retardation in previously normal children. In fact, there is substantial evidence suggesting that mercury poisoning may be one of the causes of autism and autism-like disorders.

Mercury can be found in adhesives, air conditioners, cosmetics, dental fillings, fabric softener, polishes, laxatives, paints, seafood, wood preservatives, and many more things. Mercury contamination is a particular problem in the town in which I live. For years, paper mills upriver dumped mercury into the water supply. Now there are signs posted by the docks warning people not to eat too much catfish and other bottom-feeding animals. Unfortunately, and perhaps coincidentally, the area in which I live has a higher rate of autism than any other place in North America. (See below for common symptoms associated with mercury poisoning.)

- Agitation Abdominal pain
- Vomiting
- Gastritis
- Colitis
- Excessive salivation
- Headaches
- Mood swings
- Depression and/or anxiety
- Bad breath
- Chronic fatigue and irritability
- Irritability and aggression
- Impaired face recognition
- Impulsivity
- Hyperactivity
- Stereotypic movements, such as hand flapping or rocking
- Deficits in hand-eye coordination
- Dizziness
- Clumsiness
- Loss or failure to develop speech
- Social deficits, such as shyness, withdrawal, or lack of eye contact

Fortunately, there are cheap and effective tests that can detect lead and mercury, both in your home as well as in a child's body. If you suspect that your child has either lead or mercury poisoning, please contact your doctor.

Poor Nutrition and Health Care

Other preventable postnatal causes of mental retardation are poor nutrition and health care. A person's brain keeps growing and developing well into their adolescence. Just as a baby's brain can be damaged by vigorous shaking, its development can be severely impaired by improper diet and illnesses.

This isn't to say that if you give your child a Twinkie, of if she gets the sniffles, that she is going to become mentally retarded! It doesn't work that way.

Think of children like fine, expensive automobiles. They need the proper gasoline and routine tune-ups in order to operate effectively. If children are habitually given nothing but the wrong things to eat (such as junk food), or not enough food, their bodies cannot develop adequately. Further, if they are not taken care of when they are sick, slight illnesses can become major infirmities. Again, I am not saying that a little cold or fever can cause mental retardation. But a prolonged period of excessive fever as well as chronic infections can.

Lack of Stimulation

Perhaps the most preventable postnatal cause of mental retardation is a lack of a stimulating environment. This particular cause sickens me, even as much as shaken baby and fetal alcohol syndromes. By not teaching and providing stimulating environments, we can create mental retardation in any child. I'll give you a very sad example.

When I was in college, I was sitting in my yard, sunbathing and reading a book. As I was reading, a little boy walked right up to me. I thought that this was strange because I didn't know him and he was pretty young, probably three or four years old. Moreover, there weren't any adults with him. He was by himself, and I lived on a pretty busy street.

At any rate, he asked me what I was doing. I explained that I was relaxing. He then pointed to the book and asked, "What's that?"

"It's a book," I replied rather startled.

He then climbed into my lap and took the book from my hands. Picking it up so that a cover was in each hand and the pages were pointed down, he started to blow on the pages so that they swayed back and forth. After a few seconds, he got up, dropped the book, and said, "That's stupid!" He then walked away.

It was almost as if he had never seen a book before! When I told that story in class a couple days later, the professor told me how that was not uncommon. Apparently, many students, especially those from an economically deprived background, see their first book when they enter school. I remember he even quoted some research saying that the further somebody lived from a public library, the more likely that person was to have mental retardation.

I haven't seen that research, so I don't know if it is true or not. Still, it makes sense. No matter how exceptional a child's brain is, it will not fill itself with much knowledge without help. That is why educators encourage parents to read to their children, even at very young ages. Parents should also encourage make-believe play and asking questions. The more stimulation that a child gets, the better off he or she will be. Learning, after all, is an action and it must be taught!

PREVENTING MENTAL RETARDATION

Preventing the preventable cases of mental retardation requires little more than common sense. Basically, people just have to take care of their baby before and after it is born. This means mothers should get regular prenatal examinations, eat well, and not expose the baby to any risk factors, such as cigarette smoke, drugs, alcohol, or other toxins. Mothers should also keep themselves healthy. What affects the expecting mother affects the unborn child. Other ways of reducing the risk of having a baby with mental retardation include:

- Don't smoke, drink, or take illegal drugs before or during pregnancy.
- Don't take over-the-counter or prescription medications if pregnant, without consulting a doctor.
- Don't expose pregnant mothers to potential toxins.
- Ensure regular pre- and postnatal health care.
- Children and expecting mothers should have well-balanced diets.
- Expecting mothers should gain an appropriate amount of weight.
- Provide children with stimulating and educational environments.

There are now many medical tests that can determine if potential parents are carriers for genetic abnormalities. Moreover, there are tests, such as an amniocentesis, that can tell if the unborn has a disability associated with mental retardation. We'll talk about some of these conditions in the next chapter.

SUMMARY

Hopefully this chapter has given you some answers as to what may or may not have caused your child to have mental retardation. As I said in the beginning, in most cases, we just don't know. This is especially true when a child has mild mental retardation. In such cases, the etiology of the disability could range from exposure to environmental variables, such as lead or mercury, to willful acts of child abuse, such as shaken baby or fetal alcohol syndrome, to inadequate nutrition, health care, or educational opportunity.

The more severe the mental retardation, the more likely it is probably caused by several interacting factors. Further, the more severe the mental retardation, the more likely a genetic component is coming into play.

4

CONDITIONS ASSOCIATED WITH MENTAL RETARDATION

GUIDED COMPREHENSION QUESTIONS

By the time you complete this chapter, you should be able to:

1. Name several conditions associated with mental retardation
2. Describe the general characteristics of those conditions

INTRODUCTION

In previous chapters, we talked about what mental retardation is, how it is diagnosed, and what causes it. Now I want to focus on several conditions that are *associated with* mental retardation. Notice that I stressed the words "associated with." We will be talking about many conditions that are often linked with mental retardation, but that does not mean that people with these conditions *have to have* mental retardation. For example, people with Down syndrome and autism are all at risk for having varying degrees of mental retardation. But they are also able to have perfectly normal, as well as above-average, intelligence.

When possible, I will try to denote the chances somebody with the conditions will also have mental retardation. However, keep in mind that these numbers are, at best, just "guesstimates." Statistics vary from research study to research study, so exact numbers are impossible to report. In some cases, I simply will not report any statistics since no two experts seem to agree upon them.

Also keep in mind that we will be talking about each condition in very general terms. When I discuss symptoms or causes, remember that there is a great deal of variation within each condition. One person with Aicardi syndrome, for instance, might develop microphthalmia, or have extremely small eyes. Other people with Aicardi syndrome, on the other hand, might have eyes of normal size.

Differences between my descriptions and your experiences will become increasingly problematic when conditions have several subtypes. For example, there are many different types of cerebral palsy. Some people with cerebral palsy have atonic muscles; that is, their muscles flop around like they don't have any bones. Other people have spastic cerebral palsy, where their muscles are frozen as if turned to stone.

Unfortunately, we can't discuss all of the various subtypes of each condition within this chapter. Instead, I will talk about characteristics that are more or less common among people with each condition.

Also, you might get a bit confused because several conditions have different names. For instance, Angelman syndrome is also known as Happy Puppet syndrome. And Fragile X syndrome is often called both Marker X syndrome and Martin-Bell syndrome. I will do my best to utilize the most common of these names as well as indicate alternatives that might be used.

When possible, I have listed support groups, websites, and additional resources relating to each condition in the last section of the book. These should help you learn additional information.

In this chapter we will be discussing:

- Aarskog syndrome
- Acrodysostosis
- Aicardi syndrome
- Angelman syndrome
- Autism
- Bourneville-Pringle syndrome
- Cat cry syndrome
- Childhood disintegrative disorder
- Cerebral palsy

- Down syndrome
- Fetal alcohol effects
- Fetal alcohol syndrome
- Fragile X syndrome
- Galactosemia
- Gorlin syndrome
- Hunter syndrome
- Hurler syndrome
- Hydrocephaly
- Klinefelter syndrome
- Lesch-Nyhan syndrome
- Microcephaly
- Noonan syndrome
- Phenylketonuria
- Prader-Willi syndrome
- Rett syndrome
- Rubinstein syndrome
- Sanfilippo syndrome
- Tay-Sachs disease
- Trisomy 13
- Trisomy 18
- Turner syndrome
- Williams syndrome

AARSKOG SYNDROME

Aarskog syndrome (a.k.a. Aarskog-Scott syndrome, ASS, Greig syndrome, facial-digital-genital syndrome) is an inherited condition caused by a recessive, mutated gene on the X chromosome. It is characterized by facial, musculoskeletal, and genital abnormalities. Specifically, people who have Aarskog syndrome tend to have round faces with wide-set, downward slanting eyes and sagging eyelids. The tops of their ears flop over slightly and their hairline recedes into a widow's peak.

People with Aarskog syndrome typically have unusually small, yet very broad, hands and feet. Their toes and fingers can be short and webbed up to the middle joint. Their little fingers tend to be hooked inward like a bird's claw. They also are likely to have severely misaligned teeth that will require orthodontic work.

Approximately 30 percent of children with Aarskog syndrome have mild to moderate mental retardation, with boys tending to be more severely affected than girls. Boys are also likely to be sterile. Both genders commonly experience chronic seizures.

Aarskog is usually evident by the time a child is three years old. Genetic screening can identify the mutated gene prior to the child's birth. Further, x-rays can reveal skeletal abnormalities associated with this condition once the child is born.

- Also known as Aarskog-Scott syndrome, ASS, Greig syndrome, facial-digital-genital syndrome
- Common characteristics include round face, short stature, widow's peak hairline, wide-set, downward slanting eyes, and chronic seizures
- Boys tend to be more affected than girls
- 30 percent of individuals have mild to moderate mental retardation

ACRODYSOSTOSIS

Also known as Arkless-Graham syndrome, acrodysplasia, and Maroteaux-Malamut syndrome, acrodysostosis is a congenital condition typically passed on to children by parents who were above the age of thirty-five at the time of conception. Individuals with acrodysostosis develop skeletal deformities, including progressive deterioration of the spine as well as pervasive arthritis and carpal tunnel syndrome. Consequently, as they get older, their range of motion in their backs, arms, legs, and hands will diminish.

Individuals with acrodysostosis tend to be very short in stature, have widely spaced eyes, short heads with protruding jaws, broad flat noses, and abnormal dental development. Approximately two-thirds will experience recurring middle ear infections that result in significant hearing loss. Over 80 percent of individuals with acrodysostosis will also have varying degrees of mental retardation.

- Also known as Arkless-Graham syndrome, acrodysplasia, and Maroteaux-Malamut syndrome
- Common characteristics include mild to moderate growth deficiency, hearing impairments in approximately two-thirds of cases, widely spaced eyes, protruding jaw, irregularly shaped head, short arms and legs with deformed hands and feet
- Approximately 80 percent of individuals with acrodysostosis also have mental retardation

AICARDI SYNDROME

Aicardi syndrome is a rare condition where the corpus callosum, which connects the right and left hemispheres of the brain, is at least partially absent.

Individuals with this condition experience spastic-like movements, abnormal brain development, and frequent seizures. They are also likely to have lesions on the retina, causing various vision impairments. Diagnosis usually occurs prior to five months of age.

There are fewer than 1,000 cases of Aicardi syndrome worldwide, but the prevalence rate appears to be increasing. It is thought to be genetic and carried on the X chromosome. Profound mental retardation is probable. Communication and motor skills are likely to be appreciably underdeveloped. Unfortunately, life expectancy is approximately thirty years; however, existing data is rather limited, so this figure might be inaccurate.

- Absence of the corpus callosum (the connection between the two hemispheres of the brain)
- Common characteristics include seizures, lesions of the retina, nonverbal, nonambulatory
- Tend to be female
- Profound mental retardation is probable
- Life expectancy of about thirty years
- Rare; fewer than 1,000 reported cases

ANGELMAN SYNDROME

Identified by Dr. Harold Angelman in 1965, Angelman syndrome is a neurological condition inherited from the biological mother that affects about 1 out of every 25,000 people. Because individuals with Angelman syndrome have large, protruding tongues and experience prolonged bouts of laughter accompanied by floppy hand movements, it is often referred to as Happy Puppet syndrome. I know it sounds as if I am making that up, but I am not. Basically, individuals with Angelman syndrome are said to look like a marionette jiggling up and down laughing, hence the Happy Puppet reference.

At first, newborns with Angelman syndrome appear perfectly normal. However, at around two months of age, they begin to experience difficulties feeding. Within a year, children exhibit developmental delays and by three years they are likely to have reoccurring seizures.

By early childhood, individuals with Angelman syndrome have significant deficits in verbal communication. They also tend to be hyperactive as well as have poor motor control, causing them to have difficulty sitting up and balancing. Moderate to severe mental retardation is common.

- Also known as Happy Puppet syndrome
- Common characteristics include small heads that tend to be flat on top, protruding tongues, jerky movements of the hands and arms, prolonged periods of laughter, motor deficits (particularly in regard to balance), and profound speech impairments
- Moderate to severe mental retardation is likely
- 1 out of every 25,000 children have Angelman syndrome

AUTISM

If you have ever seen the movie *Rainman*, you probably think that you understand what autism is. However, very few people can truly say that they know much about it. That is because, although frequently portrayed in the popular media, there are still many misconceptions about the condition.

For example, autism is not one condition, but an entire host of related conditions often referred to collectively as autism spectrum disorder or pervasive developmental delay (PDD). In fact, if you put one hundred people who have been labeled with autism in a room, each of them probably would have remarkably different symptoms and degrees of functioning. Some might have profound mental retardation; others can be cognitively gifted.

Generally speaking, the defining characteristics of autism are difficulty with verbal and nonverbal communication. Further, children with autism have problems socializing and do not engage in imaginary play like other children do. They also display unusual, repetitive behaviors such a rocking back and forth, hand wringing, and flapping their fingers in front of their eyes. Other common characteristics include a reluctance to be touched, sensitivity to light and sound, "parroting" what they have heard (or echolalia), and obsessive attachments to routines or objects. These obsessive attachments can be so strong that they can become physically aggressive when their routines change or the object is not within sight.

Please realize that these symptoms do not just suddenly develop in older children or adults. They must be present by age three. This is not to say that children cannot be diagnosed later on in life; they can. However, their symptoms must be evident prior to three years old in order for their condition to be autism.

It is very hard to say how many children have autism. Some studies say approximately 2 out of every 10,000 children have it. Other, more recent studies say that the number is closer to 1 out of 1,000. However, most studies agree that it affects at least five times more boys than girls.

Unfortunately, the prevalence rate of autism is increasing rapidly and nobody really understands why. Some people point to the growing amount of toxins in the environment, especially mercury. Others suggest that the measles, mumps, and rubella vaccinations are to blame. Again, nobody really knows for sure. The increase could actually be the result of changes in how autism is defined. More likely, the real reason involves a mixture of factors, rather than just one.

- Also known as autism spectrum disorder, pervasive developmental delay, and PDD
- Common characteristics include impaired social interactions, abnormal verbal and nonverbal communication skills, self-stimulating or repetitive behaviors, echolalia, obsessive commitment to routines, and physically aggressive tantrums
- Approximately 2 out of 10,000 children have autism; however, this number is increasing rapidly and may be as high as 1 out of every 1,000 children

BOURNEVILLE-PRINGLE SYNDROME

Bourneville-Pringle syndrome is a genetic condition that results in lesions of the skin and central nervous system as well as the development of multiple tumors throughout the body. Approximately 1 out of every 6,000 people has Bourneville-Pringle syndrome; however, most don't know it. This is because mild forms of this condition can produce few symptoms and can go undetected. More severe cases, on the other hand, can cause profound mental retardation, seizures, and even death.

Bourneville-Pringle syndrome has many other names, including Bourneville disease, Bourneville syndrome, Bourneville-Brissaud disease, Pringle disease, turberose sclerosis, sclerosis tuberosa, and spongioblastosis circumscripta. Perhaps this is why so few people have ever heard of this condition even though it is relatively common, especially compared to more well-known but less prevalent disabilities, such as autism and Rett's syndrome.

- Also known as Bourneville disease, Bourneville syndrome, Bournevill-Brissaud disease, Pringle disease, turberose sclerosis, sclerosis tuberosa, and spongioblastosis
- Common characteristics include lesions of the skin and central nervous system, frequent seizures, reoccurring tumors
- Only severe cases result in mental retardation
- 1 out of every 6,000 individuals has Bourneville-Pringle syndrome

CAT CRY SYNDROME

Cat cry syndrome is an interestingly named condition. Also known as *cri du chat* syndrome, 5p deletion syndrome, and 5p minus syndrome, affected individuals tend to experience slow physical and cognitive development, have small heads, wide-set eyes that are slanting downward, small mouths, malformed ears, and webbed hands or feet. But their most predominate characteristic is that they cry like a high-pitched, screaming cat. The sound is really quite unmistakable.

Approximately, 1 in 20,000 individuals has cat cry syndrome. It is thought to account for about 1 percent of all individuals with severe to profound mental retardation. Recent research has found that it is caused by a chromosomal malformation where part of the fifth chromosome is missing; however, what causes this malformation is still unknown.

- Also known as *cri du chat* syndrome, 5p minus syndrome, and 5p deletion syndrome

- Common characteristics include slow growth, small head, wide-set downward slanting eyes, small jaw, low-set malformed ears, webbed feet and hands, and an unusual, high-pitched cry that resembles a screaming cat
- Cat cry syndrome accounts for about 1 percent of all children with severe mental retardation
- Approximately, 1 out of every 20,000 children has cat cry syndrome

CHILDHOOD DISINTEGRATIVE DISORDER

Childhood disintegrative disorder (CDD) is often referred to as regressive autism; however, it is not truly a form of autism. People who have autism must exhibit symptoms prior to age three. People with CDD, on the other hand, develop perfectly normally for three or four years and then start to gradually lose previously learned skills. For example, a happy, healthy, social two-year-old might begin to forget words that he already knew. He then might stop playing with other children, talking, and responding to verbal stimulation. Eventually, he will lose bowel and bladder control and will have difficulty acquiring new skills. In short, by the time the child turns ten years old, he will appear to have severe autism.

The cause of childhood disintegrative disorder is unknown, but some researchers have suggested that it is a severe reaction to vaccinations or environmental toxins. Because it is often confused with autism, an accurate indication of its prevalence is impossible. Some sources indicate that approximately one in 100,000 children will develop CDD, but again this number is more of an educated guess than based upon extensive data.

Childhood disintegrative disorder is also called Heller syndrome and disintegrative psychosis.

- Also known as CDD, Heller syndrome, regressive autism, and disintegrative psychosis
- Common characteristics include a gradual loss of previously acquired social and motor skills and development of autistic-like symptoms that develop in children after three years of age

- Possibly 1 out of every 100,000 children will develop childhood disintegrative disorder

CEREBRAL PALSY

Much as with autism, many people think that they understand cerebral palsy (CP), but really don't. First of all, CP is not contagious. It is caused by brain damage suffered prior to, or shortly after, birth. The source of this brain damage is thought to vary. Some cases of CP may be the result of lack of oxygen while the fetus is developing. Other cases are the result of illnesses, such as meningitis or chronic infections, during infancy. Still other cases maybe the result of prematurity or low birth weight.

Secondly, CP is not progressive. That is, it doesn't get worse over time. Individuals who have CP might have good and bad days, when their symptoms are more pronounced or problematic, but their condition will not continue to deteriorate steadily throughout their lives.

Finally, people with CP don't have to have mental retardation or be confined to wheelchairs. Yes, one of the primary characteristics of CP is loss of movement or muscle control—but this does not mean that everybody with CP cannot walk. Many people are only slightly affected or are only affected in one arm or one side of their body and can walk perfectly fine. Further, only about half of people with CP have varying degrees of mental retardation.

There are many different types of cerebral palsy, and each has different characteristics. For instance, individuals with spastic CP (the most common form) experience periods when their muscles become extremely tight and rigid. Arms and legs appear to be locked into position, as if frozen. Individuals with athetoid CP, on the other hand, have the opposite problem. Their muscles frequently produce abrupt, sweeping, involuntary movements, especially of the head, arms, and legs.

In addition to poor muscle control, people with cerebral palsy are also likely to have seizures, speech impairments, and breathing difficulties. However, as with muscle control, the severity of these impairments can vary significantly from person to person.

Cerebral palsy is one of the most common chronic motor-related disabilities. Recent research has stated that approximately 2.5 out of every 1,000 children have some form or degree of cerebral palsy.

- Also called CP
- Common characteristics include full or partial loss of movement or muscle control, seizures
- Various degrees of mental retardation in approximately 50% of cases
- 2.5 out of every 1,000 children have some form of cerebral palsy

DOWN SYNDROME

Down syndrome (also called Down's syndrome) is probably one of the most well-known, and easily identifiable, conditions that is associated with mental retardation. In fact, it the most common biological cause of mental retardation that we know of. Specifically, approximately 5 percent of people with mental retardation also have Down syndrome. However, despite what you may have been told, *not all people with Down syndrome have mental retardation!* Some can have IQs well into the normal range.

People with Down syndrome tend to be short in stature and have broad hands with thick fingers and a single crease across their palms. Their faces are flat with small ears and mouths, which tends to make their thick tongues look even larger than they are. Finally, people with Down syndrome have almond-shaped eyes that are slanted slightly upwards and have a flap of skin called the epicanthic fold that droops down at their corner.

Because Down syndrome is so recognizable, as well as the fact that most people erroneously believe that all children with Down's have mental retardation, many parents are electing to utilize cosmetic surgery to make their children with Down syndrome look more "normal." Critics say that such surgery is sending the message that people with Down syndrome should be ashamed about what they look like. Proponents say that the surgeries reduce the stigma and discrimination associated with having a disability. In the end, you will have to form your own opinions.

In addition to their physical appearance, people with Down syndrome also tend to have poor muscle tone (hypotonia), hyperflexible joints, increased susceptibility to upper respiratory infections, and heart defects. As a result of their poor muscle tone and heart ailments, people with Down tend to live significantly shorter lives than does the general population; thankfully, that is starting to change.

A couple decades ago, children with Down syndrome would typically live only into their early to mid-twenties. Now, it isn't uncommon for them to live well into their fifties. Part of this increase is the result of lifesaving heart surgeries, but exercise programs have also helped. About 1 out of every 800 to 1,000 children has Down syndrome.

- Also called trisomy 21
- Common characteristics include poor muscle tone, short stature, upward slanting eyes with folds of skin drooping in the corners, small mouths with thick tongues, and broad hands with stubby fingers
- Risk of having a child with Down syndrome increases with the age of the mother
- 5 percent of kids with mental retardation also have Down syndrome
- 1 out of every 800 to 1,000 children has Down syndrome

FETAL ALCOHOL SYNDROME

Whereas Down syndrome is the leading known biological cause of mental retardation, fetal alcohol syndrome (FAS) is thought to be the leading non-biological cause. Approximately 0.5 to 2 out of every 1,000 children have FAS. Unfortunately, this rate is increasing steadily.

Children with fetal alcohol syndrome tend to be smaller in stature than their peers. They also tend to have small (microcephalic) heads with facial abnormalities, such as widely spaced eyes, small, upturned noses, and thin upper lips. Heart defects and malformed hands, feet, and joins are also likely. Moderate mental retardation is common.

The name *fetal alcohol syndrome* is a bit misleading because it can be caused not only by alcohol but also by the consumption of illegal drugs and tobacco. "How much alcohol, drugs, or tobacco does a mother have to consume in order for her baby to have FAS?" you are probably wondering. Unfortunately, nobody can really say. It depends on many factors, such as the size of the mother and the gestation of the fetus. The smaller the mother, the more effect one drink will have on her and her unborn child. Further, the earlier in the pregnancy, the more damage can occur to the fetus.

However, many studies have indicated that even social drinkers can have affected children. Further, drinking doesn't have to be prolonged. One binge episode could permanently damage the fetus's brain development.

- Also known as FAS
- Common characteristics include delayed physical development; deformed hands, feet, and joints; and facial abnormalities (e.g., small upper jaw, short, upturned nose, thin upper lip, small asymmetrical eyes)
- Moderate mental retardation likely
- Approximately 0.5 to 2 children out of 1,000 have fetal alcohol syndrome

FETAL ALCOHOL EFFECTS

Fetal alcohol effects (FAE) is a milder form of fetal alcohol syndrome. Individuals with FAE have less noticeable facial abnormalities, but are more likely to have behavioral problems, such as hyperactivity. Roughly a third will have mild mental retardation or various learning disabilities. Estimates of prevalence range from 1 per 750 live births to 3 out of 1,000.

- Also known as FAE
- Common characteristics include delayed physical development, small for age, hyperactive, inattentive, and behavioral problems
- Approximately a third have mild mental retardation
- Approximately 1 out of 750 to 3 out of every 1,000 live births have fetal alcohol effects

FRAGILE X SYNDROME

Next to Down syndrome, fragile X is the most common genetic cause of mental retardation. Also like Down syndrome, fragile X is caused by a chromosomal abnormality that is passed down from either parent. More precisely, the lower tip of the X chromosome is underdeveloped, almost as if it has been cut off.

Approximately 1 out of every 1,500 males and 1 out of every 1,000 females carry the gene that is linked with fragile X syndrome. This doesn't mean that carriers actually have fragile X or that their children will have it. It just means that their children are at risk for having fragile X. As far as actual prevalence rates, nearly 1 out of every 2,000 boys and 1 out of every 4,000 girls have fragile X. Recent medical advances have made it possible for people to determine whether they are at risk for having children with fragile X. Children who have fragile X are usually diagnosed in early childhood; however they can also be diagnosed prenatally.

Children with fragile X tend to have very prominent jaws, long narrow faces, droopy ears, and enlarged heads with elongated foreheads. They are prone to have mental retardation. Again, note that I said *are prone to* and that I didn't say *will have* mental retardation. In fact, as many as one-third of females who have fragile X are so mildly affected that they are not diagnosed with any disability at all. Those who are, are often diagnosed with learning disabilities and behavior disorders. Males with fragile X, on the other hand, tend to have more severe mental retardation than do females with fragile X. They also tend to have large, misshapen testicles that frequently render them infertile.

Behaviorally, individuals affected by fragile X frequently appear to have autistic-like tendencies. Specifically, individuals with fragile X typically have difficulty regulating their attention, maintaining eye gaze, and exhibit repetitious behaviors, such as hand wringing or flapping their fingers. They are also likely to have speech and language problems, including echolalia (repeating what has been said) and palilalia (repeating things at an increasing rate and volume). These behaviors mirror autism to such a degree that approximately 40 percent of severely affected children with fragile X are diagnosed with autism as well.

Fragile X syndrome is also known as Martin-Bell syndrome and marker X syndrome.

- Also known as Martin-Bell syndrome and marker X syndrome
- Caused by genetic abnormalities to the X chromosome
- Common characteristics include a large head, ears, and jaw; hyperactive; tendency to avoid eye contact; poor social skills

- Can affect both males and females; however, females tend to be less affected than males
- Most common form of inherited mental retardation in males
- 1 out of every 1,000 females and 1,500 males carry the gene for fragile X syndrome
- 1 out of every 2,000 males and 4,000 females actually have fragile X syndrome

GALACTOSEMIA

Also called galactokinase deficiency, galactosemia is an inherited condition in which the body is unable to fully process the sugar molecule galactose, which is found in milk. When infants with galactokinase drink milk, galactose builds up in the infant's body, causing damage to the liver, kidneys, eyes, and brain. Prolonged exposure to galactose can cause severe organ damage, cataract formation, jaundice, convulsions, cirrhosis of the liver, mental retardation, and even death.

Approximately 1 out of 60,000 children has galactosemia. However, it is unclear what percentage will have mental retardation. Given that prenatal tests can now diagnose galactosemia, early detection and avoidance of galactose can limit its negative affects.

- Also known as galactokinase deficiency
- Caused by negative reaction to milk and milk products
- Common characteristics include jaundice, poor feeding, slow weight in infants, lethargy, convulsions, liver and kidney damage, and cataracts
- 1 out of 60,000 children has galactosemia

GORLIN SYNDROME

Gorlin syndrome, or nevoid basal cell carcinoma syndrome or basal cell nevus syndrome, is a rare inherited condition in which individuals develop abnormalities of the skin, nervous system, eyes, endocrine glands, and bones. Individuals with Gorlin syndrome tend to have enlarged heads (hydrocephalus), wide-set eyes, thick protruding brows, jutting jaws with frequent cysts, and overly curved backs. They might also have seizures, sensory impairments, mental retardation, and early onset skin cancer.

Approximately 1 in 57,000 people has Gorlin syndrome. It can be detected with genetic testing, and x-rays to determine the existence of skeletal abnormalities can also aid diagnosis. As of now, there is no cure for it.

- Also called basal cell nevus syndrome and nervoid basal cell carcinoma syndrome
- Common characteristics include an enlarged head, thick brow bone, wide-set eyes, broad bridge of the nose, protruding jaw, skeletal abnormalities (e.g., scoliosis, kyphosis, etc.), and a predisposition for skin cancer
- 1 in 57,000 people has Gorlin syndrome

HUNTER SYNDROME

Hunter syndrome is an inherited condition associated with the X chromosome. It causes the chemical mucopolysaccharide to slowly build up in the body. When excessive amounts of mucopolysaccharides are present, tissue and organs become damaged.

There are two different types of Hunter syndrome, affecting about 1 out of 130,000 people. Both types typically lead to progressive hearing loss, carpal tunnel syndrome, stiffening of the joints, and enlarged heads. Early onset, or juvenile Hunter syndrome, also leads to hyperactivity, aggressive behavior, severe mental retardation, and death by the early twenties. Later onset Hunter typically results in a longer life and is not always associated with mental retardation.

- Also called iduronate sulfatase deficiency
- It is an inherited condition causing elevated levels of the chemical mucopolysaccharide to be stored in the body
- Common characteristics include a large head, stiffening of joints and carpal tunnel syndrome, progressive hearing loss, hyperactivity, and aggressive behavior

- Early onset Hunter syndrome tends to result in severe mental retardation
- Can lead to premature death before twenty years of age
- Approximately, 1 out of 130,000 people has Hunter syndrome

HURLER SYNDROME

Very similar to Hunter syndrome, Hurler syndrome is an inherited condition where mucopolysaccharides accumulate in the body and cause damage to various organs, including the heart and eyes. Newborn infants with Hurler appear normal at first, but by the end of the first year, they begin to develop cloudy corneas, progressive stiffness in their joints, thick tongues, and prominent dark eyebrows. As they get older, they lose their hearing and develop severe mental retardation.

Approximately 1 in 150,000 children has Hurler syndrome. Unfortunately, they are unlikely to live into their adulthood. Most die in their late teens from heart disease.

- Also known as mucopolysaccharidosis type I and MPS I
- It is an inherited condition causing mucopolysaccharides to accumulate in the body and damage various organs, including the heart and eyes
- Common characteristics include short stature, prominent dark eyebrows, cloudy corneas, progressive stiffness, excessive body hair, full lips with thick tongue, heart disease, and severe mental retardation
- Early onset form often leads to death by early teens
- Approximately 1 out of 150,000 people has Hurler syndrome

HYDROCEPHALY

Hydrocephaly is a condition characterized primarily by an abnormally large, often pointed, head. It is caused by the buildup of cerebrospinal fluid between the brain and the skull. This buildup creates pressure and makes the brain contract as the skull expands. Consequently, individuals can have severe brain damage and mental retardation.

It is estimated that 1.8 out of every 1,000 children have hydrocephaly. In many cases, it is congenital and can be detected prior to birth by ultrasound. Other forms, such as Dandy-Walker syndrome, occur later in life. Regardless of age of onset, hydrocephaly can be treated by implanting a shunt into the person's head. The shunt, which is basically a long tube, drains the cerebrospinal fluid into the abdomen, thereby releasing the pressure and preventing damage to the brain or skull.

Years ago, hydrocephaly would have meant certain mental retardation and death at a young age. Now, with early detection, it can be successfully treated. In fact, once as I was discussing this condition in my introduction to disabilities course, a student of mine raised her hand and said that she was hydrocephalic. Apparently, she was diagnosed shortly after being born and had a shunt implanted. She has never developed mental retardation and is presently a special education teacher in a nearby town.

- Caused by cerebrospinal fluid building up between the brain and the skull
- Characterized by an abnormally large head
- If untreated or treated late, mental retardation and early death are likely
- 1.8 out of every 1,000 babies are hydrocephalic

KLINEFELTER SYNDROME

Klinefelter syndrome is another chromosomal-related condition associated with mental retardation. Klinefelter syndrome only occurs in males and is caused by having an extra X chromosome. In other words, affected individuals have an XXY chromosomal set, rather than XY.

While individuals with Klinefelter syndrome can have mild mental retardation (i.e., approximately 10 percent of the cases), they are more likely to have learning disabilities or even normal cognitive faculties. Other key characteristics include poor expressive and receptive language skills, difficulty processing auditory information, and immature social behavior. They are also likely to have abnormal male sex organs that result in sterility. They may also develop female secondary sexual features.

Surprisingly, Klinefelter syndrome is far from being rare. Approximately, 1 out of every 500 males has this disorder. Although there is no cure, physical characteristics can be successfully addressed by hormonal treatments, surgeries, and medication.

- Chromosomal condition causing individuals to have an extra X chromosome
- Affects only males
- Common characteristics include poor expressive and receptive language skills, difficulty processing auditory information, immature social behavior, and female secondary sexual features.
- Approximately 10 percent of people with Klinefelter syndrome have mental retardation
- 1 out of every 500 males has Klinefelter syndrome

LESCH-NYHAN SYNDROME

Like Klinefelter syndrome, Lesch-Nyhan syndrome is an inheritable condition that affects 1 out of very 100,000 males. Symptoms of Lesch-Nyhan syndrome generally appear between three and six months of age. First signs typically include orange-colored crystals, much like sand, appearing in the infant's diaper after urination. This is caused by an increase in uric acid in the child's kidneys. The buildup of this acid will eventually impair the functioning of the kidneys and central nervous system.

By the end of the first year, children will exhibit delays in motor development, frequent kidney stones, as well as uncontrollable spastic movements. However, one of the most shocking features of Lesch-Nyhan is the almost compulsive, self-destructive behavior. Children with Lesch-Nyhan have been known to chew off their own fingers and lips. Severe mental retardation is likely.

- Also known as LNS
- Common characteristics include compulsive self-mutilating behaviors such as lip and finger biting and extreme head banging, crystals in urine, kidney stones, and spasticity

- Severe mental retardation likely
- Approximately 1 out of every 100,000 children has Lesch-Nyhan syndrome

MICROCEPHALY

The opposite of hydrocephaly, people with microcephaly have very small heads. There are numerous causes for this condition. For example, there are several chromosomal abnormalities, such as Down syndrome and cat cry syndromes, that will result in a person having microcephaly. But it can also be caused by malnutrition, chronic infections, prenatal exposure to toxins, and maternal drug, tobacco, or alcohol use.

Because the child's skull does not grow at the appropriate rate, development of the brain is also significantly delayed. All levels of mental retardation are possible. However, 85 percent have severe and profound mental retardation. One in every 6,000 to 8,500 children is microcephalic.

- Common characteristics include a small head and slow brain development
- High likelihood of Down syndrome, cat cry syndrome, Seckel syndrome, trisomy 13 and 18
- 85 percent of children with microcephaly have severe mental retardation
- 1 out of every 6,000 to 8,500 children is microcephalic

NOONAN SYNDROME

Noonan syndrome is a genetic disorder thought to affect at least 1 in every 2,500 children. It is characterized by physical symptoms such as webbed necks, concaved chests, wide-set eyes, droopy eyelids, small mouths, and low, oddly shaped ears. In approximately one-quarter of the cases, mild retardation is also present. Noonan syndrome was once thought to affect only males; however, it has now been determined that females are affected as well, but at lower rates than males.

- Common characteristics include short stature, webbing of the neck, sunken chests, congenital heart disease, low-set and oddly shaped ears, wide-set eyes with droopy eyelids, and small jaws
- Mild mental retardation in approximately 25 percent of cases
- Noonan syndrome affects 1 in 2,500 people

PKU

Short for phenylketonuria, PKU is a rare inherited disorder that prevents a person from breaking down the amino acid phenylalanine. Consequently, levels of phenylalanine increase within the body and, if untreated, damage the brain and central nervous system, producing chronic seizures and severe mental retardation. Individuals with untreated PKU are also likely to experience tremors, spastic movements, and chronic skin problems.

Fortunately, only 1 in 10,000 to 15,000 infants has PKU. Further, it can easily be detected by a simple blood test. Diets low in phenylalanine have been found to reduce the risk of mental retardation by 75 percent. However, such treatments must be introduced by the first month after birth in order to have any affect.

- Also known as phenylketonuria
- Inherited disorder that prevents a person from breaking down the amino acid phenylalanine
- Common characteristics include a small head, jerking movements (especially in arms and legs), tremors, seizures, hyperactivity, chronic rashes, and poor social skills
- Approximately 1 out of every 10,000 to 15,000 people has PKU

PRADER-WILLI SYNDROME

Prader-Willi syndrome is a condition caused by damage to the fifteenth chromosome. In fact, part of the chromosome is missing completely. Individuals with Prader-Willi experience delays in motor and cognitive development and often have mild to moderate mental retardation. However, the principal characteristic of individuals with Prader-Willi is that they have insatiable appetites that, coupled with their short statures, results in morbid obesity as well as non-insulin-dependent diabetes mellitus. Their appetites are so strong that they compulsively overeat and will even devour unappetizing objects, such as dirt, wood, garbage, and even nails or glass.

Prader-Willi typically progresses in two stages. The first is an infantile hypotonic stage in which infants with Prader-Willi experience periods of hypotonia. That is, they do not exhibit much muscular tone and flop around like a rag doll. The second stage, which often begins by their second birthday, is called obesity stage. At this time, the child begins to routinely gorge him- or herself to such a degree that his or her life can be threatened, if not significantly shortened.

Approximately 1 out of every 16,000 to 20,000 children is born with Prader-Willi. Some reports indicate that this rate is increasing. However, current data is still lacking.

- A condition caused by damage to the fifteenth chromosome
- Infants with Prader-Willi syndrome are hypotonic (floppy muscle tone) and have difficulty eating
- By age two, children with Prader-Willi syndrome exhibit an insatiable appetite and become morbidly obese
- Other characteristics include almond-shaped eyes, short in stature, highly social personalities, and delays in motor and cognitive development
- Often leads to mild to moderate mental retardation
- 1 out of every 16,000 to 20,000 children is born with Prader-Willi

RETT SYNDROME

Rett syndrome is a progressive neurological condition usually caused by a mutation in the X chromosomes. It only appears in females, and even then both chromosomes must be compromised. Consequently, only about 7 to 10 in every 100,000 females have Rett. Males with the mutation are spontaneously aborted during early pregnancy.

Individuals with Rett syndrome develop normally during their first few months. However, by approximately six months of age, infants will exhibit hypotonia (floppy muscles, almost as if they were a rag doll). The child's physical growth, especially the head, will then begin to slow. By the end of the first year, the child will begin to regress intellectually. By three years of age, individuals with Rett's will appear to have autism. They will demonstrate repeated, stereotypic movements, such as hand wringing and rocking, as well as severely impaired communication skills.

- Caused by a mutation in the X chromosomes
- Appears only in females
- Characterized by normal development as an infant, hypotonia, small head, loss of previously acquired skills, seizures, severely impaired receptive and expressive language skills, and autistic-like behavior
- 7 to 10 children out of 100,000 have Rett syndrome

RUBINSTEIN SYNDROME

Rubinstein syndrome, also called Rubinstein-Taybi syndrome or RTS for short, is a rare condition affecting approximately 1 in 125,000 people. It is caused by a genetic mutation and results in an array of physiological characteristics, including short stature, downward slanting eyes, very large or small head, low-set irregular ears, excessively hairy bodies, and extra fingers or toes. Children with Rubinstein syndrome experience delayed motor and cognitive development and are likely to have mild to moderate mental retardation. Roughly 40 percent have life-threatening heart defects that require surgery.

- Also known as Rubinstein-Taybi syndrome and RST
- Rubinstein syndrome is caused by a mutation in the person's genetic material
- Common characteristics include short stature, very large or small heads, low-set ears, downward slanting eyes with droopy eyelids, excessive body hair, six or more fingers or toes, heart defects, and poor motor development
- Approximately, 1 out of 125,000 children have Rubinstein syndrome

SANFILIPPO SYNDROME

Sanfilippo syndrome is a condition closely associated with Hurler and Hunter syndromes. All three conditions are associated with a difficulty in breaking down the chemical mucopolysaccharide. As with Hurler and Hunter syndromes, individuals with Sanfilippo syndrome tend to have heavy brows, thick lips, and stiff joints. Although they begin life developing normally, by three years of age, their mental and physical abilities start to deteriorate. By six years old, they have underdeveloped motor skills and profound mental retardation. However, unlike in Hurler and Hunter syndromes, individuals with Sanfilippo do not have cloudy corneas and they are more likely to live to adulthood. One in 25,000 people has this condition.

- Also called mucopolysaccharidosis type III, MPS, or MPS type III
- An inherited condition making it difficult for the body to process the chemical mucopolysaccharide
- Closely associated with Hurler and Hunter syndromes.
- Common characteristics include short stature, deterioration of gait, thick lips, stiff joints causing limited range of motion, normal cognitive abilities until age two, then slow decline leading to severe mental retardation.
- Can lead to death by early adulthood
- 1 out of 25,000 people has Sanfilippo syndrome

TAY-SACHS DISEASE

Tay-Sachs disease (TSD) is an inherited condition characterized by a deterioration of motor and cognitive skills, dementia, sensory impairments, and paralysis. It is caused by a deficiency of hexosaminidase, which is an enzyme that helps process gangliosides (chemicals found in nerve tissue).

There are three general types of Tay-Sachs—infantile, juvenile, and adult onset. Infantile onset is the most common. Unfortunately, it is also the most detrimental. Infants with Tay-Sachs begin experiencing symptoms between three and six months. Motor, cognitive, and communication skills deteriorate rapidly until the child has profound mental retardation. Death usually occurs by age five.

Juvenile Tay-Sachs occurs between the ages of two and ten years old. Children will begin to lose speech, coordination, and cognitive abilities. They are also likely to develop seizures, mental retardation, and blindness. Most die by the age of seventeen years.

Adult chronic Tay-Sachs is the least common. Further, its progression is much slower than infantile and juvenile subtypes. Adults will not lose their motor functions, but nearly half will develop psychiatric conditions, such as depression, bipolar conditions, and schizophrenia.

Tay-Sachs disease can be found among all populations. However, it is mostly associated with people of Ashkenazi Jewish populations. One out of every 3,600 Ashkenazi Jews has Tay-Sachs disease. One in every thirty Ashkenazi Jews is a genetic carrier for the condition.

- Also known as TSD
- Caused by a deficiency of an enzyme that helps process chemicals found in nerve tissue
- There are three types of Tay-Sachs disease; the most common is typically the most severe
- Common characteristics include a loss of motor skills, hearing and vision impairments, seizures, paralysis, deterioration of cognitive and communication skills, and dementia
- Some forms of Tay-Sachs disease are fatal
- It is found in all populations, but predominately in families of Ashkenazi Jewish ancestry
- 1 out every thirty Ashkenazi Jews is a genetic carrier for Tay-Sachs disease
- 1 out of every 3,600 Ashkenazi Jews had Tay-Sachs disease

TRISOMY 13

Also called Patau syndrome, trisomy 13 is caused by an extra thirteenth chromosome. It is very common and occurs in approximately 1 out of every 5,000 births. Individuals with trisomy 13 have small heads, cleft lips or palates, extra fingers, close-set eyes and rather tiny, low-set ears, and seizures. Approximately 80 percent have congenital heart disease; the majority of these die by the first month of life. Nearly all individuals with trisomy 13 have profound or severe mental retardation.

- Also known as Patau syndrome
- Trisomy 13 is caused by the presence of an extra thirteenth chromosome
- Common characteristics include a small head, skeletal abnormalities such as extra fingers or toes, cleft lip or palate, very close-set eyes, low-set ears, seizures, and congenital heart conditions
- Many infants with trisomy 13 die within a month after birth
- Severe and profound mental retardation is highly likely
- 1 out of every 5,000 infants has trisomy 13

TRISOMY 18

As you might have guessed, trisomy 18 (a.k.a. Edwards syndrome) is a condition caused by the presence of an extra eighteenth chromosome. As with trisomy 13 and trisomy 21 (Down syndrome), trisomy 18 is pretty common. Roughly 1 out of every 3,000 children has this condition, although it tends to affect females three times more often that males.

Individuals with trisomy 18 tend to have low birth weight, small heads, low-set ears, small mouths and jaws, and clinched hands with underdeveloped fingernails. They are also at risk for heart and kidney abnormalities. Fifty percent of children with trisomy 18 die within the first week of life. Some have lived into adulthood, but this is more of an exception than a rule.

- Also known as Edwards syndrome
- Trisomy 18 is caused by the presence of an extra eighteenth chromosome
- Common characteristics include a small head, low-set ears, small jaw, clenched hands with underdeveloped fingernails, congenital heart and kidney abnormalities
- Half of infants with trisomy 18 die within the first six months
- Severe and profound mental retardation is highly likely

- Affects females three times more than males
- 1 out of every 3,000 infants has trisomy 18

TURNER SYNDROME

Turner syndrome is very much like Klinefelter syndrome, except that it occurs in females. Whereas Klinefelter involves having an extra X chromosome, individuals with Turner are missing an X chromosome. So, rather than have the normal XX set, females with Turners have just an X, or what is often referred to as an XO chromosomal pair.

Approximately 1 in 2,500 live female births has Turner syndrome. However, considering that 95 percent of fetuses with Turner are naturally aborted, the actual occurrence of the condition is much higher.

As with Klinefelter syndrome, individuals with Turner syndrome are more likely to have learning disabilities and behavior problems than mental retardation. Typically, individuals with Turner syndrome have difficulty with memory, attention, mathematical calculations, spatial relationships, and social interactions. Physically, they tend to be short and lack secondary sexual features, making them sterile.

- Caused by an absent X chromosome
- Occurs only in females
- Common characteristics include short stature, a lack of secondary sexual characteristics, poor memory, inattentive, difficulty with mathematical calculations and spatial relationships, immature social skills
- Most fetuses with Turner syndrome are aborted naturally
- 1 out of every 2,500 females has Turner syndrome

WILLIAMS SYNDROME

Williams syndrome is a genetic disorder caused by a malformation of the seventh chromosome. Individuals with Williams syndrome tend to have small upturned noses that appears further away from the upper lip than what is usually considered normal, stiff joints, concaved chest, and drooping eye lids. Three-quarters of individuals with Williams syndrome have some degree of mental retardation, usually mild to moderate. The remaining individuals are likely to have learning disabilities and behavior disorders. Due to congenital heart defects, high blood pressure, and other ailments, people with Williams syndrome tend to have shortened lives, though many live well into late adulthood. Williams syndrome occurs in 1 out of 20,000 births

- Also known as Williams-Beuren syndrome
- Genetic condition caused by a malformation of the seventh chromosome
- Common characteristics include short stature, progressive stiffness of joints, inappropriately friendly, heart defects, delayed language development, flattened facial features
- Likely to have mild to moderate mental retardation
- 1 out of 20,000 children have Williams syndrome

SUMMARY

Well, we certainly covered a lot of conditions associated with mental retardation! And there are many, *many* more that we haven't covered. Keep in mind that we only talked about each of these very briefly and in pretty general terms. If you would like additional information on any of these conditions, please look in the back of this book. I have tried to list organizations, books, websites, and other resources that may help you.

Further, keep in mind that many of these conditions are just *associated* with mental retardation. Not everybody who has Down syndrome, autism, or cerebral palsy, for example, has to have mental retardation. They could have average intelligence or even be gifted!

Just think about the importance of this for a moment. Image that you were misdiagnosed with mental retardation, just because you had one of these conditions that are associated with mental retardation! Think about how different your life would be. This is why all of the stuff on assessment that we talked about in chapter 2 is so crucial. Without proper diagnosis, all can be lost!

"But what if my child doesn't have *any* of the conditions that we covered in this chapter?" You are probably asking yourself. "What is mental retardation like for my child?"

This is a good question, especially since most people with mental retardation don't have any particular syndrome or genetic condition. If you want to understand more about the characteristics of mental retardation, keep reading! It is the topic of our next chapter.

5

TYPICAL CHARACTERISTICS OF MENTAL RETARDATION

GUIDED COMPREHENSION QUESTIONS

By the time you finish reading this chapter, you should be able to

1. Identify key motivational, self-regulatory, learning, social, and physiological characteristics commonly attributed to people with mental retardation
2. Identify strategies to address these characteristics of mental retardation

INTRODUCTION

In chapter 4, we talked about a whole lot of different conditions that are associated with mental retardation. Remember that I said *associated with* mental retardation. Not all of the conditions that we discussed have to result in mental retardation. For example, many people with autism and cerebral palsy can have very high IQs!

Moreover, most people who have mental retardation don't have any of the conditions that we discussed. The typical child with mental retardation doesn't have a small head or droopy eyelids or any kind of obvious physical characteristics. They don't have a genetic condition, and their mother wasn't drinking or taking drugs while she was pregnant. The typical child with mental retardation simply looks like a normal kid who happens to have a low IQ and poor adaptive skills.

For this reason, I want to talk about what mental retardation is like aside from the various ancillary conditions that might cause it. As always, try to keep in mind that we are talking in generalities. Some of what we will be talking about might not apply to your child or student. For instance, although most children with mental retardation have underdeveloped social skills, your child might be very polite, well mannered, and a joy to be around. Still, there are probably many things that we are going to explore that will sound exactly like what you are experiencing. Specifically, we will be talking about the following:

- Motivational characteristics
- Self-regulatory characteristics
- Learning characteristics
- Social characteristics
- Physiological characteristics

Rather than merely outlining what the typical child with mental retardation is like in these five areas, I want to also give you some practical suggestions on how to address the issues that we are going to discuss. So, after each section, I will give you some ideas on how to improve your child's motivation, self-regulation, learning, social skills, and appearance. Let's begin!

MOTIVATIONAL CHARACTERISTICS

Perhaps the most critical, and most detrimental, characteristics of mental retardation involve motivation. You are doubtless scratching your head and wondering where I am heading with this. After all, you probably thought that I would start off by talking about how people with mental retardation have limited intelligence or something like that.

True, as we discussed in the first chapter, people with mental retardation by definition have subaverage intelligence. But, as we also discussed, they *can* learn. However, in order to learn anything, they have to be willing to try first!

Think about that for a moment. No matter how intelligent somebody is, no matter how well she does on a standardized IQ test, she can't learn very much if she doesn't try. So, in essence, how well somebody learns is secondary to whether or not she wants to learn to begin with. In other words, motivation to learn is probably one of the most important characteristics that anybody can have.

Unfortunately, people with mental retardation typically have problems with motivation. Please don't think that I am saying that all people with mental retardation are lazy, sluggards, or whatever. I'm not saying that at all. It is just that people with mental retardation usually have certain characteristics that hamper their ability to self-start activities as well as motivate themselves to do their very best. Let's talk about these characteristics, and hopefully, this topic will become clearer.

External Locus of Control

"Locus of control" involves how we see our lives and who is in control of it. If you believe that you are in complete control of everything that happens to you, then you have a very strong internal locus of control. If you think that everything happens because it is "fate" or the will of God or because of something outside of your influence, then you have a very external locus of control.

I would guess that most people have a kind of mixture of the two. Certainly, there are some things that we can control. For example, in some cases we can avoid being fired by working hard and being a good employee. Those are things that we have power over. However, we can't completely control the economy or business trends. So, if your employer is laying off people because they are about to go out of business, you won't be able to keep your job even if you are the best employee of them all. In other words, you are in control of some things, but not others. Make sense?

People with mental retardation tend to have very external loci of control. For example, if they do well on a spelling test, they often believe that it is because the teacher "liked" them that day or because it was luck or random fate. They don't see the connection between their own hard work and the outcome of the test. They don't understand that their studying improved their spelling ability, and that doing well on the test was largely in their own hands.

Learned Helplessness

In addition to believing that they aren't the masters of their own destinies, individuals with mental retardation often display what is called "learned helplessness." That is, they expect to fail before they even try. So, in many cases, they don't even attempt to do the work or they don't try very hard. This, unfortunately, leads them to do poorly, which in turn creates a greater expectation of future failure. This behavior creates a vicious circle, or a "self-fulfilling prophecy."

Remember, individuals with mental retardation already think that things are out of their control. So, trying harder or employing another strategy to complete a task successfully usually doesn't occur to them. They believe that failure is predetermined by some outside force that they can't change; so, they tend to just give up before they start.

I'll tell you a story that, regrettably, illustrates this point too well. It involves a student of mine named Nate. I talked about him earlier and will mention him throughout this book. He became a very good friend of mine and taught me more than most of my college professors.

When he was a senior in high school, I got Nate a job at a McDonald's. He was hired to clean the lobby, take the trash out, greet customers, and so forth. I thought that he would be perfect for the position. He loved McDonald's, was very social, but in an appropriate way, and he seemed motivated to earn money to support his hobby of buying model cars. Everything indicated that the job was a good match for him.

On the first day of work, I brought Nate to the restaurant and began showing him what he was supposed to do. I showed him where and how to clock in and out, where his supplies were, introduced him to his coworkers, and so on.

When I showed him how to clean a dirty table, he looked at me blankly and said, "I can't do that."

In my positive, reassuring, teacher voice, I said, "Sure you can!" I then proceeded to show him how to swipe the crumbs into a pail with a damp towel.

As I was bent over the table, showing him how to clean it, he looked down at me, shook his head slightly and repeated, "I can't do that."

"Sure you can!" I said again even more positively. "See. Just do what I am doing! Take your spray bottle. Spray the dirty table. Then wipe everything up with your pail! It is easy! Here, try it!"

"I can't do that."

By then I started to get a bit annoyed. My Pollyanna-ish teacher voice was starting to waiver. I forced a smile and asked politely, "Why don't you think that you can do it? You haven't even tried."

Nate looked back at me, shrugged, and then said, "I have mental retardation. I can't do that."

That was how Nate was. Actually, it was how most of my students were. They didn't believe that they could do anything, and getting them to try something new was a monumental undertaking. As I said at the very beginning of this book, most of my students were more disabled by how they perceived themselves than by their actual mental retardation.

Dependence

Let's think about all of this from the perspective of the person with mental retardation for a moment. Maybe that will help you appreciate the importance of this topic.

Imagine that you have a history of failure. Every time you try to do something, you get it wrong or somebody else does it quicker and better than you. Further, you usually don't try, and you don't attempt more effective ways of succeeding because you think that your fate is controlled by something other than yourself. You are a leaf being blown by the wind, whether you like it or not. So, what do you do?

If you were like most kids with mental retardation, you would give up and have other people do things for you. Further, because people like helping "poor retarded children," it would be pretty easy for you to find all the help that you need. Can't do your homework? Raise your hand, look pathetic, and say, "I can't do it." Then the teacher or aide or parent will "help" you—

which usually means that they will do the work for you rather than teach you how to do it yourself. Let me give you an example.

When I was an aide in a special education classroom, we had a student named Henry. Every day was the same routine. Henry would come to school and stand by the door. The teacher would then take Henry by the hand and lead him into the room. Once inside, Henry would walk over to the row of hooks on the wall where everybody hung up their coats and backpacks. He would then stand there until the teacher took off his coat and hung it up for him. After his coat was taken off and hung up, Henry would stand by the cubical where his books and supplies were kept. The teacher would hand him his things. And so it would go every day.

I should point out that Henry could walk into the room without any assistance if he wanted to. He could take off his backpack and coat and hang them on the appropriate hook. He had no physical limitations of any kind. Further, he understood exactly what to do and when. In fact, if we hung up his coat on the wrong hook, he would calmly retrieve his coat and put it where it belonged. If we gave him the wrong folder or notebook, he would get what he needed on his own. But for some reason, if we did nothing for him initially, if we just let him stand outside the room at the beginning of the day without helping him inside, he would just stand there for hours like a prehistoric bug trapped in amber. If we didn't lead him to the lunchroom or to recess or to the bus at the end of the day, he would sit at his desk waiting.

Many of my students were like Henry. They were completely and utterly dependent on us to tell them what to do. Again, it wasn't because they couldn't do the task or because they didn't want to do the task. They simply didn't do tasks for themselves. They were like robots who needed constant programming. If we didn't give them the proper instructions or initiate the launch sequence each and every day, they didn't function.

Students with mental retardation not only develop a dependence on people for help, they also rely upon the environment for clues to tell them what to do. While this might sound like a good thing, it often isn't. Let me give you an example.

Imagine that you are a young student again. Maybe you are in first grade. The teacher walks up to the chalkboard and writes "1 + 1," then "1 + 2," then "1 + 3," and so on up to "1 + 10" all the way from left to right across the chalkboard. When she points to "1 + 1," she says "1 + 1 = 2" and everybody in the class repeats it. When she points to "1 + 2," she says "1 + 2 = 3" and everybody repeats that. And so forth, down the line of problems.

The next day, the teacher goes to the chalkboard and writes "2 + 1," then "2 + 2," and so on from left to right all across the board. When she points to the first problem, "2 + 1," she says, "What is this? Do you remember from last time? It is the same as 1 + 2."

If you are an average student, you might recall that "1 + 2" yesterday was "3." So you would raise your hand and say enthusiastically, "The answer is 3!"

If you have mental retardation, however, you would probably remember that the answer to the first question that the teacher wrote to the far left on the board was "1 + 1." Further, you might remember that the answer was "2." So, you would likely think that this answer was "2" as well.

In other words, nondisabled students will look at the problem and focus on the numbers. They will look at "2 + 1," see that it is the same as "1 + 2," and get the correct answer.

Students with mental retardation, on the other hand, will look where the question is written on the board. They remembered that when the teacher pointed to the far left, the answer was 2, a little bit to the right, the answer was 3, and so on. In other words, the student with mental retardation relies on the question's location on the board for the answer, or the color of the chalk that was used to write it, not the numbers involved in the problem. Make sense?

Stated another way, students with mental retardation often don't know what stimuli to pay attention to. Should they remember how a problem is written? Where it is written? What color shirt the teacher is wearing? The time of the day? They don't understand which variables are directly related with the problem at hand, so they frequently lock onto environmental clues, such as where on the board things were written.

Improving Your Child's Motivation

Hopefully, you understand how paramount of an issue motivation can be. If your child isn't motivated to learn or do new things, his experiences and learning will be limited as will his future. So, how can you combat this formidable problem? Here are some suggestions.

Clear and Manageable Goals

One reason why people with mental retardation frequently fail is because they are given tasks that are too grand and challenging for them. Remember, these kids have difficulty acquiring new skills, and they may need additional time to process information. If you expect them to accomplish the same tasks as soon as a typical child, both you and the child will probably become disillusioned very quickly.

Rather than teaching an entire skill all at once, break it down into clear, manageable steps. For instance, rather than expecting a child to learn how to cook an entire meal, focus on specific tasks, such as how to turn the stove on and off or how to measure ingredients. Once one step is mastered, teach the next step. This is called "chaining," and we will talk about it in greater detail in later chapters.

Breaking larger tasks into smaller and more manageable steps is important for two reasons. First, it divides information into more meaningful chunks. This will help the child learn, which should increase the chances of the child mastering the overall task. Secondly, by focusing on the small steps within a larger task, the child experiences more opportunities for success. In other words, rather than focusing on the big picture of cooking a meal, the child can be successful at getting the ingredients out of the refrigerator, measuring them, putting them all together, utilizing the stove safely, and so on. That is to say, the child will experience multiple successes rather than just one. The more success a child experiences, the less the likelihood they will begin to expect failure.

Frequent Recognition of Success

Giving children with mental retardation opportunities to succeed is certainly important, but you also have to help them realize that they are making progress and that their progress is the result of their own hard work. Without appreciating this, they won't develop an internal locus of control. So, how do you help them make the connection between their effort and their success?

First of all, you have to be blatant. You can't be subtle with kids who have mental retardation. They will often miss your hints. You also have to be very repetitive. Saying something once most likely won't be effective. Every time your child succeeds at something, stop and say, "See! You did it! All that hard work paid off! You couldn't do that yesterday, but now because of all of your hard work, you can!" Again, you have to be very clear. Keep hitting on the fact that (1) they succeed at doing something, (2) they couldn't do that task before, but now they can, and (3) that their hard work was what made the difference.

In addition to you repeating this, try to get others to provide the child with similar feedback. If enough people are constantly saying, "Hey! You are learning new things, and it is all because you are trying your best!" then your child may start believing it.

You might also want to devise a system where your child can keep track of his or her successes. For example, many teachers have "word walls" where they post all of the new words that students learn to spell or write. This is a constant visual reminder of the student's progress. Maybe you could keep a list of new accomplishments on the refrigerator door or on the wall of the child's bedroom. Then refer to it often. Make a big production when there is an addition to it.

Again, the bottom line is you have to make sure that your child draws the connection between his accomplishments and his effort. In order for him to make this connection, you are going to have to be very repetitive and overt. Keep hitting him over the head with it, and the idea will eventually sink in!

Promotion of Self-Reliance

The purpose of any teaching should be to enable the child to eventually do something for himself or herself. If you don't eventually wean your support away from the child, you are just creating dependency. I know this sounds mean, but please realize that giving too much help is not a good thing. Gradually lessen the amount of support that you are providing. Allow your child to do things on her own—even if that means that she struggles a bit. Mistakes are often our best teachers. Don't deny your child the experience of learning on her own. But also take care to make sure mistakes are corrected and turned into successes!

SELF-REGULATORY CHARACTERISTICS

Okay, so you are going to have to work on your child's motivation and his locus of control. If you can get your child to see that hard work pays off, then you have made a huge difference in his life! Not only will he try harder and experience greater success, but he will also be more in control of his own destiny! Now I want to move on to another very important topic—your child's self-regulatory skills.

Self-regulatory skills involve the ability to control one's behavior. You might think of it as not only being able to distinguish right from wrong but also taking responsibility for your own actions. Unfortunately, kids with mental retardation often do not regulate their own behavior very effectively. This isn't to say that they are "evil" or that they don't know how to act appropriately. It is just that many kids with mental retardation give little thought to how their actions affect others. Further, they put very little energy into monitoring what they are doing.

Let's put this issue of self-regulation and motivation together. They are, after all, very much interrelated. Then maybe you can better understand why your child acts the way he or she does.

As we discussed in the last section, people with mental retardation tend to have external loci of control. That means that they see things as beyond their ability to change. So, if they get in trouble at school, they often see their predicament as the teacher's fault, not their own. Or, if nobody wants to play with them, they believe it is because the other kids are mean, not because their behavior bothers the other kids. See how those two characteristics interplay?

Children with an external locus of control won't look at their own behavior when things go poorly (or when things are going well, for that matter). So, if they get into a fight or are yelled at by a teacher, they don't think, "I got in trouble because of how I was behaving." They think that they got in trouble because of something that they can't control, such as how the teacher was feeling or how mean the other kids are. Consequently, they don't attempt to prevent future situations by acting differently. Why would they? After all, they aren't to blame for getting in trouble. Everything is beyond their control! Or, so they think. Is the picture becoming clearer? Let me tell you yet another story.

I was working with a high school student named Josh, for whom I got a job as a groundskeeper at Purdue University. Josh was a really great guy. He was lovable, friendly, and very inquisitive. He was curious about everything. He would take things apart and conduct various "experiments." Of course, this meant that a number of things were never put back together and his "experiments" would often put him in harm's way.

For instance, Josh had a cart that contained all of his tools and supplies. It was like a shopping cart with holders for his rakes, shovels, garbage bags, and so forth. Well, anyway, one day while he was cleaning out a flower bed, Josh got it into his head that he wanted to push his cart in front of a bus that he saw coming down the street. The bus was going about 35 miles per hour at the time. Needless to say, there was quite the commotion!

The bus hit the cart dead on and ran right over it. The cart ripped apart the bus's grill and did extensive damage to the underside of the vehicle. I can't remember for sure, but I believe that there was more than $10,000 worth of damage. As you can imagine, the people at the city's transit authority were livid! Absolutely livid!

When I talked to Josh about what had happened, he was honest as always. He said that he saw the bus coming and wondered what would happen if he pushed the cart into the street just before the bus passed—which, of course, he did. He wasn't apologetic, just amazed that he saw sparks flying as the bus dragged the cart underneath it for half a block.

Throughout our discussions, Josh kept saying over and over that it wasn't his "fault." When I asked whose fault it was, he just shrugged and looked blankly at me the way most of my students did when I asked them such questions.

This was more than just adolescent denial. Josh genuinely didn't see the connection between his actions and the resulting damage to the bus. It was almost as if he thought, "I didn't hit the cart with the bus; therefore, I didn't play any part in how the bus or the cart got damaged."

Further, he didn't believe that he could control his actions. The idea of self-restraint was completely foreign to him. From his perception, he was like a knee being hit by a little rubber hammer. He got the idea to push the cart in front of the bus, so he had to do it. He had no choice. It wasn't his fault. People just do whatever comes into their minds, and then they react to whatever circumstances that arise. At least, that is what he believed.

Now, you would think that this kind of thing would only happen once, right? Well, it didn't! A couple of months later, Josh pushed his new cart in front of a moving passenger car. Luckily, the driver was able to swerve out of the way in time and nobody was hurt.

Again, not only did Josh fail to see the connection between his behavior and the resulting consequences, he also didn't take responsibility for what he did. His learned helplessness that he so frequently demonstrated in the classroom seemed to take over all aspects of his life. I could almost hear him think, "Bad things happen. Bad things will always happen. I can't stop bad things from happening, so I might as well not try to make things better."

I should point out that after the second incident Josh was fired from his job as a groundskeeper. When I asked if he understood why he got fired, he said with the same blank face as before, "Because Carl [his supervisor] didn't like me."

When I asked why he thought Carl didn't like him, Josh just shrugged. When I asked what he could have done differently so that Carl liked him more, Josh just shrugged again. And so it went.

Again, the problem with Josh, as well as many other kids with mental retardation, is that he didn't think that he had any control of his behavior or responsibility for what he did.

Please don't think that this is a natural outcome of having mental retardation. It isn't. It has nothing to do with intelligence or adaptive behavior. It is something that we actually teach them.

Whenever we lower standards of behavior for students with mental retardation, we are subtly (and not so subtly) saying, "That's okay. You have mental retardation. We don't expect you to behave appropriately." We treat kids with mental retardation differently, so they act differently. Here is another example.

We used to bring our students to a community recreation center for teenagers during the summer. It was kind of like a Boys' and Girls' Club. One of my students, Benny, had a propensity for grabbing the butts of teenage girls. He would walk up to them and grab two handfuls of their rear ends. The girls were, understandably, very upset by this, but they usually didn't do anything about it. And when they did, they just lectured Benny about how it wasn't appropriate to act that way. But Benny kept going around grabbing the young girls' butts.

When the other teenage boys, who did not have mental retardation, saw Benny getting away with this, they started grabbing, too. But when they touched a girl improperly, the girl would turn around and slap them. The boys without mental retardation then stopped.

When I asked one of the girls whom Benny liked to grab why she didn't respond to Benny the same way as she did with the other boys, she said it was because he was "mentally retarded." Benny never did stop grabbing women inappropriately. I often imagine how his life is now. He is probably close to thirty years old. I picture him walking down the street, grabbing every female that he passes. I wonder if he will be arrested for assault. I am not advocating violence against kids with mental retardation or anybody else, mind you, but I bet that Benny would have stopped his behavior if one of the girls had slapped him across the face like they did to the other boys.

The point is, how can people with mental retardation be expected to develop self-regulatory behaviors when they aren't expected to control themselves? If you want your child to develop appropriate self-regulatory skills, you must expect her to control herself. This means you have to set rules. But that isn't as easy as it sounds.

Remember, kids with mental retardation often have difficulty with abstract concepts, so knowing when various rules apply and when they don't is hard for them. For instance, I have worked with numerous females who have been told over and over again, "Never let anybody touch your private areas." Unfortunately, this rule became so engrained into their minds that the girls were unwilling to let doctors examine them.

The same is true for "Don't talk to strangers." I have had a couple of students who refused to talk to *any* strangers, no matter the situation. They were not able to order food in unfamiliar restaurants, ask clerks or cashiers questions, or even go up to police officers for help if they need it.

So, before you begin setting down all kinds of rules, be sure that your expectations are very overt. If there are exceptions to the rules, make sure that you child understands them. For example, "no running in the house" might be followed by "unless there is a fire or you are being chased by a stranger." Moreover, focus on rules that only need to be addressed. Too many rules can be overwhelming!

In addition to setting a handful of clear, easily understood rules, you will also need to enforce these rules consistently. Consistency is important for any child; however, it is even more so if the child has mental retardation. Variations in how the rules are interpreted and enforced will likely cause confusion.

Another way to promote self-regulatory behavior is to encourage age-appropriate peer interactions. As with your rules, talk to your child frequently about what is considered proper playing and teasing and what is not. Kids with mental retardation often model behavior from other kids, so it might be very helpful for you to have your child play with older, more mature and responsible children. Remember, you are not the only effective teacher in your child's life!

Finally, if you want to build your child's self-regulation skills, you will also have to increase his internal locus of control, which we talked about earlier. You can't expect your child to take responsibility for his actions if he thinks that his actions are out of his control!

LEARNING CHARACTERISTICS

Of course, other primary characteristics of people with mental retardation involve learning. We have already discussed what intelligence is thought to be; that is, it is a measure of how well people learn, not how much they know. However, we really haven't discussed how "subaverage intelligence" affects the learning of students with mental retardation. So, let's do that now.

Inefficient Learners

As I have said before, having subaverage intelligence doesn't mean that people can't learn. They can! However, people with mental retardation do not learn as efficiently as do other people.

"What does that mean?" you might be wondering. "What does 'efficiency' have to do with learning?"

Efficient learners acquire information quicker than do inefficient learners. Not necessarily because they are smarter, but because they are better able at focusing upon relevant information and systematically analyze data. They can also retain and retrieve correct data more readily than do other people. Let me give you an example.

Remember when we discussed a student with mental retardation thinking that where a math question was written on the board dictated the answer? That is an example of ineffective learning. You see, all the students in the class noticed where the problem was written on the chalkboard, the color of the chalk, time of day, and what the teacher was wearing. But most of them were able to screen out these inconsequential stimuli and focus on the relevant details.

Students with mental retardation, on the other hand, often do not know what to focus their attention on when they are trying to figure out something new. They dwell on meaningless details and disregard key pieces of information. Consequently, they struggle at putting bits of information together in order to see the bigger picture.

Maybe I can illustrate this concept with a riddle. Read the following passage and see whether you can come up with the answer. But don't read too far. Really try to figure out the riddle before you go on.

Alive without breath,
As cold as death;
Never thirsty, ever drinking,
All in mail never clinking.

I got that from J.R.R. Tolkien's *The Hobbit*, so if you read it, you probably know what the answer is. But if you don't, take a few moments and try to solve it. Maybe show it to some of your friends or even your students or kids. See if they can come up with the answer quicker than you can.

If you are struggling to come up with the answer to this riddle, it isn't because that answer is something that you aren't familiar with or that the words in the riddle are beyond your comprehension. If you are having difficulty, it is probably because you are focusing on the wrong details or you are misinterpreting some of the lines. For example, after reading the last line, you might be thinking of things that wear armor, such as knights or a tank. But that is leading you in the wrong direction. So, in a sense, you are not deciphering the riddle as "efficiently" as some people who focus on other clues, such as "never thirsty, always drinking," and then get the answer almost automatically.

Something that you probably are doing is identifying the riddle's keywords and phrases, such as "without breath," "cold," and "ever drinking." For example, you might have thought to yourself, "What is something that is cold, always drinking, but doesn't have a breath?"

Inefficient learners wouldn't utilize this kind of problem solving strategy. They would merely keep reading and rereading the words until the answer came to them. They are very passive and will rarely change problem-solving strategies, even when the strategy that they are using isn't working.

Have you figured out the riddle yet? If you began thinking about things that are cold and live in water, you probably arrived at the answer a long time ago. The answer, of course, is "fish!"

If you didn't get the answer until just now, don't worry. It doesn't mean that you have "subaverage intelligence" or mental retardation. It just means that you weren't picking up the relevant clues and then thinking about them in the right way for this particular exercise. In other words, you weren't processing the information in the riddle very efficiently.

If you had mental retardation, most things would be like this riddle. You would probably focus on the wrong details and have to take longer to arrive at the correct answer. Again, I am not saying that people with mental retardation can't solve riddles; they certainly can. However, they will probably take longer than people with average or above-average intelligence.

So, let's summarize a little bit. People with mental retardation are very passive learners. They don't seek out new and effective ways of acquiring information. They tend to wait for answers to magically appear in their heads. Further, they tend to focus on the wrong details, so their learning is slowed down. But there is more!

Memory

Another learning characteristic of individuals with mental retardation involves memory. If you can't recall basic facts or information, learning is going to be tough for you. Unfortunately, people with mental retardation usually have very poor short- and long-term memories. That is to say, they have difficulty retrieving data that they have already mastered. As you can imagine, this slows their learning down ever further.

I should point out that there *are* people with mental retardation who have incredible memories. For example, one of my students with autism had a photographic memory, just like the character in the movie *Rainman*. He remembered everything that he read. It was really quite fascinating.

Once, he walked up to me in the hallway, quoted my full name, address, social security number, and the name of my cat and then walked away. It left me very puzzled. But then I remembered that on the weekends he worked at our local humane society where he typed files into their computer. I had adopted a cat a year or so before and he must have entered my information into their system!

Although you have probably have heard similar stories, children with mental retardation usually don't have exceptional memories. Such circumstances are pretty rare.

"So what can I do to improve my child's memory?" you ask. Well, first you need to understand why their memory is so bad.

First of all, you probably recognize when you will need to remember specific information. For example, if you park your car in a huge parking lot, you probably think to yourself, "Boy! I better remember where I parked or I will be walking home!" Or, if you meet somebody important, such as a potential friend or somebody during a job interview, you think to yourself, "I better remember her name!"

People with mental retardation often don't distinguish important information from unimportant information. For example, they don't know whether to memorize the person's name or what their face looks like or what they are wearing or what the person might have said, such as "It is a nice day, isn't it?"

Further, people with mental retardation tend to focus on the here and now, not the future, so it never occurs to them that they are going need to remember something for later. They don't think to themselves, "I better try to remember this because it might help me in a few days!" As a result, what they tend to remember is almost accidental. They just happened to remember things without proactively trying to do so.

Moreover, when they do try to remember things, they often associate information with meaningless variables. For example, rather than looking at a sign that says where in a parking lot they parked (e.g., section 3 D), they might try to remember that they parked next to a white minivan, not realizing that there may be dozens of white minivans in the lot or that the white minivan might be gone when they come back.

Okay, so let's go back to the original issue of how to improve your child's memory. First of all, you need to teach him that remembering things is important. Tell him what he has to remember and why. Also tell him what is not important and can be forgotten.

It is particularly important to educate students with mental retardation about future events since this often doesn't come naturally to them. For example, you might say, "What homework do you have this weekend?" And then add, "So what materials will you need to remember to bring home with you today so that you can do the homework this weekend?"

Next, teach them strategies that minimize the energy required to remember things. For example, I strongly encourage teachers to use daily logs when working with kids with mental retardation. As soon as an assignment is given, I suggest that teachers make their students write it down in their daily log. That way, the student doesn't have to waste energy remembering what is due and when. Parents can use the same strategy for helping children remember daily chores or activities.

Also teach students strategies that help them recall things quickly. For example, have them repeat things three times to themselves and a couple times out loud. So, when they meet somebody and want to remember their name, the student can say something like, "It is nice to meet you, Rob." "So what do you do for a living, Rob?" They then can imagine the name "Rob" written or echoing in their head.

You can use flash cards and other devices the same way. If you want a child to remember vocabulary words or math facts or something like that, keep drilling them over and over. Again, kids with mental retardation need plenty of practice to master tasks. So don't be afraid to overdo it! Show them the same flash cards day after day! Eventually, they will get it. Then return to what they have learned periodically so that they get into the habit of recalling the information from their long-term memory.

Also encourage your children to pair relevant and related variables. For example, suppose that Rob has red hair. They can use the "R" in "red" to remember the "R" in "Rob."

Most importantly, you have to get your child into the habit of remembering things. Memory is like a muscle. If you don't use it, you lose it. Unfortunately, children with disabilities too often become dependent on other people constantly reminding them of everything, so they never build the sense that remembering information is important. They just assume that people will always tell them what to do and when. Further, their ability to recall information decreases.

A parent of one of my students once told me that she was getting sick and tired of telling her child when his favorite television programs were on. So I just said, almost flippantly, "Then don't. Make him remember for himself." So, she did. Every time the child asked, "When is such and such on?" the mother would say, "I don't know." If the child wanted to see the show, he had to look it up in the *TV Guide* and remember it for himself. He became so motivated to remember when his shows were on that he bought a watch with an alarm. He then set the alarm to go off whenever various programs were about to air.

Generalization

In addition to having difficulty learning new information and recalling old information, people with mental retardation also have problems applying information, especially to novel situations. Let me give you some examples.

When I was teaching high school students, we focused a great deal on teaching life skills, such as how to wash clothes. Each week, we would have students bring in some dirty clothes that they would wash in the "home economics" room. We went to extreme lengths to break the task down into small, manageable steps (which is called a "task analysis"). We had picture boards with each step clearly illustrated. We even practiced each step many, many times. Eventually, my students were able to use the washer and dryer independently . . . but *only* the washer and dryer in the home economics rooms!

You see, there are many different types of washers and dryers. Some require you to put clothes into the machine from the top, others from the front. Some have dials that you need to turn before it will start. Others have buttons that need to be pushed. And so forth.

My students became experts at washing their clothes on the particular kind of machine that we had at school. However, they had extreme difficulty trying to figure out how to use the machines at their own homes or in the local laundromats. Even when the machines were very similar, they had problems applying what they learned at school to other environments. For instance, one student got upset because, at school, there was a white cabinet next to the washer where the detergent was kept, but not at home. Another student couldn't wash clothes at home because we used a liquid detergent and his mother used a powder.

We also dedicated a great deal of time to teaching our students how to use money. We even had a classroom store where they used Xerox copies of dollar bills to "buy" supplies, such as pencils and paper. But, as you might guess, they didn't apply what they learned in the classroom to the community. One of the biggest problems was that they couldn't get used to the idea of using real money. They knew what the Xeroxed money meant, but not real money!

So, what can you do to build generalization skills? First and foremost, teach everything in a variety of different environments, especially the one in which the skills are going to be employed! If you are going to teach a child how to use a washing machine, teach them how to use several different models in different places. For example, use the machines at school, in local laundromats, and—if possible—at their homes.

Point out the commonalities that all of the models have and teach the child how to problem solve by utilize various clues to figure out how to perform each step. For example, at the laundromat where I eventually started bringing my students, all of the machines had places to insert change. Some had vertical slots into which you drop coins. Others had horizontal trays onto which you placed the coins. You would then push the tray into the machine. In both cases, there was usually a picture of coins or a "$" sign. I got my students used to looking for the slots. I had them say out loud, "Now where do I put the money?" Eventually they got the hang of it.

Also, use actual materials rather than replicas. Toward the end of my high school teaching career, I began using real money rather than the Xeroxed copies. My students not only learned quicker, but they also didn't have to transfer what they learned about fake money to real money. Cutting out that middle step made all of the difference in the world!

SOCIAL CHARACTERISTICS

Individuals with mental retardation tend to have very underdeveloped social skills. This isn't to say that they can't be polite and charming. Some certainly can! Many of my students could charm you into doing anything that they wanted! I just mean that they often have difficulty interacting appropriately. For example, they might tell a joke when they should be serious or interrupt a conversation at the wrong time—that kind of thing.

Appropriate social skills are very hard to master. Think about it. Think about all of the skills that you need to carry on an appropriate conversation with a stranger. You need to be able to read nonverbal cues, such as facial expressions, body language, and posture. You also have to be able to understand what is being said and then make a relevant response. You have to take turns and allow others to speak. You can't constantly interrupt. And so forth.

As a result of these many complexities, kids with mental retardation often do not fit in socially. They tend to have difficulty gauging the mood of an interaction. For example, they might joke when people are being serious. They might also be overly informal or have difficulty adjusting to changing expectations.

Let me tell you a quick story about how kids have problems adjusting to changing expectations. When I taught middle school and high school, I would frequently get students who were overly "clingy" and "touchy." They would always want hugs and to be kissed on the head and picked up and held and so forth.

There are a number of problems with this behavior. First, it is inappropriate, especially since I am a male teacher. Nowadays, male teachers can't go around touching students, let alone kissing them! It just is not acceptable. It is a lawsuit waiting to happen!

Second, as we discussed, kids with mental retardation tend to have problems generalizing. So, if I let them hug and kiss me, they will likely go around hugging and kissing all kinds of strangers and adults at inappropriate times or places—such as on their job site.

Finally, such behavior puts people with mental retardation at extreme risk for sexual exploitation. They will go up to the wrong person, kiss and hug them and that person will slowly turn that innocent behavior into something very disgusting. (See boxed discussion 5.1 for more details about the sexual exploitation of kids with mental retardation.)

Now please understand, I am not saying that kids with mental retardation shouldn't be friendly or affectionate. I am just saying that sometimes you have to teach them when and where and with whom! But let's get back to my story regarding changing expectations.

It was really puzzling that all of our kids came to us thinking that it was appropriate to be kissed and hugged all the time at school. Then we found out that in the elementary schools from which our students came the teachers routinely used "physical" praise. Again, this is fine for little kids, but probably not for teenagers and young adults—especially when we want them to start acting their age! And remember, kids with mental retardation often don't realize that one set of behaviors is fine when they are one age and a completely different set of behaviors is expected when they get older.

In the end, we had to get together with the elementary school teachers and come to an understanding regarding how children with mental retardation should be treated. The kindergarten and early grade-level teachers still praised physically. But the fourth-, fifth-, and sixth-grade teachers started to wean the students off of it. Further, when they got to our school, we replaced the hugging and kissing with high fives and handshakes, which is more age appropriate.

The Sexual Exploitation of People with Mental Retardation

This topic probably deserves its own chapter, but we just don't have that kind of time. Still it is *extremely* important. So please consider the follow data.

According to the ARC (formally called the Association for Retarded Citizens), every year, approximately 20 percent of females and 5–10 percent of males with mental retardation are sexually abused. Each year, between 15,000 and 19,000 people with mental retardation are reported raped. It is estimated that 39–68 percent of girls and 16–30 percent of boys will be sexually abused by their eighteenth birthday. By the end of their lifetime, nearly 90 percent of all people with mental retardation will be sexually abused at some point. Unfortunately, the frequency of reported rape and sexual abuse is increasing.

People with mental retardation are obvious targets for sexual offenders. They are easily confused and distracted. They often don't know what kind of sexual contact is appropriate or inappropriate, so they may not report incidents. Finally, they have poor memories, so they are bad witnesses for police and prosecutors.

What to look for if you suspect sexual abuse:

- Unexplainable bruises, especially in genital areas
- Genital discomfort
- Sexually transmitted diseases
- Changes in personality, such as depression, anxiety, or withdrawal
- Sudden atypical attachment to people
- Reluctance to go somewhere or be with somebody
- Sexually graphic language or play
- Sleep disturbances

If you suspect that somebody, with or without mental retardation, is being sexually abused, do not bathe the person or wash his or her clothes, since this may destroy evidence. Contact the police *immediately*. You can also contact the National Task Force on Abuse and Disabilities at 1-310-391-2420 or at abuses@soca.com.

How To Build Your Child's Social Skills

It is very easy for me to sit here and type all kinds of stories and facts about how people with mental retardation have poor social skills. But the real issue is, "How do you improve them?" Here are some suggestions.

Have Clear and Consistent Expectations

As we discussed before, kids with mental retardation really need clarity and consistency. So, it is very important that your expectations don't keep changing. For example, if you expect no name calling or teasing, then you have to make sure that you follow through on your expectations as much as possible. That means frequently reinforcing appropriate behavior and addressing inappropriate behavior. We will be talking about rewards and punishments in the next chapter.

So, before you start disciplining and rewarding your child, sit down and think about how you want him or her to act. Make a list of some of the behaviors you want to stop and what behaviors you want to replace them with. Pick two or three behaviors, such as defying authority and hitting other kids, and focus exclusively upon those. Then, once those behaviors have been modified, pick another two or three behaviors to address. You don't want to work on too much too fast. You could overwhelm your child.

There is a great deal to know about behavior modification. There are several good books on the market that you might want to read, including *Enhancing Your Child's Behavior: A Step-by-Step Guide for Parents and Teachers*. It is available through the publisher of this book as well as at www.amazon.com and www.barnesandnoble.com. Other resources are listed in the appendix.

Model Appropriate Behavior

Once you have decided what social skills you want to address, you have to model the appropriate behavior. Keep in mind that telling kids with mental retardation what to do isn't the best way to teach them. They need to see things in order to process them. So, *show* them how to act. Frequently explain to them why you are acting a certain way and why other behavior is not appropriate.

Because children with mental retardation tend to imitate the behavior of people around them, I highly recommend that they interact a lot with older kids—*but only if the older kids are well behaved and responsible.* There are several programs that pair older students with younger kids with disabilities. I participated in one when I was in high school called "CrossAge." Basically, I tutored kids who were in special education. It is what made me become a teacher. The Boys' and Girls' Clubs and many YMCAs often have similar programs. The idea is to expose your child to as many good role models as possible.

You also should limit the number of bad influences that your child is around. This includes what children watch on television and in movies! I'll give you an example.

A few years ago, there was a cartoon program that was really popular with kids. For the life of me, I can't remember what it was called or what it was about, but it had a lot of martial arts moves in it. I think the main characters were ninjas or something.

At any rate, my students would watch this show and start imitating everything that they saw. They would come to class and try to karate chop their desks in half, do roundhouse kicks, and go flying through the air with legs and arms flailing around. I can't even guess how many students got hurt and how many things, especially pencils, got broken in two!

When we started sending notes home to parents requesting that they monitor what their children were watching, things started to change drastically. They no longer were trying to kill each other or break through brick walls. I think that they started watching Pokémon. As a result, other, far less violent, behaviors emerged.

The point is that kids with mental retardation learn by watching other people, so you have to really be conscious of who and what they are being exposed to. I'll give you another quick example. This one might disgust you, so be prepared.

As I told you before, I used to get jobs for my older high school students. Further, we often got them jobs at fast food places like McDonald's and Burger King. One of my students, let's call him Richard, was a cook. He really loved his job, however, he kept getting in trouble by his boss for not doing things the "company way."

For instance, according to the company's training videotapes, hamburger patties were supposed to be on the grill for a certain number of minutes. You were supposed to put the patties on the grill, push a button, and when the alarm went off, you flipped them over. You weren't supposed to remove them beforehand.

That was the company way. What everybody actually did was, they would put the patty on the grill, push it down with the spatula, flip it, and then push it down again. Apparently, pushing the meat down made it cook faster or something. Hamburgers were finished in half the time.

I taught Richard to cook the "corporate" way. We watched the videos, practiced on a grill, and everything was fine. After a while, he was able to cook completely independently. But soon, I started getting calls from his boss. Apparently, Richard was going against the rules.

So, one day, I went in and watched Richard work and sure enough, he was searing the food and rushing it through before it was completely cooked. But then I watched the other cooks (teenagers without disabilities). They were doing the same thing. In effect, they modeled behavior that undid everything that I taught Richard!

Now if that doesn't disgust you a little bit, I am sure that this will. As I watched Richard, one of the teenage cooks dropped a hamburger on the ground, picked it up, put it on a bun, and sent it to the cashier! Ugh! But what shocked me even more was that, minutes later, I saw Richard drop a hamburger on the ground (apparently on purpose) and do the *exact* same thing!

If you are wondering, I made sure that neither hamburger got to the customer. I told the manager what I saw. He wasn't surprised that Richard would do such a thing. After all, that is why Richard was getting in so much trouble. However, he couldn't believe that the other, nondisabled, cook would be so disgusting. Apparently, he was the best cook the manager had.

This raises an important point. You see, Richard was modeling the behavior of the other cook, but he didn't have the skills to know when to behave appropriately and when not to. Richard would drop a hamburger on the floor right in front of his manager, pick it up, and send it to the cashier without knowing that he was going to get in trouble. The nondisabled cook, however, was able to avoid getting in trouble because he could change his behavior when the boss was watching!

Because nondisabled kids are able to "change their spots" when being observed, it is really important to make sure that you are letting your child play with kids who can be trusted. As we discussed a few pages back, people with mental retardation are very prone to being abused. Before you allow your child to play with other kids, before you get a babysitter, or before you enroll your child in an after-school program, you should really check out the people with whom you are entrusting your pride and joy. Ask for references. Do background checks. Get as much information as possible before finding role models!

Build Age-Appropriate Vocabulary and Grammar

Something else that you can do to develop your child's social skills is to teach him or her how to speak like an adult. Too often, my high school students spoke like little babies. They will say things like, "Me not like that!" or "Me be sorry." Perhaps it is just a pet peeve of mine or something, but I honestly believe that it is hard to treat people like adults when they sound like children. Moreover, kids with mental retardation are not going to be able to be socially integrated with their peers if they can't sound and act like their peers.

So, teach your child how to speak correctly. Don't let baby talk carry on longer than what is appropriate. Being able to speak well will help your child socially, professionally, and academically. Plus, if you enlarge his vocabulary early, his comprehension of new ideas will be enhanced and he may learn quicker later in life.

Practice! Practice! Practice!

Finally, if you want to build your child's social skills, you have to make her practice, practice, *practice*! This means making sure that she has plenty of opportunities for appropriate social interaction. Getting her involved with groups like the ones that we discussed before or even regular after-school activities can help immensely. Just because a child has mental retardation doesn't mean that he or she can't play little league baseball or join clubs or go to the YMCA and play with other kids. The more exposure to social situations that children with mental retardation have, the better!

In addition to getting your child enrolled in various sports and clubs and other group opportunities, you can also teach social skills by role-playing. What's role-playing? Well, think of it as a game where you and your child act out various situations. It is kind of playacting. For example, sit down with your child and act out a situation where somebody is trying to give them drugs. Teach your child how to say no.

I used to role-play job interviews with my students. I would have them get all dressed up and come into my office, shake my hand, and then explain why they wanted a job. It really helped them for the real thing!

We even role-played dating situations! We would set up the classroom like a nice restaurant and eat lunch. The students had to say things like, "Please pass the soda pop!" And "Why, thank you. I had a wonderful time. Let's do this again!"

It may sound kind of funny, but the practice really does help. I mean, how else are they going to be prepared for such events? Again, the main idea is to give children with mental retardation frequent opportunities to learn how to act appropriately. Without these opportunities, how do you expect them to learn?

PHYSIOLOGICAL CHARACTERISTICS

Talking about the physiological characteristics of people with mental retardation is very difficult. First, as within any population, there are a great many differences between people with mental retardation. Secondly, the vast majority of kids with mental retardation look like any other "normal" child. Kids with mental retardation don't have hunched backs or a big bull's-eye painted on their chests. They are like everybody else.

As soon as I say that, however, I also have to point out that there are some physiological issues that are more common among the people with mental retardation than the nondisabled population. Specifically, I want to briefly address three very general topics:

- Seizures
- General health, and
- Overall appearance

Seizures

We already discussed seizures a little bit in chapter 3, when we discussed causes of mental retardation. However, because chronic seizures are so prevalent among people with mental retardation, it is something that we should dedicate more time to. Moreover, untreated chronic seizures can cause extensive brain damage, thus decreasing a child's functioning abilities.

Seizures are like electrical storms in the brain, and they affect people in different ways. Some seizures, such as tonic-clonic seizures, result in violent convulsions. Others, such as absence seizures, cause people to stare ahead as if daydreaming.

- *Absence seizures (a.k.a petit mal seizures).* Individuals experiencing an absence seizure look as if they are staring off into space, much like they are daydreaming, but they will not respond even if you wave your hand in front of their face. They might blink frequently or their head might bob up and down, but other than that, they will have a vacant expression. Absence seizures will usually only last a few seconds; however, most individuals will have frequent seizures per day.
- *Myoclonic seizures.* Myoclonic seizures are characterized by sudden jerking motions of a single muscle or group of muscles. For example, their hand might twitch violently or their upper body might swing forward and then back. Myoclonic seizures should not be confused with normal muscle spasms or Tourette syndrome.
- *Atonic seizures.* People having atonic seizures will suddenly lose all muscle tone, as if they were rag dolls.
- *Tonic seizures.* Tonic seizures cause people to go rigid, as if frozen in stone.
- *Tonic-clonic seizures (a.k.a. grand mal seizures).* Tonic-clonic seizures begin with the person becoming very rigid (see tonic seizures). Their body then convulses as if it is being shocked. They will fall to the ground, repeatedly arch their backs, jerk their arms and legs, and roll their eyes back into their heads. They might also urinate, defecate, and foam at the mouth.
- *Frontal lobe seizures.* Individuals with frontal lobe seizures may experience a strange twitching or odd feeling in their face, hands, or legs.

Sometimes their heads will turn to one side or one of their arms will stiffen. In some cases, their bodies will display a series of bizarre movements. Unlike tonic, clonic, absence, or tonic-clonic seizures, people with frontal lobe seizures are aware of what is transpiring.

- *Parietal lobe seizures.* Parietal lobe seizures are characterized by a tingling feeling that may spread throughout the body. Individuals may feel like they are moving, sinking, or being choked.
- *Occipital lobe seizures.* Individuals who are experiencing occipital lobe seizures will temporarily lose part or all of their vision. They might see flashes of light or have hallucinations. Vision will return to normal after the seizure is over.

Epilepsy is a condition in which people experience frequent seizures, unless the seizures are controlled by medications. In the general population, less than 1 percent of people have epilepsy. However, between 20 and 30 percent of children with mental retardation have epilepsy. If you have a child with mental retardation, there is a good chance that you will see a seizure at some point in your child's life.

So, what do you do if your child is having a seizure? Good question! First of all, remain calm. There is nothing that you can do that will stop a seizure, so don't even try.

Second, look at the time. You will have to be able to tell how long a seizure lasts so that you can see if they are getting worse. This is particularly important if your child is on medications. Noting the duration of the seizures will give you and your doctors an idea of whether the medications are working.

Third, do *not* call an ambulance *unless*:

1. your child has never had a seizure before,
2. the seizure goes on for longer than usual,
3. your child keeps having one seizure after the other, or
4. if you child is hurt while having a seizure.

If you call an ambulance, the operator will likely ask you how long the seizure has been going on. So, make sure you look at the clock as soon as possible.

Fourth, get your child on the ground, if he or she isn't already there. Cushion the head with something such as a folded shirt or a purse. You don't want the child to bang his or her head against the ground or to pull things on top of himself or herself, so move everything out of the immediate area.

Fifth, *never, ever* put anything in their mouth! Years ago, it used to be standard operating practice to put things in people's mouths so that they don't "swallow" their tongue. But it is physically impossible to swallow a tongue. Even if the tongue swells up and fills their mouth, the seizuring person can still breathe through his or her nose. Further, people have incredibly strong bite reflexes! So, if you put something in their mouth, they are likely to bite it off! Story time!

My father worked in a factory in the 1960s. At that time, everybody was told to put a spoon in people's mouths if they were having a seizure. So, one day, as you might guess, an employee fell to the floor and started convulsing. When somebody put a metal spoon in his mouth, the worker bit right through it! Seriously! Right though the metal!

So then the worker was choking on the broken spoon that was stuck in his throat! Apparently everybody started to panic, which is understandable given the situation. Without thinking, somebody reached in and tried to retrieve the broken spoon, but the seizuring worker bit down and cut off his index finger!

So now the worker has part of a metal spoon and half of a human index finger lodged in his throat. People were really starting to panic to say the least! The way my father tells it, the worker was turning blue and looked like he was suffocating.

Finally, somebody got the idea to grab the worker by the feet and hold him upside down like in the cartoons or the *Three Stooges*. This probably wasn't the smartest thing to do, but it did the trick. As the worker dangled upside down, still convulsing, the finger and metal spoon came out! The moral of the story? *Don't put anything in the mouths of people who are having a seizure*!

Sixth, as your child is seizuring, try to make him or her as comfortable as possible. Loosen his clothes, take off his glasses. If he is wearing a tie or something around his neck, try to take it off. Then wait. Again, there is nothing that you can do other than make the child safe and comfortable.

Once your child comes out of a seizure, she might be confused and disoriented. You might have to explain where she is and what had happened. Further, she probably urinated or defecated on herself, so she might have to get cleaned up. If you are a teacher, you should have extra clothing handy in your classroom. If you are a parent, keep extra clothes in the trunk of your car, just in case you are away from home when the seizure hits.

Let the child rest, but whatever you do, don't leave the child alone, even if he seems like he is fine. Don't leave him alone. Seizures are like earthquakes. They typically happen in pairs or groups. Sit with the child and see if another seizure ensues.

Also, do *not* give the person anything to eat or drink until you are sure that he or she is fully alert. The last thing you want to happen is to have the person have another seizure when he has food or water in his mouth.

Next, check to make sure that the person isn't hurt. He might have bruised or cut himself during the seizure. Treat as needed. If you think that he hit his head and has a concussion, get him to a doctor.

Finally, document everything. Write down how long the seizure lasted, what the person did during the seizure, whether the person complained of anything unusual right before the seizure hit (e.g., hot flashes, cold sweats, tingling feelings, etc.). Let your doctor know everything. Below is a quick summary of what to do when your child is having a seizure.

1. Remain calm
2. Notice the time
3. Get the person to the floor
4. Cushion his or her head
5. Clear the immediate area
6. Make the person comfortable
7. Call 911 *only* if this is the person's first seizure, if the seizure is longer than normal, if the person keeps having seizures, or the person is hurt
8. Reorient the person after the seizure is over
9. Allow the person to rest, if needed
10. Don't leave the person alone for at least an hour after the last seizure

General Health

Perhaps the greatest injustice for people with mental retardation is their poor health and short lifespan. As we discussed at the very beginning of this book, the average life expectancy for a person with mental retardation is a little over sixty-three years. The average life expectancy of a person in the general population, on the other hand, is just about seventy-seven years. That is nearly fifteen years longer than people with mental retardation! Moreover, the more severe the mental retardation, the shorter their lifespan will most likely be.

There are several reasons for the lack of longevity for people with mental retardation. One is that people with mental retardation often have other conditions, such as heart defects or immune deficiencies. Another is that they tend not to get proper health care.

But probably the biggest factor contributing to the short life of people with mental retardation is their lifestyles. People with mental retardation are not active. They tend to do very few physical activities. Further, they tend to be overweight and have very poor diets.

So, what can you do? Well, first of all, make sure children with mental retardation eat well. Apparently, good eating habits start very early. If you feed children fruits and vegetables when they are young, they have a greater chance of liking fruits and vegetables when they get older.

Also, get your child off the sofa. Turn off the television! Have your child outside running around! Sign her up for team sports and group activities. Have him join a gym or the YMCA. In addition to improving their health, it might also improve their social skills and make them happier.

General Appearance

I am hesitating to write about this topic. I am afraid that I am going to sound negative or to stereotype people with mental retardation. Further, I could find no research studies or data-driven facts about this topic at all. However, after consulting with other teachers, I have decided to talk about something that might appear superficial, but I think is very important.

You see, while most people with mental retardation, especially mild mental retardation, have no physiological symptoms, they are often easy to pick out of the crowd. For whatever reason, most of my students, always dressed, well . . . like nerds. They wear clothes that are either too big or too small. They wear white socks with dark dress shoes, as well as pants that are several inches too short. They wear glasses that are unflattering. They have haircuts that went out of style in the 1950s or are just plain bad. I could go on and on, but I think that you get the picture.

Now please, keep in mind that I didn't say all people with mental retardation are like this. Further, I am basing this entirely upon my own observations and the comments made by other teachers that I know. Maybe every student with mental retardation outside of my hometown dresses with perfection and is the top of style. Maybe they are setting the fashion trends! But somehow I doubt it.

Why is this important? Who cares how kids with mental retardation look? Well, for one, I hope that they do. And, for another, I know that their nondisabled peers do.

Have you ever listened to a group of teenagers talk? Even preteenagers! There is such an emphasis on appearances. Kids can't hope to fit in if they look different. Unfortunately, the way that many kids with mental retardation dress, they might as well hang a sign on their back saying, "Don't play with me! Don't treat me as an equal!"

I guess what I am trying to say is that I see how regular education students treat kids with disabilities, especially mental retardation. They tease them, sometime cruelly. But they don't tease them because they have mental retardation or because they "aren't smart." Kids honestly don't care if other students are smart or not. As a matter of fact, the smart kids tend to get teased for knowing too much!

When I walk up and down the hallways at school or watch during recess or lunch period, I see kids with mental retardation getting picked on because of how they look. They don't get teased because of their droopy eyelids or oddly shaped heads. They get teased because they aren't wearing the right clothes or have the correct backpack with popular characters on them! I'll give you an example.

A few days ago, I was in a high school observing a student teacher of mine when I noticed a girl with mental retardation getting ready to go home. She had a Hello Kitty backpack, a lunch box with the Powder Puff Girls on it, and her folders had pictures of Smurfs! She even had a cute little outfit on that would have be perfect if she were in first grade, but she wasn't. She was probably eighteen or nineteen years old!

My point is, if you want your child to act like a normal kid, if you want your child to be treated like a normal kid, if you want your child to have friends . . . then try to have them look like a normal kid! Make sure that they wear the up-to-date fashions. Be sure that they have good hairstyles. Buy them school supplies that are appropriate for their age.

Now, in all honesty, I know nothing about teenage trends. I personally think that low-cut, tight-fitting jeans that show underwear look awful! But I also know that, if I were a teenager again, that is exactly what I would be wearing. And if I didn't, I know that I would be feeling self-conscious and I would probably get picked on.

If you don't know what is hip nowadays, go the mall. Watch an episode of whatever television program is popular. Ask the teenie-bopper down the street. But please, don't dress your child as if he or she has mental retardation. Dress your child for success!

SUMMARY

Throughout this chapter, we discussed various general characteristics of people with mental retardation. We covered motivational issues, such as learned helplessness and external locus of control. We covered issues related to self-regulation and how people with mental retardation often do not monitor or attempt to change their own behaviors. We went into different learning problems that children with mental retardation often have, such as generalizing information from situation to situation. Finally, we addressed social and physiological issues, including health concerns and factors that might make them social outcasts.

Although we have discussed various strategies for dealing with each of these issues, we haven't gone into detail about how to teach children with mental retardation. We haven't talked about overall teaching strategies, or the philosophies that are now commonly held in schools. Fortunately, these are the topics for our next chapter!

6

PHILOSOPHIES AND TIPS FOR TEACHING INDIVIDUALS WHO HAVE MENTAL RETARDATION

GUIDED COMPREHENSION QUESTIONS

By the time you finish reading this chapter, you should be able to

1. Identify three components of effective teaching
2. Discuss educational philosophies that might affect your child
3. Utilize teaching strategies that might enhance your child's learning

INTRODUCTION

Okay, by now you should have a good idea about what mental retardation is, what causes it, the conditions associated with mental retardation, and the common characteristics that individuals with mental retardation tend to have. I suppose that if there has to be only one thing that you have learned thus far, I want it to be that kids with mental retardation *can* learn. Like the title of this book says, "Mental retardation doesn't mean 'stupid!'"

"But how do I teach kids with mental retardation?" is probably your next question. "Is it like teaching other children? Or, do you have to use special techniques and strategies?"

These are great questions! Fortunately, in this chapter, I want to talk about the philosophical foundation of working with students who have special needs. I also want to go over a few very general teaching strategies that are very useful for educating kids who have mental retardation in particular. But, before we move on, I want to make a couple very important points.

First, by and large, teaching kids with disabilities, whether mental retardation or learning disabilities or whatever, is basically the same as teaching anybody without a disability. Yes, there are certain considerations that you need to make. For instance, if a student is blind, you probably don't want to use a lot of visuals when teaching that student! But, in a general sense, effectively teaching all students involves three things:

- exposure to new ideas,
- time to process what the new ideas mean, and
- activities that allow the new ideas to be applied.

Exposure to New Ideas

If people aren't exposed to new ideas or skills, they can't learn them. This is just common sense. People with mental retardation tend to need more exposure than do other people. So, rather than just seeing or hearing something once or twice, people with mental retardation often require four or five or ten times before they can master new ideas. Keep this in mind when teaching your child.

Time to Process What New Ideas Mean

Just as people with mental retardation need more exposure to ideas, they also need more time to process new information. For example, in regular education, there is something called "the five-second rule." Basically, regular educators are taught to wait at least five second after asking a question before they call on a student for the answer. This gives their students time to think about what has been asked and formulate the correct response.

Students with mental retardation process information much slower than their nondisabled peers. They may require ten or fifteen seconds, if not longer, to arrive at their answer. So, make sure that you don't rush your child. Waiting for your child may make you feel impatient, and you will probably feel compelled to "help" him along, but don't! Give children with mental retardation the time that they need, and don't expect them to learn as quickly as everybody else!

Activities That Allow New Ideas to Be Applied

Effective teachers allow their students to apply what they have learned. Whether it is a math or science problem, a spelling or vocabulary word, or a physical activity such as playing the piano or writing their names, people usually need to utilize new knowledge before it truly sinks into their brains. Without this application, students are likely to soon forget what they have "learned."

As you can probably guess, kids with mental retardation need more numerous opportunities to apply new knowledge before it becomes committed to long-term memory. Further, kids with mental retardation need hands-on activities in order to fully comprehend abstract concepts, such as time or math. So, give your child several tasks that will enable her to employ the lessons that you are trying to teach. Further, make sure that the tasks are as real to life as possible. The more times they partake in these activities, the more likely they will learn the underlying skills.

PEOPLE FIRST LANGUAGE

Now that we talked a little bit about the overall mechanics of teaching, I want to cover some of the important philosophies and strategies that are associated with special education and mental retardation. The first topic that I want to discuss here is "people-first language." Very simply, people-first language means that you say things like "child with mental retardation" or "individual who has mental retardation." In other words, when talking about people with disabilities, you emphasize the person first, and then mention their diagnosis.

Initially, this topic might seem a bit meaningless or just a matter of semantics. Some of my college students roll their eyes when I correct their "disability-first language," especially when they say "retarded kids" or "disabled students." I suspect that they think I am being overly politically correct or something.

But the fact is, words can hurt people. What we say and how we say it conveys hidden messages. If you don't believe me, just think about the many racially charged words and phrases that are out there. I won't use any here, so you will have to guess at the ones that I mean. If what we say and how we say it isn't important, we wouldn't be so careful about how we discuss racial issues. We don't say certain racial words, not because it is "politically correct," but because we, as a society, have realized that certain words have served to repress entire populations of people.

By saying "mentally retarded child," we are focusing upon the disability. It is like we are covertly saying, "This isn't a real child . . . this is a *mentally retarded* child." Perhaps that is not what people mean to imply, but it is often how the words are interpreted or internalized.

So the bottom line is this: When you are talking about people who have mental retardation or any other conditions, emphasize the person first and then say the disability. It is a subtle, but very important, way that you can treat people who have disabilities with respect. And without showing respect, you can't be an effective teacher.

DIGNITY OF RISK

"Dignity of risk" is a philosophy to which many teachers and parents of kids with mental retardation have difficulty adhering. Its underlying principle is that failure is usually our greatest teacher. Unfortunately, we too often shelter kids with disabilities from failure. So, in the end, they wind up missing out on this critical aspect of their education.

Think about it for a moment. As soon as things start to get a little tough for kids with mental retardation or they start to struggle, what do we do? We jump in and begin helping them!

In and of itself, this isn't a bad thing. It's great that people want to help. But what our helping ends up teaching the child is that he doesn't need to try. All he has to do to get something done is look at an adult with a confused look and shrugged shoulders and then the adult will do the desired activity for him. In essence, this is the root to the learned helplessness that we discussed earlier.

So, what the dignity of risk philosophy is more or less saying is that we should allow people with mental retardation to make mistakes and learn from them. I am not advocating that we should not give kids with mental retardation *any* help. I am just pointing out that too much help can often actually hurt the child. You have to strike a good balance between helping and allowing the child to work at their own pace, even if that means they don't succeed initially. Perhaps an example might help.

One of the teachers with whom I have been working was really perplexed by the lack of progress that her students were making throughout the semester. She has taught for many years and has a good idea what kids can and can't do. But for some reason, this particular group of students was not progressing *at all*! No matter what strategies she tried or how much time she spent on a topic, her students as whole were simply not learning, and she was utterly flabbergasted.

Then one day she noticed something that made her understand. Students would raise their hands, looked really sad at the classroom aide, and the aide just gave them the correct answers! In other words, what the kids had learned wasn't math and English, but how to manipulate the teacher's aide.

Now before you start minimizing the impact of the aide's "kindness," keep in mind that this went on for the better part of a school year. So, the students weren't learning what they should have been. They were falling further and further behind their peers. Moreover, they were learning bad habits that would affect them for the rest of their lives.

Again, I am not suggesting that the aide shouldn't have helped the students. I am not saying that she should have turned her back on the students whenever they raised their hands and said that they were confused. What the aide should have done was figured out why the students were having problems and *taught* them the skills needed for accomplishing the task. If the aide needed to go over a problem to show how it is done, she should have made up a problem different from the ones the students were working on.

For example, if they were working on math and students claimed to be stuck on the problem 5 + 5, the aide should have demonstrated what addition was and how to apply it to their problem. Maybe teach them how to figure out what 5 + 4 was and then have them apply it to 5 + 5.

Again, the issue is to have individuals with mental retardation do their own work. If they fail or get the wrong answer, you then help them figure out why it is wrong. Of course, you should also help them figure out why their answers are correct, too! By allowing them to do their own work, even though they are risking failure, you are teaching them that they are expected to try.

NATURAL CONSEQUENCES

If "dignity of risk" is difficult for parents and teachers, utilizing the philosophy of "natural consequences" is even harder. As a matter of fact, I am guessing as soon as I start discussing it, you might get kind of offended and start saying "Yeah, but . . ." So, before you throw this book away in disgust, let me explain what the concept of natural consequences is, when it should apply, and when it shouldn't.

As you might have already guessed, "natural consequences" means that individuals with mental retardation should experience the same results from their actions as they would if they didn't have a disability. In other words, if they don't bring the permission slip home for their parents to sign, then they don't get to go on the field trip, no matter how much they beg, plead, cry, or look sad. If they don't show up for work on time, they should get fired and won't get a paycheck or see their work friends anymore. If they lose a library book, they have to pay the fine. And so on.

As with "helping" people with mental retardation do their work, many parents and teachers have great difficulty allowing kids with mental retardation to experience the natural consequences of their actions. As a result, kids with mental retardation do not learn that their actions, or inactions, are often tied to various outcomes. They also learn that they don't have to be responsible for their own behavior.

In essence, we make mental retardation even more debilitating than it actually is. After all, people with mental retardation don't naturally have learned helplessness or an external locus of control. We teach them to be dependent upon other people and not to look at their own actions.

Now, I am not saying that you should let your kid run out into a busy street and get hit by a car! What I am suggesting is that you treat your child as if he or she doesn't have mental retardation. If your child does something that will have unexpected or unpleasant consequences, do whatever you would do if your child had an average IQ.

Again, how you treat your child will often affect them for the rest of their lives. If you do everything for your daughter, she will soon learn that she doesn't have to do anything for herself. If you don't make your son responsible for his actions, he will soon stop caring about how his behavior affects himself or others. As I have been saying all along, people with mental retardation aren't stupid. They learn what we teach them. Sometimes, they learn what we don't want them to know!

SYSTEM OF LEAST RESTRICTIVE PROMPTS

Whenever I talk to my students about "systems of least restrictive prompts," I think of an episode of *Happy Days*. If you are as old as I am, or watch cable television late at night, you might remember it. In this particular episode, Fonzie is trying to teach somebody how to change a carburetor, but his student just can't get it right. Fonzie keeps explaining each step over and over, but no matter how slowly he talks or how many times he repeats himself, Fonzie is unable to teach the student how to replace the carburetor.

Finally, Fonzie walks behind the student, puts his hands on top of the hands of his student, and then makes him change the carburetor. Gradually, he pulls his hands away and the student does it by himself. That is an example of a "system of least restrictive prompts."

If you need a more formal definition, a system of least restrictive prompts is a strategy by which you gradually fade away the support that you give to students. For instance, you might literally do "hand-over-hand" instruction, where you are doing the work, but using the student's hands. Then you gradually lessen the physical interventions and rely more on verbal or gestural prompts. The idea is to eventually get the student to do the task completely independently.

There are many different ways to give support. Below, we will discuss several examples. You can even combine them. For instance, you might point to an object (i.e., a gestural prompt) and say, "pick that up and open it" (i.e., a direct verbal prompt).

When teaching children using a system of least restrictive prompts, begin by using the least restrictive method that results in reoccurring success. Then take away a little support. Children might falter a little bit and that's okay. Once the child has mastered the task with less support, fade a little more. Again, as we discussed above, the idea is to get to the point where your child is able to perform the activity without any help whatsoever.

- *Full Physical Prompt.* Taking the student by the hand and "making" them perform the action even though you are probably doing all the actual work.
- *Partial Physical Prompt.* Guiding the student's hand to where it should be, such as putting it on the pencil with which she should be writing.
- *Visual Prompt.* Having a picture of what the next step should look like or modeling what to do.
- *Gestural Prompt.* Making a gesture, such as pointing, to something that should clue the child into performing the next step of the task.
- *Verbal Prompt.* Saying something that would clue the child into performing the next step of the task.
- *Direct Verbal Prompt.* Saying something explicit, such as "Put the peanut butter on that side of the bread."
- *Indirect Verbal Prompt.* Giving a verbal hint or saying something subtle, such as "What do you think you should do with the butter knife?"

TASK ANALYSES

As we discussed in the very first chapter, people with mental retardation *can* learn, but they often need tasks broken down into more manageable units. One very effective way for breaking tasks down into smaller steps is to create a task analysis. A task analysis is a list of all of the steps needed to complete something. The example that I always use when training my college students is how to make a peanut butter and jelly sandwich.

Think about all of the steps that you have to perform in order to make a peanut butter and jelly sandwich. You have to get your ingredients and supplies—the peanut butter, jelly, bread, and knife. You have to open the jars, stick the knife in the peanut butter, pull the knife out with the right amount of peanut butter on it, and spread it evenly on one side of the bread. You then have to repeat all of those steps for the jelly and put the two slices of bread together so that the peanut buttered and jellied sides are facing each other. There are a lot of steps to remember and master!

What a task analysis does is enable you to teach each stage separately. Again, the average child could look at all of those steps once or twice and perform them correctly, as well as in the proper order. A child with mental retardation may need a long time to learn each specific step.

Further, using task analyses help you figure out what parts of the task your child can and can't do and why. For example, look at the task analysis presented in table 6.1. In the far left-hand column, you can see the steps that we just discussed. All of the other columns display data collected each time the child tried to make a peanut butter and jelly sandwich. If the child was able to complete the step without help, an "I" for "independent" was put in the corresponding box. If the child was able to complete the step, but needed to be reminded of what to do or how to do it, an "H" for "help" was listed. If

Table 6.1. Task Analysis for Making a Peanut Butter and Jelly Sandwich

Step	*Try #1*	*Try #2*	*Try #3*	*Try #4*
1. Get the ingredients and supplies	H	H	H	I
2. Open the jars and bag of bread	X	X	X	X
3. With a butter knife, scoop out a lump of peanut butter	H	I	I	I
4. Spread the peanut butter over one side of one piece of bread	H	H	I	I
5. With a butter knife, scoop out a lump of jelly	H	I	I	I
6. Spread the jelly so that it covers one side of the other piece of bread	H	I	I	I
7. Put the two pieces of bread together (peanut butter and jelly touching)	H	I	I	I
8. Put all ingredients away and the dirty butter knife in the sink	H	H	I	I
9. Eat the sandwich!	I	I	I	I

Note: "I" indicates that the child was able to perform this step independently (i.e., without any clues or prompts). "H" indicates that the child was able to perform this step with minimal help (e.g., with a verbal prompt or reminder). "X" indicates that the child was not able to do this step without receiving a physical help (e.g., somebody had to do it for him or her).

the child couldn't complete the task, even with verbal help, an "X" was put in the box.

Let's talk about the task analysis presented in table 6.1 for a moment. Now, if you only look at the task as a whole, you can tell that the student *cannot* make a peanut butter and jelly sandwich independently, correct? After all, she can't get past the second step, even with assistance.

But, if you look at each of the individual steps, you learn a great deal more about her abilities. Specifically, after a few tries, she is able to do everything independently—except open the peanut butter and jelly jars. That is a big difference from saying she can't do *any* of the steps! We now have a better picture of what she can and can't do! Further, we now know where to focus our attention!

But what do we do now? Well, we have to teach her how to complete the second step or figure out a way around it so that she can complete the entire task by herself. Before we can do this, we have to determine why she is having problems in this one area. Of course, it would help if we actually were there watching the child performing each step, but we can't. So, we will just have to guess.

Let's suppose that the student couldn't open up the jars because they are too big for her hands, or she is weak, or maybe has some fine motor deficits. Based upon these assumptions, we could get her jars with smaller lids, we can teach her exercises to strengthen her hands, or we can buy a device that will make it easier to open the jars up. We can even buy the peanut butter and jelly in squeeze bottles so that she doesn't have to unscrew the lids!

The idea that I am trying to illustrate is that task analyses give you valuable information. They tell you what your child can and can't do. They also help you determine what problems your child is having and why. Based upon this information, you can change your teaching strategies, get adaptive equipment, or develop accommodation that will help your child succeed!

CHAINING

We talked about "chaining" a long time ago, but I want to touch upon it again. Chaining is a way of teaching a series of skills that can be built upon each other to accomplish a bigger goal. It is much like teaching each individual step in a task analysis.

You can chain skills together in two ways. You can start at the very beginning, teach the first step (e.g., getting supplies out), and then move on to the next (opening jars) once the first has been mastered, and so forth until all of the steps are taught. This is called "forward chaining."

Or, you can start with the last step and go backwards until the student has mastered the entire task. For example, using the peanut butter and jelly sandwich task analysis that we already discussed, you would perform all of the steps except for the last one (i.e., eating the sandwich). Then once that step is mastered (which probably wouldn't take long!), you move on to the second to last step (i.e., putting everything away), and so forth until you go backward to the very beginning. As you might have guessed, this is called "backward chaining."

The advantage to backward chaining is that it tends to work well with students who are motivated by seeing the final product. In other words, if they want to have a sandwich, but not do all of the work, you can start at the end of the process. If they do the last step, they can have the sandwich. And then next time, they have to do the last two steps to get the sandwich. And so on.

DIRECT INSTRUCTION

The term "direct instruction" means many different things to many different people. What it is exactly is often debated by pointy-headed academics, such as myself. However, I won't go into those discussions here. For our purposes, direct instruction can be thought of as a teaching strategy that provides students with frequent, often repetitive, practice and immediate feedback. You might have heard it referred to as "drill and kill."

An example of direct instruction might involve the teacher chanting with her students "One times one equals . . . one! One times two equals . . . two! One time three equals . . . three!" And so on, over and over until the students master the material. Often students clap or snap their fingers rhythmically as they say each word. If a student makes an error, the teacher immediately corrects it. It is also often used for learning vocabulary and spelling words.

There is a lot of research suggesting that many students benefit from direct instruction, especially those who need considerable exposure to material before they are able to process it. Consequently, it is frequently used for children with mental retardation.

MULTISENSORY TEACHING

There are many different ways that our brains receive information. We see things. We hear things. We smell things. We taste things. We feel things. The more ways that we can get our brains to experience something, the faster we will learn it and the easier it is for us to recall from our memory.

Multisensory teaching involves engaging as many different senses and learning styles as possible. For example, rather than just explaining that 2 + 2 = 4, have them see it. Have them say it. Have them pick up two blocks, add two more, and then count all four blocks out loud as they touch each block.

When teaching the alphabet, don't just show flashcards. Have your child draw the letters on a piece of paper or in sand. Have them say the letter and think of a word that starts with it.

Multisensory teaching is important for all learners, but it is especially important for kids with learning difficulties and mental retardation. These students need to "overlearn" information. They need to be inundated with what they are learning in order to retain the information. They have difficult learning passively. They learn by doing. So, when teaching your child new things, have him actually do the task. Have him talk about it. Have him see it. Have him hear you explain each step. Try to utilize as many senses as possible, over and over again!

REINFORCERS AND PUNISHERS

The secret to effective teaching often involves knowing how to motivate your pupil. Of course, this is often easier said than done, especially when you don't know what is motivating to your student. However, if you watch, listen, and even ask your child, you usually can figure out what she likes and doesn't like.

The problem with most parents and teachers is that they only know two ways to motivate kids. The either spank them when they do something wrong or say "good job" when they do something right. Unfortunately, these don't always work. Thankfully, there are many other ways for reinforcing good behavior and punishing bad behavior.

Before we go on any further, I need to clear up a few things. You see, many people seem to think that "reinforcement" means "being nice to the child" and "punishment" means "being mean." But being nice or mean doesn't have anything to do with reinforcement or punishment. As a matter of fact, your emotions shouldn't even enter into the picture! You are simply following through on what you told your child would happen if a certain behavior did or did not occur. So, what does "reinforcement" and "punishment" mean then? Good question (I am trying to reinforce your desire to ask questions!).

Reinforcers

The primary function of reinforcers is to *increase* appropriate behaviors, or what are often called "target" behaviors. There are two primary ways of doing this.

One way is to give somebody something that they want, such as a dollar or extra free time, if he does what he is supposed to. This is called "positive reinforcement." Think of "positive" in terms of "addition," not in terms of a value judgment of quality.

Another way to gets somebody to perform an appropriate behavior is to take away something that she don't want. This is called "negative reinforcement." Think of "negative" in relation to "subtracting" something. This second option might be a bit confusing, so let me give you a few examples.

With positive reinforcement, you would give something to your child as a reward for conducting the desired behavior. For instance, if your child cleans his room, you will give him an extra hour of curfew or you will give him a new computer game. Make sense? Of course, we are assuming that the child wants to have an extra hour of curfew or a new computer game. If he doesn't want these things, then they aren't reinforcers.

With negative reinforcement, you are taking away something that a child doesn't like if they conduct the desired behavior. For instance, if your daughter gets all *A*'s, then she doesn't have to do her household chores for a week. Again, we are assuming that your child doesn't want to do household chores.

Keep in mind that what is reinforcing for you might not be reinforcing to your child. For example, when I was a teenager, my mother used to always say "Way to go! I knew that you could do it!" whenever I did well in school—which wasn't very often. I hated that she made such a big deal about my grade. It wasn't reinforcing to me. Actually, it was probably more of a punisher. I didn't want to listen to my mother. I just wanted to be left alone. Plus, being told "I knew that you could do it!" sounded too much like "I told you so!" Which was another way for my mother to say, "I know better than you do!" Her effort to praise me wasn't reinforcing and, when I did well, it was in spite of my mother's efforts, not because of them.

There are two keys to using reinforcers. First, the desire for the reward has to be more than the desire not to do the appropriate behavior. In other words, in order for the reward to be successful, it has to mean more to your child than the hassle of doing what he is supposed to do.

Think about it. What would you do for $1? Would you smile at somebody? Probably. Would you clean my entire house? Probably not. Why? Well, in economic terms, a dollar is worth more than smiling, so you see the trade as being in your favor. Whereas cleaning my entire house is more costly. It simply isn't worth your time and energy for a single dollar.

See what I am getting at? If you are going to use reinforcers to promote a certain behavior, you have to make sure that the rewards and behaviors are "priced right." Otherwise, the rewards will not be strong enough to be motivating.

Secondly, the best kind of reward is one that is naturally occurring as a result of the behavior. After all, you don't want to have to pay your child to do everything! They should be able to do some things simply out of the need to do them.

This isn't to say that you shouldn't use artificial rewards, such as food or tokens or money. These are fine, especially when you are first trying to get the good behavior started. But, eventually, you need to fade away the rewards so that the behaviors stand on their own.

For instance, imagine that your son is very argumentative and "unpleasant" at school. In order to increase his good behavior, you make him a deal.

If he goes the entire day without getting in trouble at school, he gets $5. This should get his attention! After all, $5 is probably pretty motivating, especially if he can get it every day!

So, let's suppose that your son's teacher reports that his behavior is starting to improve. Whereas before he had "bad days" four out of five days of the week, he now only has bad days once a week. Time to up the ante!

Now you tell your son that he can earn $25 a week, but he has to go all five school days without getting in trouble. So, if he has one bad day in the week, he doesn't get the reward that he wants. But when he does earn the rewards, you add a secondary, natural reinforcer. You start pointing out that his classmates seem to like him more and that they are more willing to play with him now that he is behaving so well.

In this situation, you have accomplished several very important feats. First, you have increased what is expected of him; that is, moved from one day of good behavior to five consecutive days. You are setting the stage for even more personal growth later on.

Second, you have started to delay gratification of the reward. You have now begun to make him work for things that are in the near future. He will start to realize that his current behavior affects future outcomes. Kids with mental retardation often have difficulty learning this on their own, so this is a very important concept for you to help them realize!

You might have to take things kind of slow, especially if your child has a very hard time understanding the connection between his behavior and outcomes. But, by gradually increasing the expectations, and slowly decreasing the artificial rewards, hopefully the appropriate behavior will take root and become a habit.

Third, you are pairing the artificial reinforcer (i.e., the money) with the natural reinforcer (i.e., being able to have good relationships with peers). Eventually, you can gradually fade away the money and let the behavior be completely motivated by its own rewards.

Again, this is a very important concept to teach kids with mental retardation. As we discussed before, people with mental retardation are often externally focused. They see their locus of control as being outside of themselves. They also become very dependent upon other people.

By utilizing a reward system, such as the one described above, children with mental retardation learn that receiving a reward is not dependent upon other people's behavior, but their own. They realize that they are in control. If they want to earn the reward, they have to act a certain way.

In order for this type of reinforcement system to work, however, you must enact it consistently. You can't give in and allow the child to get the reward without the behavior. If you do, he or she will have trouble seeing the link between the actions and the consequences.

Punishers

If you are like most parents, when you hear the word "punishers," you probably think of men in dark hoods standing next to guillotines! Maybe you think of shock therapy or spanking or time-outs. Yes, all of these could be considered punishers, but there's far more to them than that.

Whereas reinforcers increase the desired behavior, punishers *decrease* undesired behaviors. There are two ways to accomplish this. The first, of course, is presenting an adverse consequence whenever the inappropriate behavior occurs. This is called "presentation punishment" or "classical punishment." An obvious example of this is spanking, assuming, of course, that the child doesn't like to be swatted on the butt!

The second way to decrease undesired behavior is to take away something the child likes every time the behavior occurs. This is called "response-cost punishment." An example of this could be taking away a minute of free time every time your child talks back to you. Or, you could take away a half an hour of television for every uncompleted homework assignment.

As with using reinforcers, there are some general guidelines that you should follow when using punishers. First, make sure that the consequence of behavior is known beforehand. You don't want to take away all of your child's toys when she didn't know that what she had done was wrong!

A good way to make sure that children understand your expectations and the consequences of inappropriate behavior is to develop a behavioral contract. Basically, you sit down with the child and write up a "contract" between the two of you. State, in writing or pictures, what will happen if certain behaviors occur. Then post the contract where your child can see it. Refer to it frequently.

Secondly, use punishment in conjunction with reinforcement. You don't want to just decrease inappropriate behaviors. You also want to increase appropriate behaviors. Behavior changes far more quickly when there are both negative and positive consequences.

Third, you have to be very consistent when punishing your child's behavior. If you sometime punish the behavior and other times don't, your child will get confused. After all, kids with mental retardation have a hard enough time figuring out when to behave a certain way and when not to. The more consistent the better!

Try to have the punishment fit the crime. This gets back to what we talked about earlier with "natural consequences." Sometimes the most effective punishment is what naturally happens as the result of the behavior. For example, if a child gets upset and throws his toy against the wall, the natural punishment is that he can't play with the broken toy anymore.

You also have to make sure that the punishment isn't too strict or too lenient. For example, imagine being grounded for a year for the smallest infraction! Then ask yourself, "What are they going to do if I act out again?" In other words, with everything gone, the child has nothing left to lose!

On the other hand, imagine that you steal your parents' car and all that happens is that they shake their head and wag their finger at you. Would that stop you from stealing the car again? Probably not.

Finally, make sure that the punisher is actually a punisher. We talked about this earlier when we discussed reinforcers, but the same is true here. What you think is a punisher probably isn't a punisher to your child. For example, during my first year of teaching, I used to yell a lot. I thought that if I raised my voice, my students would somehow decide to behave themselves. It didn't work. They thought that getting me mad was funny. It was rewarding to them to see the veins bulge in my neck!

I also used to add to my students' homework if they misbehaved. For instance, if they weren't in their seats or quiet when the bell rang, I would walk over to the board and start writing page numbers to read. For most of my students, this was *extremely* effective. As soon as I picked up the piece of chalk, they sat down and kept quiet.

However, I had several students who never did their homework anyway. So, the threat of being assigned more meant nothing to them. Once, as I was trying to get the class to quiet down, one of these students walked up next to me and wrote on the board, "Do problems one to a zillion." He then looked at me and said, "I don't give a shit!" Again, in order for a punisher to work, the student has to not want it.

SUMMARY

In this chapter, we covered many extremely important topics. Specifically, we talked about how the goal of effective teaching is to get your child to be able to do something independently. Then we talked about various philosophies that are currently prevalent in the field of special education. Finally, we finished up by discussing strategies for teaching and motivating your child.

In the next chapter, we are going to talk more about special education programs and your rights as a parent of a child with mental retardation. I think that this will be very important and useful information for you to have. So, take a break and then get ready to learn a great deal!

7

AN OVERVIEW OF YOUR RIGHTS AND SPECIAL EDUCATION

GUIDED COMPREHENSION QUESTIONS

By the time you finish reading this chapter, you should be able to

1. Define "special education"
2. Discuss the six main components of IDEA
3. Outline the special education process
4. Define IEP
5. Identify the require part of IEPs
6. Contrast other formal plans with IEPs for individuals with mental retardation

INTRODUCTION

If you have a child with mental retardation, you either are, or will be, well acquainted with special education programs and personnel. Consequently, you should know something about what special education is and isn't, as well as what your rights are as a parent of a child with disabilities. Please keep in mind that the legal history and legalities surrounding special education could fill several volumes of books. We are only going to go into some of the key issues. If you want additional information, please access the resources at the end of this book.

WHAT IS SPECIAL EDUCATION?

Special education is a federally mandated entitlement program that gives qualifying students an appropriate, individualized education. There is a lot packed into that sentence. So, let's pick it apart a bit.

Federally Mandated

First of all, "federally mandated" means that all states in the United States are required to have special education programs by a series of complicated national laws. This isn't to say that states don't have some say as to how special education is carried out in their schools; they do. They get to decide what forms have to be filled out and what terms are used. For instance, the phrase "mental retardation" isn't used in all states. In Wisconsin, we use "cognitively disabled," whereas in Illinois people with mental retardation are said to be "developmentally disabled."

Still, the main point here is that all public schools in the United States must provide special education services to qualifying students. Who "qualifies" for special education? Great question! But before we get to that, let's talk about what an "entitlement program" is.

Entitlement Program

As I said before, special education is an "entitlement program." That means that children who qualify cannot be denied access to special education services. No matter how severe somebody's disability, no matter how inappropriate her behavior, if she qualifies for special education, she automatically get services. But we'll talk more about that later. Now let's talk about who "qualifies" for special education. I am sure that you are dying to know!

Qualifying Students

In order to qualify for special education you must meet several criteria. First, you must have one of ten different types of disabilities (see table 7.1). Since you have a child with mental retardation, you don't have to worry about this. Mental retardation is the third most common disability served by special education. Learning disabilities and communication disorders are first and second, respectively.

If your child has mental retardation, he or she *might* qualify for special education, but not necessarily. In addition to having mental retardation, they must also be between the ages of three and twenty-one. So, if your child is younger than three years old or older than twenty-one, she is not eligible for special education services. She is eligible for early intervention or adult services, but these are completely different from special education.

Let's suppose that you have a child with mental retardation (which is one of the ten disabilities accepted into special education) and she is between the ages of three and twenty-one. Does your child qualify for special education? No, not yet. In addition to having mental retardation and being the right age, her disability must also "adversely" affect her ability to get an "appropriate education"—which is usually the case if somebody has mental retardation. "What is an appropriate education?" you ask. Well, keep reading!

Table 7.1. Ten Disabilities Served under IDEA

Disability	*Number of Students*	*Percent of Students in Special Education*
Specific Learning Disabilities	2,748,497	51.0%
Speech and Language Impairments	1,065,074	19.8%
MENTAL RETARDATION	**602,111**	**11.2%**
Emotional Disturbance	454,363	8.4%
Other Health Impairments	190,935	3.5%
Multiple Disabilities	106,758	2.0%
Hearing Impairments	69,537	1.3%
Orthopedic Impairments	67,422	1.2%
Autism	42,487	0.8%
Vision Impairments	26,015	0.5%
Traumatic Brain Injury	11,895	0.2%

An Appropriate and Individualized Education

Okay, so your child has one of the ten disabilities listed in table 7.1. Plus, she is between the ages of three and twenty-one. The final criterion to qualify for special education is that her disability (e.g., mental retardation) must adversely affect her ability to receive an "appropriate" education.

Defining "appropriate" education is very difficult and would require a great deal of time. In fact, there really isn't any one completely accepted definition. The courts tend to decide on a case-by-case basis. However, if a student is not succeeding in the general education curriculum because of his disability, then he probably qualifies for special education.

"What about individualized education?" you might be thinking. "What does that mean?"

Unlike regular education, which is based upon a school-identified curriculum, special education focuses upon the individual needs of its students. So, if your child needs help with reading, then the special education services are designed to help him to learn how to read. If your child needs to learn acceptable social skills, then that is what special education will focus on. In other words, the services provided via special education address the unique needs of each child. Sometimes those needs are academically oriented. But, frequently, they focus on other areas, such as emotional or social development.

Summary of "Special Education"

Okay, let's tie all of this together. Special education is a program that federal laws make available in all public schools. If a child is between the ages of three and twenty-one, has one of the ten specified disabilities, and that disability prevents the child from getting an "appropriate" education, then he qualifies for special education. Moreover, if a student qualifies for special education, he cannot be denied access or kicked out of special education.

THE IDEA BEHIND SPECIAL EDUCATION

So, that is what special education is. Now let's talk a little bit about the legalities behind special education. As you can imagine, this is a very broad and complicated topic. There are many books written exclusively on special education law. But, at the very least, I want you to understand your rights as a parent of a child with mental retardation. If you require additional information, please access some of the resources listed at the end of this book.

There are a great many laws and court cases that involve special education. But the biggie is IDEA, or the Individuals with Disabilities Education Act. If you hang around any special educators for very long, you will undoubtedly hear about it. There are six main components of IDEA that you need to know about.

- Zero Reject
- Nondiscriminatory Identification and Evaluation
- Free and Appropriate Public Education (FAPE)
- Least Restrictive Environment (LRE)
- Parental and Student Participation
- Procedural Due Process

Let's talk about each of these in turn.

Zero Reject

We already talked about this in passing; however, it is important enough to go over again. Basically, IDEA says that if a student qualifies for special education (i.e., is between three and twenty-one years old, has one of ten disabilities, and that disability prevents the child from getting an appropriate education), the student cannot be denied access to special education services. So, no matter how "disabled" a child is, or how violent her behavior, or even if she has a highly communicable disease, children who qualify for special education *cannot* be turned away.

Nondiscriminatory Identification and Evaluation

The second key component of IDEA involves how kids are assessed. According to federal law, students must be evaluated in a fair manner. As we discussed in an earlier chapter, children must be assessed by multiple devices, over an extended period of time, and by several individuals. Further, the instruments used cannot be biased against the student's ethnicity or culture. This means that all tests must be administered in the child's native language. So, if the child primarily speaks Swedish or Hmong or Spanish or whatever, the school must get an interpreter who is qualified to translate that particular language.

Moreover, all assessments are free to the parents. Schools cannot charge parents for evaluating their child. Nor can schools make parents go to outside evaluators and charge their insurance companies. Any services used to diagnose a child must be paid for by the school district.

"What if the school tests my child and I disagree with what they do or their conclusions?" you might be wondering. If this is the case, you can have an independent, third-party evaluation paid for by the school district. Now, if you disagree or don't like the independent evaluation, then you are on your own. Schools don't have to keep paying experts to evaluate your child forever. Basically, you get the first evaluation done by the school and, if you want another, you can have somebody from outside the school do another. But you can't keep demanding that the school pay for assessment after assessment until you get the results that you like. Well, you could . . . but you are not legally entitled to getting them paid for.

I should probably point out that assessing students for disabilities isn't a one-time shot. Once a child is enrolled in special education, he or she must be reevaluated at least every three years. After all, it may be that the student no longer has a disability. Maybe he or she has learned effective strategies for retaining information and now is able to get an appropriate education without special services.

In addition, this part of IDEA also requires that schools actively look for kids with disabilities. School officials can't just sit back and wait for kids to identify themselves. They have to have programs in place that proactively seek out children who might have disabilities that adversely affect their education.

Free and Appropriate Public Education (FAPE)

The third component of IDEA is something that we already hit upon. It is called FAPE, or free and appropriate public education. As you probably know, public education up to twelfth grade is free in the United States. So, if you have a child in special education, his or her education is provided at no expense to you. Schools cannot charge you for your child's education (with the exception of extracurricular activities, such as going on field trips or being on a sports team).

In addition to getting a free education, children are guaranteed under IDEA an "appropriate" education. We already talked about this a little bit, but I really need to drive this important point home. You see, your child is not entitled to the "best" education possible. Your child isn't even guaranteed a "good" education. He or she is guaranteed an "appropriate" education.

So, let's suppose that you have a child in special education who is getting some services and doing pretty well in her classes, but you think that she could do even better if she had additional help. Maybe you want her to get an aide who will follow her from class to class and provide extra tutoring. Does the school have to provide you with these services?

No! Schools only need to provide your child with the services that she needs to obtain an "appropriate" education. So, anything above "appropriate" is at the discretion of the school. Again, the main point here is that IDEA guarantees an "appropriate" education, not the best!

So, what happens if the school says that your child is getting an "appropriate" education and you disagree? That is where procedural due process comes in, which we will discuss in a few moments. But, before we go on, I want to talk about some services that may or may not be a part of your child's FAPE.

Whenever I am brought in to mediate a dispute between schools and parents, one of the key areas of contention involves summer school. Many parents want their child to get a jump on the next year's curriculum by attending summer school or getting a tutor over the summer, which is often a logical way of doing this. However, many times schools refuse to pay for such things. So, who wins?

There are numerous court cases on this subject. The general consensus is that, if parents can show that their child would regress considerably over the summer without additional education, then the student is entitled to free summer school. However, if the parents just want the additional education so that their child gets a leg up or for day care services, then they have to pay for it out of their own pocket. So, if your child will lose most of what he or she has learned from the previous year as the result of being out of school during the summer, then yes, you can get summer school paid for by the school. Otherwise, the school is not obligated to provide any services over the summer.

Another area of contention often involves the school to which a child should go. This is a little tougher to answer since there are different court rulings based upon variation in cases. However, generally speaking, the courts usually require that students attend their local schools. So, let's suppose that you live on one side of a city and you want your child to attend a school on the other side. Maybe you think that school is much better. Usually, you have to send your child to your neighborhood school.

There are exceptions. For example, suppose that your child had a rare condition or combination of conditions, such as being deaf and blind. If your local school doesn't have the personnel who are trained to work with those disabilities, then students are often bussed, at the school's expense, to a school that does.

Least Restrictive Environment (LRE)

Perhaps one of the most important concepts in IDEA is "least restrictive environment," also called LRE. (If you haven't already guessed, there are a lot of acronyms in special education!) The least restrictive environment clauses of IDEA are frequently misunderstood, so I want to spend some extra time discussing them.

According to IDEA, students in special education must be taught alongside their nondisabled peers *as much as appropriate*. Some people have interpreted that to mean that *all* children with disabilities have to be included in regular education classes, but that is simply not the case.

IDEA mandates that there has to be a continuum of placement options available for students in special education. For instance, children with mental retardation might be placed in regular education with very few supports for the entire school day. They can also be placed in a residential facility completely apart from their nondisabled peers. It all depends upon their unique needs. Below is a list of some of the LREs that are available to students in special education.

- Fully included in regular education classes with minimal support
- Fully included in regular education classes with a great deal of support (e.g., full-time aide)
- Mostly in regular education classes, some classes in a resource room
- Some classes in regular education, most classes in a resource room
- All classes in a special education classroom
- Home-based instruction
- Separate academic facility
- Separate residential facility
- Hospital or treatment facility

Now, take a look at table 7.2 for a moment. Notice that nearly half of special education student spend most of their day in the general education classroom. This is compared to only 11 percent of students with mental retardation.

By and large, students with mental retardation are taught either in classrooms completely separated from their nondisabled peers or in a mixture of regular and resource rooms. This, however, is changing. Lately, more and more students with even severe mental retardation are being taught in inclusive environments.

Some people are extremely bothered by this trend. They say that having kids with mental retardation in regular classrooms is disruptive and takes the teacher's time away from students without disabilities. Other people feel that including kids with mental retardation in general education classes is not only beneficial for them but also their nondisabled peers, who learn how to relate to individuals with disabilities. In the end, you will have to make up your own mind.

Table 7.2. Percent of Special Education Students in Various LREs

LRE	*Students with Mental Retardation*	*All Students in Special Education*
General Education Classroom	11%	46%
Resource Room	28%	27%
Separate Classroom	54%	22%
Separate Education Facility	6%	3%
Residential Facility	0.5%	0.7%
Home/Hospital	0.5%	0.7%

Who decides where a child's LRE is? The short answer is the "IEP team." What is an IEP? Don't worry. We will get to that very soon. Basically, a group of people involved in your child's education get together to decide what your child should be taught and where. Keep in mind that you know your child better than anybody, so you should be on that team too!

Your next question is probably, "How does this IEP team determine where my child's LRE is?" There is no magical answer to this. However, there are definitely some very wrong ones!

The child's needs should be the first and primary factor used to determine where his or her LRE is. What you need to do is start with the least restrictive environment possible (i.e., the regular education classroom with minimal supports) and ask yourself, "Could my child get an appropriate education here?" If the answer is "yes," that is the child's least restrictive environment. If the answer is "no," then you go to next least restrictive environment on the continuum, such as being in regular education full-time with a classroom aide. You keep asking yourself the same question until you come to an environment in which your child could receive a FAPE (i.e., free and appropriate public education).

Now, there is a little more to consider here, such as your child's effect on the learning and safety of the other students. I taught a lot of kids with behavior disorders who were *extremely* smart. They could easily do the work in a regular education classroom. However, they were violent. Several of my students were sexual predators and could not be left alone with other children. Others killed people. I had one student who killed members of his family with a hatchet!

As you probably agree, these students shouldn't have been taught in the regular education classroom, even though they could get an appropriate education there. They needed constant supervision, which could not reasonably be provided in a regular education setting. As a result, their LRE was in a lockdown residential facility for juvenile offenders.

Again, LRE is *not* always in the regular education classroom. However, the regular education classroom must be the first place that is considered. If a child can't learn effectively in the regular education classroom, or her behavior is severely inappropriate, then her LRE is elsewhere.

I should probably point out that there are school officials out there who do not adhere to this aspect of IDEA. For example, I have been at schools where all kids with mental retardation were taught in one room, all kids with learning disabilities were in another room, and so forth. I have been told by principals of these schools that the teachers "specialize" in individual disabilities and this is the best way for kids with disabilities to be educated. When I point out that this violates IDEA, some will argue with me. Some become very cold and distant.

Placement in a LRE is based upon the needs of the individual child, *not* the child's disability label! Certainly, some children might benefit from being in a room exclusively for kids with mental retardation. However, placing all kids in one type of placement violates the law.

The same is true when I go to schools where all kids with disabilities are "mainstreamed" into regular education. Yes, a great many students in special education probably should be in regular education full time. However, to place everybody in regular education without thought to the student's unique situation also goes against IDEA's mandate.

Parental and Student Participation

The fifth major component of IDEA involves parental and student participation. According to federal law, parents and students must be directly involved in educational planning. This means that you, as the child's parent, have considerable input as to what services are going to be provided, what goals your child is going to work on, where your child is going to be taught, and so forth. Schools *must* invite you to meetings that involve your child. Further, you should be given access to any information about your child, including what is in the school's file.

Procedural Due Process

So, what happens when you, the parent, disagree with the school or they do not allow you to participate in the planning of your child's education? Well, then you take them through procedural due process, which is the last component of IDEA.

According to IDEA, parents can appeal any decision made by the school. For example, let's suppose that you want your child to be taught functional math (e.g., using money and basic counting), but your child's teacher wants to emphasize community living skills instead. After meeting several times, trying to work out some sort of compromise, you two just can't come to an agreement. What do you do?

The first step is to file a formal grievance with the school district. If the school doesn't resolve the issue to your satisfaction in a timely manner (your state board of education will have specific timelines that the school has to follow), then the issue is taken to an independent due process hearing officer. The hearing officer will hear both sides and then make a ruling. If you do not like the ruling, and the issue involves some sort of violation of law, you can then bring the matter to the courts.

If you ever find yourself in a disagreement with school officials about your child's education, you might want to follow these suggestions:

1. Try to understand the school's perspective. Very few school officials will willingly act against the best interests of their students. Maybe the school has a valid point.
2. Try to make your case without emotion. I think that a lot of times messages get lost because people react negatively to the emotions behind the messages. I have been at a lot of meetings between parents and schools where both sides had great ideas, but nobody was willing to listen to each other because of the passion involved. I have even attended meetings where profanity was used and push literally turned to shove.
3. Document everything! Get things in writing! If a school says that they will do something for you or your child, have them write it down. Or bring a tape recorder to the meetings! However, out of politeness, make sure that you inform everybody at the meeting that you are taping the conversation.
4. If you have tried to resolve the difference, but the school isn't paying attention to your request or isn't following through on what they say, get an advocate. An advocate is somebody who is familiar with special education law and has worked with schools before. The advocate can act as your personal support network as well as give you advice about what to do. Some will even sit in on meetings with you, just so you don't feel alone. Contact support groups listed at the end of this book. Many of them can recommend people in your state who will act as advocates for parents.

THE SPECIAL EDUCATION PROCESS

Okay, we have talked about some of the legal aspects of special education. Now, let's fill in the picture by talking about the special education process itself. In most, if not all, cases, the special education process follows a fairly predictable series of steps:

Step #1: Detection of a problem
Step #2: Prereferral strategies
Step #3: Nondiscriminatory evaluation
Step #4: Enrollment in special education
Step #5: Development of an Individualize Education Plan (IEP)
Step #6: Implementation of the IEP
Step #7: Evaluation of the IEP and the student

Let's go through each step one at a time.

Step #1: Detection of a Problem

The first step down the special education road obviously involves somebody noticing that the child is having a problem learning. When this occurs depends largely upon the type and severity of the disability. Children with severe and profound mental retardation usually are identified shortly after birth, sometimes even before. Children with mild mental retardation are typically diagnosed around third or fourth grade.

Why the difference in ages? Well, as we discussed in previous chapters, the more severe the mental retardation, the more likely there are multiple conditions interacting. Further, individuals with severe disabilities are likely to have physiological or genetic conditions that can be detected through chromosomal testing, such as Down syndrome.

Kids with milder forms of mental retardation usually appear just like everybody else, so they are harder to identify. They usually start "looking" different from their peers around the middle of elementary school because that is when fairly abstract concepts, such as higher ordered math, begin being taught.

Moreover, social expectations and norms begin to change around this time. Kids are no longer "young children." They are expected to control their emotions and regulate their behavior with greater effectiveness than at earlier ages. As we discussed earlier, this is often difficult for individuals with mental retardation.

So, coupled with their academic delays and social immaturity, teachers tend to realize that children have mild mental retardation when they are about nine to ten years old. Unfortunately, by this time, they are usually already very far behind their peers in terms of basic academics. They have also learned a number of inappropriate behaviors.

Step #2: Prereferral Strategies

Once somebody realizes that a child is "different," the special education teacher is usually contacted. Keep in mind that this only applies if a child is of school age. If the child is younger, he or she doesn't qualify for special education. Children who are diagnosed with mental retardation before they enter school enter the special education process at step #4. But, for now, let's assume that a child is in school and somebody, probably the regular education teacher, notices that something is different about the child.

The regular education teacher will then contact the special education teacher and ask for help. The special education teacher would then make suggestions to help correct whatever difficulties the student is having. At this stage, the emphasis is on changing the environment or the regular educator's teaching strategies, not the student. It is presumed that the child doesn't have a disability; instead, there is something in the environment that is interfering with his or her learning. So, maybe the special educator will recommend that the child be moved to the front of the classroom. Or, maybe the special educator will recommend that the regular educator should start using more visual examples while presenting new information.

If these recommendations work, then great! The process ends right here. But if the student continues to have problems, then we go to the third step in the process.

Step #3: Nondiscriminatory Evaluation

After it is evident that the environment and the teaching strategies of the regular educator are not to blame, attention begins to be focused on the possibility that the child might have a disability. But, before a nondiscriminatory evaluation is able to take place, the school must get permission from the child's parents. If the parents refuse to give their informed consent, the special education process stops here, and the child continues in regular education without any services.

Informed consent involves more than just saying that the school can test your child. The school must tell you, in advance, what tests will be given, by whom, and for what purpose. Further, they must also tell you when the evaluation will be over. You consent is always time-limited, usually three months. Consent cannot be in perpetuity. Finally, if you ever want to withdraw your consent, you can do so at any time.

If you give your consent, the school will start assessing your child for a variety of conditions. If they suspect that your child has mental retardation, they will most likely begin by administering several IQ tests and adaptive behavior scales. As we discussed in chapter 2, you should fill out some of the scales. You, after all, know your child better than anybody!

Step #4: Enrollment in Special Education

Okay, so let's recap a bit. Somebody notices that your child is a bit different than his peers. Maybe a regular education teacher sees that your child is having difficulty learning new skills or is socially behind everybody else. The first thing that the regular educator should do is talk to the special educator. The special educator then will observe the class and make recommendations for improving the situation.

If the recommendations don't change the fact that your child is still doing poorly, then the special education teacher will ask for your permission to test your child. The special education teacher should explain to you why he or she wants to assess your child, as well as what tests are going to be given and when.

Let's suppose that the school officials give your child an in-depth, comprehensive, nondiscriminatory evaluation, and they determine that your child qualifies for special education. That is, he has one of the disabilities covered under IDEA, the disability adversely affects your son's ability to get an appropriate education, and your child is between the ages of three and twenty-one.

Now, you have to decide whether to enroll your child in special education. Of course, only you can make this decision. But be aware that there are both good and bad aspects of any program, including special ed. For example, special education can provide your child with individualized instruction that can't be found in regular education. However, there is also a certain stigma to receiving special education services. Again, only you can make the decision to enroll your child in special education.

There is probably something that you need to know before you decide. Although enrolling your child in special education is purely your decision, taking your child out of special education isn't. It may seem a bit strange, but pulling your child out of special education is considered a "change in placement," which requires the approval of the entire IEP team. Once a child is in special education, he is there until the team decides that services are no longer necessary.

I have known several parents who have tried to get their kids out of special education, but the rest of the IEP team refused. In the end, they chose to move to a different school district where they enrolled their child in regular education. It may sound like an extreme situation, but it really isn't that uncommon.

Not to sound melodramatic or anything: But, please realize that enrolling a child in special education is a big decision that may affect your child for the rest of his or her life. Before you commit to anything, you might want to do some research.

Only about 30 percent of children referred to special education make it this far. In other words, 70 percent of students who have problems in school either do not have disabilities that qualify for special education, or they have qualifying disabilities, but their parents decline to enroll them.

Step #5: Development of an Individualize Education Program (IEP)

If you do decide to enroll your child in special education, the next step is developing an Individualized Education Program, or IEP. An IEP is a legally binding document between the school and parents. It outlines the goals and objectives that the student will be working on during the school year as well as the services the school is going to furnish.

The IEP is developed by the IEP team, which consists of you, your child's teachers (both regular and special education teachers), and anybody else who might be involved with your child's education. Sometimes the principal or some other school administrator is also involved.

We'll go over IEPs in detail in a little while. However, for now just realize that developing the IEP should be a team process, a team of which you are an integral member. If a school official comes to a meeting with the IEP already developed, you don't have to sign it. You can disagree, insist upon changes, and even write your own draft. If the team cannot come to an agreement about what should be included in the IEP, then you or the school could call in a due process hearing officer to mediate the disagreement.

Step #6: Implementation of the IEP

Once the team agrees on an IEP, it is ready to be implemented. Basically, what that means is that the teachers begin to teach whatever the team thinks your child needs to learn. Data is also collected to determine whether progress is being made.

For example, let's suppose that you and the rest of the IEP team feel that your daughter needs to improve her ability to read basic sight words (e.g., "stop," "go," "up," "down," etc.). The first thing that needs to be done is to figure out what the child knows. To do this, the teacher or school psychologist or somebody will assess your daughter's reading ability. (This will probably be done as part of your child's nondiscriminatory evaluation.) Then the teacher will begin to teach the sight words in a way, hopefully, that she will learn them. Periodically, through the school year, data will be collected to see if she is progressing. You should be informed regarding their findings.

Step #7: Evaluation of the IEP and the Student

Creating and implementing an IEP isn't the final step of the special education process. You see, an IEP is only good for one calendar year, or twelve months. At the end of that time, you and the rest of the IEP team has to get together and create another IEP. Of course, things have probably changed during the previous year, so your new IEP might look completely different from the one before. Or, maybe your child never accomplished her goals from last year, and you want to continue working on reading this year too. That's okay. The point is, IEPs have to be recreated *at least* every year.

Can an IEP be rewritten sooner than a year? Yes! As a matter of fact, very few of my students had their IEPs last an entire year. Most of them had a new IEP every three or four months. For instance, many of my students completed their goals early, so we would have to create a new set of things for them to work on. Or, sometimes, their situations change. For example, maybe you realize that reading isn't your child's biggest issue. Maybe she is starting to menstruate, and she needs to learn how to address that need more than anything else.

In other words, students in special education must always have a valid IEP. IEPs can last *up to* a year, but they can be changed or rewritten by the IEP team at any time. If you want to make a change to your child's IEP, all you have to do is contact the special education teacher. In most states, the teacher will have thirty days to reconvene the IEP team and address your concerns.

In addition to reevaluating the IEP, students must be reevaluated at least every three years. This is to determine whether or not they still have a disability that adversely affects their ability to achieve an appropriate education. As with IEPs, you can certainly request to have this reevaluation done earlier.

THE ABCS OF IEPS

We have been throwing around the term Individualized Education Program, or IEP, a great deal in this chapter. It is an extremely important topic, so let's give it a little more attention.

As we have already discussed, IEPs are legally binding documents between the school and the student's parents. According to IDEA (the Individuals with Disabilities Education Act), IEPs must have the following components:

- Present level of performance (PLOP)
- Annual goals
- Special education and related services
- Projected dates, duration, frequency, and location of services

- Least restrictive environment (LRE)
- Modifications for state and districtwide assessments
- Parental notification
- Transition planning

Present Level of Performance (PLOP)

Also called the "Present Level of Educational Performance," or PLEP, this section of the IEP discusses how the student is doing in various areas of life. For example, it will list the results of academic or social functioning tests. You might think of it as a "snapshot" of how your child is doing right as the IEP is being developed.

It is very important that your child's PLOP is thorough and accurate. Future teachers will be reading it to see how much progress your child has made. Inaccurate information might give false impressions and, thus, send teachers in wrong directions. Let me give you an example.

A few years ago, a new student named Greg came to our school and was placed in my class. I read his past IEPs and learned that (according to his previous teachers) he had very inappropriate behaviors around younger female students. So, as a result, I started working with him on this.

Over the course of the semester, I didn't see anything out of the ordinary. Greg was just a typical kid with mental retardation. He often misread situations, and was a bit nutty sometimes, but nothing that would warrant a great deal of attention. But, then again, I didn't want to take any chances. The past IEPs seemed to suggest that he might do something sexual, and I didn't want to risk an incident. So, I made sure that there was always an aide with him wherever he went.

To make a long story short, I eventually found out that Greg tried to kiss a girl on the playground when he was in fourth grade. For some reason, each teacher from fourth grade on kept writing about this "incident" (I taught him when he was in high school). It only happened once, and he never displayed any other inappropriate behavior of that nature. However, the story kept getting relayed to the point where it sounded like Greg was a potential sexual predator!

When I think of all the time and resources that I wasted trying to teach Greg to act appropriately around girls, I have to cringe. I could have been teaching something that he really needed, such as job or independent living skills. What is even worse, nearly every teacher from fourth grade to high school also wasted a lot of time working on his "inappropriate behavior with females"—all because some information in his PLOP was incorrect.

The moral to the story is, make sure that whatever is written about your child (in the PLOP or elsewhere) is accurate! Teachers first get to know your child by reading his or her school file. If there is information that is misleading or incomplete, then have it taken out of the file or have it explained better!

Annual Goals

The annual goals section of the IEP describes the general areas that your child will be working on during the school year. For example, maybe your son needs to work on writing, reading, following oral directions, or controlling his emotions, or whatever. This is not to say that teachers will only be teaching your son the things stated in his IEP goals; they will also be working on a whole bunch of other things. But what is listed in the goals will be the main thrust of that year's educational services. So, if there is something really important that you want to make sure that your child works on over the course of the year, make sure that there is an annual goal addressing it in the IEP.

Short-Term Objectives

Up until a few months ago, IDEA required that all IEPs have short-term objectives. However, when IDEA was reauthorized in 2005, this component was dropped. Still, many states haven't changed their regulations. So, your child's IEPs might still have short-term objectives.

Whereas annual goals are statements outlining the general areas that your child will be working on over the course of the year, short-term objectives are the steps that will be used for your child to accomplish the annual goals. Unlike goals, short-term objectives are very specific and measurable. Teachers will gather data on whatever is written in the objectives in order to see if they are being accomplished. Below is an example of how goals and objective interplay.

Annual Goal #1:	Mary will increase her reading abilities to a third-grade level as measured by weekly reading quizzes, annual standardized tests, and completion of her short-term objectives.
Short-Term Objective #1.1:	When shown flash cards with third-grade vocabulary words written on them, Mary will say the word correctly 95 percent of the time.
Short-Term Objective #1.2:	When given a reading passage written at the third-grade level, Mary will read it aloud with fewer than two errors.
Short-Term Objective #1.3:	After reading a story written at the third-grade level, Mary will correctly answer at least four out of five comprehension questions.

Special Education and Related Services

If you think about the PLOP as being a picture of where your child is right now, goals are where you want her to be in a year from now and objectives are the route that she is going to take to get there. Moreover, special education and related services involve the help that the school will give to your child so that she can accomplish her goals as well as receive a free and appropriate public education. Examples of special education and special services include, but are not limited to:

- Speech therapy
- Occupational therapy
- Physical therapy
- Counseling
- Social work
- Assistive technology
- Transportation to school

The school must provide the services that are listed in the IEP—so, if you want your child to receive certain services, such as counseling or speech therapy, then make sure that those services are included in this section of the IEP. If they aren't, then schools are not obligated to provide them.

Projected Dates, Duration, Frequency, and Location of Services

In addition to listing the special education and related services, the IEP must also state when those services will be given, for how long, and where. For example, an IEP might say, "Susie will receive tutoring in science for an hour during her homeroom three times per week in room 210 for the rest of the semester."

It is very important that such things are clearly indicated in the IEP; otherwise, a misunderstanding might arise. For instance, you might think that your daughter is going to get counseling every week, when in reality she only gets it once.

Least Restrictive Environment (LRE)

By now, you should know that all students in special education must be taught alongside their peers as much as appropriate. This doesn't mean that *everybody* has to be in regular education every moment of every day! Some kids might be in a resource room for part of the day. Others might be in a self-contained classroom for everything except for lunch or gym. Still others might live and learn in a residential lockdown facility.

This portion of the IEP specifically states where your child will be and when. So, you should know *exactly* when your child is in regular education and when he is in the special education room.

Modifications for State and Districtwide Assessments

With the passage of the No Child Left Behind Act, schools more than ever are being held accountable for documenting their students' progress. Consequently, most states and school districts are now requiring that all students be tested at various grades. For instance, my school district requires a school-readiness examination in first grade, a reading test at fourth grade, a comprehensive skills test at seventh grade, and a U.S. Constitution test at twelfth grade. All students are supposed to take these tests in one form or another, even students with mental retardation.

If your child needs certain accommodations when taking state and districtwide tests, this is the part of the IEP that lists them. For example, maybe your child needs to have the directions read to him. Or, maybe he needs to take the tests in a quiet environment with frequent breaks. If these accommodations are in the IEP, the school must furnish them.

Parental Notification

Earlier, we discussed how IDEA mandates that parents be fully involved in the planning of their child's education. In this section of the IEP, you and the school officials must come to an agreement as to how often and via what method you will be contacted about your child's progress. For instance, you could have a notebook sent home every Friday. Or, perhaps you would prefer to be contacted by e-mail. The only hitch is that the school must contact you *at least as often* as the parent of a child in regular education, which is usually about four times a year.

Transition Planning

In my opinion, this is probably the most important IEP component. You see, IDEA requires schools to prepare kids with disabilities for their life after high school. That means that, *by age fourteen*, IEPs must address postschool outcomes, such as employment, residential living, continuing education, and so on.

Notice that I emphasized "by age fourteen." IDEA specifically says that transition can be addressed earlier. As a matter of fact, I advocate that all IEPs, even those in first and second grade, should prepare children for their future. After all, isn't that the purpose of education? Moreover, if an annual goal or short-term objective doesn't help a child get ready for adult life, then why waste time working on it?

There are numerous other reasons why children with mental retardation need to be prepared early for their future. First, as we have discussed earlier, children with mental retardation take longer to learn things than other children. Even if a child with mental retardation stays in school until he is twenty-one, the seven years from age fourteen to twenty-one often will not be enough to teach him everything that he needs to succeed in the adult world.

Secondly, there are frequently very long waiting lists for adult services. For instance, in my hometown, there is an eleven-year-long waiting list for people to get into group homes. So, if you wanted your child to live in a group home after he graduates high school, you would have to put him on the list in second grade. If you want your child to get a job through a supported employment program, you would have to put her on the waiting list in middle school.

Do you see my point? If you want to prepare your child for the future, you have to start as early as possible. Don't wait until her fourteenth birthday. Start planning now! And if the school officials say, "I'm sorry but we have to wait until high school to do that," tell them that they are wrong and that you want to start planning today.

There is a great deal else that can be said about transitioning children with disabilities to adult life. Unfortunately, we don't have the time to do so here. I would recommend that you read the book *Preparing Children with Disabilities for Life* or any of the others that are listed in the resource section of this book. They will cover the topic in greater depth than we have here.

OTHER FORMAL PLANS

In addition to IEPs, there are several other formal, written plans that might affect your child's life. These include

- Individualized Family Service Plan (IFSP)
- Individualized Health Care Plan (IHCP)
- Vocational Career Plan
- Individualized Program Plan (IPP)
- Individualized Written Rehabilitation Plan (IWRP)

Individualized Family Service Plan (IFSP)

Individualized family service plans, or IFSPs, are just like IEPs, except that they are for children who are too young to be in special education (i.e., under three years old). Further, in addition to focusing upon the needs of the individual child, they also address the needs of the family as a whole. Children who are in birth-to-three programs, or "early intervention programs," will have IFSPs.

Individualized Health Care Plan (IHCP)

Often students with mental retardation will have special medical needs. For instance, they may need to be fed through a "g-tube" (gastrointestinal tube), or may be in a wheelchair and need to be positioned so that they don't get pressure sores. In such cases, an individualized health care plan (IHCP) would be created.

An IHCP is a formal document that spells out exactly what is going to be done, by whom, and when. Sometimes, they are included as part of the actual IEP. Other times, they are developed in a separate meeting.

Vocational Career Plan

Many schools, especially middle and high schools, have vocational programs where kids with and without disabilities can learn a trade, such as how to become a mechanic or a computer programmer. Students in these programs have a vocational career plan.

Vocational career plans are not legally binding, as are IEPs. They are simply agreements between the school and the student that outline the student's vocational goals and course of study.

Individualized Program Plan (IPP)

Many students with mental retardation will enter adult service programs (e.g., supported employment or sheltered workshops) once they leave high school. When in these programs, they will have an individualized program plan, or IPP. IPPs are much like IEPs in that they spell out the person's goals, as well as what services are going to be provided, by whom, and when. However, they are not legally binding.

Individualized Written Rehabilitation Plan (IWRP)

If an individual with mental retardation is receiving services through vocational rehabilitation, he or she will have an IWRP, or individualize written rehabilitation plan. As with IPPs, these plans are very similar to IEPs, but they are not legally binding.

SUMMARY

In this chapter, we talked about what special education is, what it is supposed to do, and what it is not supposed to do. We also briefly covered issues related to the Individuals with Disabilities Education Act (IDEA), the special education process, and individualized education programs.

By now, you should understand that special education only guarantees a free and appropriate public education, not the best education possible. Further, you should have a good feel for your rights as the parent of a child with mental retardation. If you ever disagree with school officials, you are able to take them to mediation. Finally, the term IEP should be less scary now than it was when you started this chapter.

In the next chapter, we are going to discuss issues related to life after your child leaves high school. This is an incredibly important topic. After all, it is what you are preparing your child for, the end product of all your labors. So, when you are ready, read on!

8

LIFE AFTER SCHOOL

GUIDED COMPREHENSION QUESTIONS

By the time you finish reading this chapter, you should be able to

1. Discuss differences between special education and programs for adults with mental retardation
2. List potential employment programs available to your adult child
3. List potential residential programs available to your adult child
4. Identify ways of improving your child's vocational, residential, social, and physical life

LIFE WITHOUT YOU

The final topic that I want to talk about is, well . . . your death. Or, more precisely, the topic of this last chapter is your child's life after you are no longer alive.

Sorry for being so grim, but it is a fact of life. Some day—hopefully far, far into the future—you will die, and your child will be living without you.

Unfortunately, many people with mental retardation are just not prepared for being without their parents. After all, their parents have been with them their entire lives and have provided a great deal of support over the years.

Okay, I want you to do something for me. I want you mark your place in this book and put it down for about ten minutes. And I want you to close your eyes and think about your child's life once you are gone. Think about what you want it to be like. Ready? Go.

If you are like most of the parents with whom I have worked, one of two things probably came to your mind when you closed your eyes. Either you said to yourself, "I want my child to be happy." Or, you didn't have a clue about your child's future without you, simply because you have never thought about it before. Both are good places to start; however, if we are going to help build your child's future, we are going to need a better picture of where we are heading.

Unfortunately, without a picture, your child will probably end up like most adults with mental retardation. If you don't remember from our first chapter, the typical adult with mental retardation either lives in an institution (e.g., nursing homes) or with family members (e.g., siblings or distant relatives). They don't work much, if at all. They don't have fulfilling social lives. And they tend to die very young. Not a very happy picture, eh?

Well, that is why we are here! We are going to lay the groundwork so that your child can have a bright and wonderful future. Specifically, I want to talk about four pillars to a good life (at least, according to my way of thinking). They include, in no particular order of importance:

- Work life
- Home life
- Social life
- Healthy life

Each of these facets of adult existence interrelates. For example, people who work on a regular basis can afford a nicer home, meet more people, and are generally healthier than people who don't work and sit at home all day. So, it is important that you consider each of these four areas when contemplating your child's future.

In addition to employment, residential options, social skills development, and promoting healthy living, we will also be discussing several other issues in this chapter. For example, we will touch upon guardianships, powers of attorney, and trust funds. By the time you finish this chapter, you will have a lot to think about!

VOCATIONAL REHABILITATION AND ADULT SERVICE PROGRAMS

Before we start talking about employment, residential, and other issues, I think that we need to talk about vocational rehabilitation and adult service programs that will likely provide your child with services. I want you to understand that they are completely different from special education. They are like night and day!

Vocational Rehabilitation

Vocational rehabilitation (VR) programs are available in every state. Just look in your local phone book. They are usually listed in the government section or under "Department of Vocational Rehabilitation" or "Office of Vocational Rehabilitation."

In a nutshell, VR is a federal- and state-funded program designed to help people with disabilities become employed. This program also helps people who have jobs to keep them. It offers employment training, vocational assessment, job placement, follow-along support, and many other services. To say that it is helpful is an understatement!

Perhaps the best recommendation that I can make to you is that you should contact your local Department of Vocational Rehabilitation a year or so before your child leaves high school. This is very important! As soon as you contact them, they will assign your child a vocational rehabilitation counselor. The counselor will develop an individualized written rehabilitation plan (IWRP), which is much like an IEP, and then refer your child to various agencies for services. By contacting them early, you can make sure that there isn't a delay in services after school ends. They can also ensure that your child is put on all the correct waiting lists.

If your experience with VR is going to be a productive one, you will need to understand that it isn't like special education. As a matter of fact, VR is as different from special education as you can get! (See table 8.1.) Need some examples? Okay here we go!

First of all, special education is an entitlement program and has a zero reject policy. If you qualify for special education, you can't be denied services. Vocational rehabilitation is *not* an entitlement program. You might qualify for services, but you can be kicked out for any number of reasons, such as failure to comply with the IWRP. You can even be denied services because the VR has run out of money, which has happened several times in my state.

Second, to qualify for special education, you need to be between three and twenty-one years old, have one of ten disabilities outlined by IDEA, and the disability has to adversely affect your education. To qualify for VR, you have to have a disability that hinders your ability to work. Sometimes, such as the case with mental retardation, people can qualify for both. Other times, you can qualify for one but not the other. For example, a person with carpal tunnel syndrome could be eligible for VR, but not special education.

Third, unlike IEPs, IWRPs are not legally binding and VR counselors do not have to place your child in the least restrictive environment. They can

Table 8.1. The Difference between Special Education and Vocational Rehabilitation

	Special Education	*Vocational Rehabilitation*
Type of Program	Entitlement. Those who qualify can't be rejected	Not an entitlement. Eligible people may be turned away for many reasons
Eligibility	Must have certain disabilities, be between 3 and 21 years old, and the disabilities must affect education	Can have almost any disability that impedes working
Program Plans	IEPs, legally binding	IWRPs, not legally binding
Focus	Education	Employment
Role of Parents	Participation is mandated by law	Secondary to the role of the adult with mental retardation
Placement in LRE	Required by law	May be a goal, but not required

place your child in a sheltered workshop even though she wants to be employed in the community.

You are probably thinking, "If IWRPs aren't legally binding, then what is the point? Can't VR counselors just do whatever they want?"

Well, not exactly. You see, VR counselors are evaluated by their bosses based upon how quickly they fulfill people's IWRP goals. So, it is in their best interest to provide services that will get people employed and stay employed.

In contrast, special educators aren't affected at all if their students don't accomplish their IEP goals. They are evaluated more on whether paperwork is completed correctly and on time, whether the legalities of IDEA are adhered to, and many other things.

For many people, the most disconcerting difference between VR and special education is how parents are treated. If you recall, parents of special education students are guaranteed certain rights by IDEA. Specifically, it is mandated that they be allowed to participate in developing the IEP. Further, they can take schools to due process if they don't agree with them.

Many VR counselors, however, don't even let parents sit in on IWRP meetings! It isn't that they are being mean or rude; they aren't. It is just that they have a different viewpoint of your child than do special education teachers. Special education teachers see your child as a kid. By the time a VR counselor gets into the picture, your child is an adult, and that is how the VR counselor should treat them. Think about it! Would you want your parents with you if you were having a meeting?

Of course, parents might attend some of the meetings; it depends on the situation and the individual counselor. But the main point here is that VR counselors are encouraged to work directly with your child, rather than with you. So, please don't feel like they are being disrespectful. Quite the opposite! They are respecting the fact that your child is now an adult.

Adult Service Programs

Adult service programs encompass a wide variety of agencies and organizations that provide services for adults with disabilities. These include county boards of mental retardation, the ARC (formally known as the Association for Retarded Citizens), Special Olympics, sheltered workshops, supported employment, group homes, and so on. If you want to find out what programs are available in your hometown, just look in the phone book, talk to your child's teachers, and network with other parents. You might be surprised by how many programs are actually out there.

As with vocational rehabilitation, adult service programs are not guaranteed. That is, they aren't entitlement programs like special education—so your child *can* be declined services!

This is a very critical point for you to understand. Once your child leaves high school, he is not entitled *any* further services. All programs after high school are affected by availability, funding, and many other considerations. So, make sure that you get as much out of special education as humanly possible! Once children with mental retardation exit school, they may be on very long waiting lists. Consequently, it would be wise for you to contact the adult service programs in your hometown at least a year before your child leaves school. That way, time without services can be minimized.

THE IMPORTANCE OF EMPLOYMENT

Let's now move to issues related to employment. Becoming employed is probably one of the most important characteristics of adulthood. Why? Well, think of all the things that being employed gives people. Yes, there is the money. That is a biggie. With money, people can buy things that they want. They can also pay their rent, food bill, or utilities. Basically, without money, it is very difficult, if not impossible, to live an independent life.

But, being employed gives people with and without disabilities more than the financial resources required to live on their own. Having a job enables people to have a purpose and something to do with their time. It also enables them to make friends and to socialize. Keep in mind that the majority of people tend to meet their future spouses either at work or through friends!

Think about it in this way. Imagine that you didn't work (and by the way, raising a family and running a household *is* work!). Image how different your life would be. You probably would be under considerable financial constraints. You probably wouldn't interact with many people, at least not on a day-to-day basis. And, unless you volunteered your time or had a lot of hobbies, you probably would start to feel a bit bored.

So, in other words, employment can be a very significant component in people's lives. Unfortunately, as we discussed in the first chapter, few adults with mental retardation are gainfully employed. Why? It isn't because they can't do the job. There are thousands of people with even severe mental retardation who work every day. More than likely, most adults with mental retardation do not work because of three reasons. One is lack of opportunity. It is difficult to find a job as it is. Now try when people think that you are stupid and can't do anything!

The second is lack of training. As we have discussed, kids with mental retardation need frequent opportunities in order to learn tasks. Unfortunately, most special education programs do not focus enough time or attention on teaching employment-related skills. They tend to begin addressing such things during the last year or two of high school as the student is being "transitioned" out into the "real world." But this simply isn't enough time for average students, let alone students with mental retardation!

The third reason why adult with mental retardation are unemployed is because they are unaware of vocational programs that can assist them. One of biggest problems with special education services is that that they stop when a child leaves school. There is often very little guidance for parents and students about what comes next, which is why I am writing this chapter.

IMPROVING YOUR CHILD'S EMPLOYMENT PROSPECTS

So, how can you improve your child's employment future? The first, and most critical, step is to teach your child, from the earliest age possible, that he will be expected to be productive citizen when he grows up. This means that he will have to get a job or volunteer or do something other than sit around for the rest of his life watching television. He has to make a positive contribution to his community.

Of course, engraining this concept into a child's psyche will take time—so start early! Encourage your children to play make-believe. Have them pretend that they are doctors or lawyers or teachers (or writers!). Talk to them about different careers and encourage exploration. Take them to your place of employment and show them what you do for a living. When they are watching television, and they see a show about an athlete or a police officer or a musician, ask them if that is something that they would want to do when they grow up. In other words, treat them like any other kid! The worst thing that you can convey to your child is that she can't live a normal life because she has mental retardation.

Another thing that you can do to help your child's employment potential is to make sure that *all* IEPs, even those from first grade on, have something to do with teaching employment-related skills. I am not saying that you should insist that your child's first-grade teacher should teach welding or carpentry. But every IEP goal should address some sort of skill that will help your child obtain or maintain employment. For example, I would propose that you try to integrate these skills and behaviors into all of your child's IEPs:

- Pride in one's work
- Following written and oral directions
- Assessing one's own work
- Problem solving
- Asking for help when needed
- Self-awareness and personal safety
- Basic math, reading, and writing skills
- General hygiene and self-care
- Getting along with others

The last skill is probably the most important. Researchers have found that the majority of adults with mental retardation lose their jobs not because they can't do the tasks, but because they often have very poor social skills and don't get along well with others. Further, if an individual takes pride in what he does, and genuinely tries hard, keeping a job will be a lot easier. In fact, he would probably end up being a better employee than most nondisabled workers!

Something else that you can do to improve your child's employment future is to create employment opportunities where your son or daughter can gain valuable experiences. Certainly, you can create activities around the home or school that will be beneficial. For example, giving your child weekly or daily chores will go a long way toward engraining some of the skills that we mentioned above. However, you can also develop job opportunities in the community that will provide even more valuable experiences.

The trick to finding a job in the community is to realize that the job market is infinite. That is to say, where there is a need, there is a potential job. Let me give you an example.

One of my biggest success stories was with a student name Donald. Donald had profound mental retardation, autism, was nonverbal, had limited mobility, and—at times—was very aggressive. He actually put one of his aides into a coma! Needless to say, he was a challenging student with whom to work. But what made him even more challenging was that his mother wanted us to get him a well-paying job, in the community, where he could work alongside nondisabled workers with minimal support from us. Sounds impossible, eh? That is what I thought!

For nearly a year, I got Donald various jobs in the community cleaning restaurants, hotels, and similar situations. He hated all of them and often refused to go to work, no matter what reward or punishment programs we set into place. I was about to give up hope. I looked in the want ads and couldn't find anything that seemed to suit his skill levels or his interests. Finally, one day, I had a brilliant epiphany (if I do say so myself)!

I was sitting in a my doctor's office, waiting for a checkup, when I realized that nurses were walking around, taking the files of patients that the doctors had already seen, and bringing them down to the records office. As I sat there, it occurred to me that the nurses could be using their time and energies doing something far more valuable. So, I suggested to the doctor, "Why don't you hire somebody to go around, pick up the files, and deliver them to the records office? That would free up the nurses to do other things."

The doctor replied, "Who would want to walk around all day grabbing files and putting them away?" I smiled and, a couple days later, introduced him to Donald.

It was perfect for Don. It was a nice quiet environment with lots of female nurses. (Don was a typical teenage male in many respects. He loved being around girls and would try to do anything to get them to smile!) Further, all he had to do was walk around the hospital with a cart, take the files that had already been used, and deliver them down to the records office in the basement. The nice thing about it was that there were lines on the floor of the hospital so that Don couldn't get lost. Plus, he used the cart to support himself, kind of like a walker, so he was able to be more mobile.

I think the greatest part of the job for Donald was that he made a lot of friends. The nurses would cheer him on and tell him that he was doing a great job. The doctors would let him wear a white lab coat that he really liked. It was a good, supportive, friendly environment with little stress. But most importantly, he was doing something of value that needed to get done. I think, at the time, minimum wage was around $3.75 or something like that. Donald made close to $6.00 an hour and earned benefits! It has been about ten years since I got him that job and, as far as I know, he is still working at the hospital with very little outside support!

The point that I am trying to make is that there are jobs out there that need to be done. You just have to be creative and identify areas of need that your child could help fill. However, you have to have a clear picture of your child's skills and interests. This leads me to another wonderful story about a student named Nate. I think that I mentioned him before.

Nate was one of my high school students with Down syndrome. He was a great kid who would do anything to please anybody. He was very social and friendly and desperately wanted to get a job. The problem was, he couldn't really tell us where he wanted to work.

I would ask Nate, "Do you want to work at McDonald's?" And he would say "Yes!" very enthusiastically. Then, when I got him a job at McDonald's, he would obviously be unhappy. Getting him to tell me what he wanted to do was nearly impossible. He would only tell me what he thought that I wanted to hear.

So, one day, I brought Nate home from a job interview. As always, he invited me into his house and showed me his bedroom. As I looked around his room, I noticed that he liked cars. Actually, I couldn't help but notice! He had literally *hundreds* of model cars, and they were all over the place! He had posters of cars on his wall, toy cars stacked in boxes, even an elaborate slot-car racing game that circled the entire room. All of this gave me an idea.

"Hey Nate," I said to him. "I see you like cars. Want to work with cars?"

To my surprise, Nate actually said "no."

"I don't like cars," he said. Then he added with a big grin, "I like Chevys!"

To say that Nate was obsessed with Chevys would be a *huge* understatement! He knew everything about them and their history. He memorized the stats on every model of Chevy since the 1960s. He knew their engine sizes, tire sizes, length, weight, *everything*! He even knew what colors they came in and what equipment was standard!

I asked Nate's mother how he got so preoccupied with Chevys. She told me that her husband, Nate's father, loved Chevys, too, and used to refurbish them in their garage. He even let Nate help him. After his father died a few years before, Nate really latched onto everything that had to do with Chevys. I suppose it was his way of remembering his father.

During our conversation, Nate's mother mentioned that Nate was really friendly with a guy in the neighborhood, mainly because he worked at the local Chevy dealership as a sales manager. Well, everything just fell into place!

I had Nate introduce me to his friend, and I made him a proposition. I told him that if he would hire Nate to wash and detail the cars on his lot, I would train him. The sales manager agreed. Moreover, he was even willing to take Nate to and from work!

For two or three years, Nate washed and detailed every single car on their lot. He did an incredible job. Even during the Indiana winters, Nate was always out there making sure that "his" cars were free of snow and looked their best!

Then something happened. Nate was out on the lot, cleaning away, when a couple walked up to him and asked where they could find a certain model of car. Being the extremely friendly person that he was, Nate walked them to part of the lot where those cars were parked. In the meantime, he chattered on about how great that model was. He quoted things that he had heard from television commercials and the sales manager. He stated—very accurately, mind you—all of the key facts and figures. He was so charming and helpful that the couple went into the showroom, told the sales manager that they wanted to buy a car, but *only* if Nate got the full commission!

Nate is now a junior sales associate! He actually sells cars! And he does pretty well, too. The last that I heard, he won some sort of sales award and had his picture in the newspaper.

It just goes to show you that there is a perfect job for everybody. Sometimes you just have to ask the right questions and find out what your child really *loves* to do. Nothing is impossible. Just ask Don and Nate!

VOCATIONAL OPTIONS AVAILABLE TO ADULTS WITH MENTAL RETARDATION

There are many different vocational programs available to help individuals with mental retardation find their dream job. In addition to those that are also available to individuals without disabilities (e.g., headhunters, temporary agencies, and simply applying for jobs found in the newspaper), there are also several programs exclusively for people with mental retardation and other disabilities. These include

- Sheltered workshops
- Supported employment
- Work adjustment
- Competitive employment

Sheltered Workshops

Sheltered workshops are programs designed to provide "employment" experiences for people with severe disabilities while in environments that are segregated from nondisabled people. I put employment in quotes because there is considerable disagreement as to whether these programs are actually beneficial. Let me give you a few examples.

I once worked at a school that had a sheltered workshop. The students were bussed to a kind of warehouse where they sat at tables and did what was supposed to be "vocational" activities. Unfortunately, what they really did was sort screws all day long. They would separate the screws according to length and then, when they were all done, the screws were dumped into buckets and mixed together. The students then had to sort them again! I am sure that the whole affair drove my students crazy!

To be fair, I have also seen sheltered workshops that have actually taught students some employable skills. For example, I visited one workshop in Indiana that taught students how to use power tools. They built various arts and crafts that were sold to the community. From what I was told, their work was pretty popular.

Another workshop in Missouri taught students how to refinish old furniture. It was really amazing. They could take old, donated furniture, and turn them into beautiful works of art!

Still, many people are very critical of sheltered workshops because they segregate people with disabilities away from the community. Further, as we discussed earlier, research has found that people with mental retardation often do not generalize what they learn in one setting to another. So, when supported employees learn something in workshops, they are often unable to apply those skills to jobs in the community.

Another criticism of sheltered workshops is that they usually do not pay their employees very much. For example, my students used to make a few cents every day. I remember having to cut checks for 30 cents! It probably cost more to print the checks than to actually cash them.

The upside to sheltered workshops, according to some people, is that they provide daylong activities to people with mental retardation in secure and safe environments. Moreover, sheltered workshops are highly regimented and supervised, unlike supported employment programs, which we will discuss next. So, they often appeal to individuals who need a great deal of structure.

Supported Employment

There are several different types of supported employment programs, but, generally speaking, they all have the same three characteristics in common. First, they attempt to get people with disabilities employed in the community along side other, nondisabled workers. Second, unlike in sheltered workshops, supported employees do actual work. If the supported employee didn't do it, somebody else would. Finally, supported employees get paid, usually at or above minimum wage.

There are four main types of supported employment approaches:

- Individual placements
- Enclaves
- Mobile work crews
- Entrepreneurial

Individual Placements

The individual placement approach to supported employment is probably the most common of the four. With this approach, a person with disabilities is found a job in the community. A job coach then helps train the supported employee at the job site. Then, gradually, the job coach fades his or her support, leaving the supported employee to work as independently as possible.

One advantage to individual placements is that supported employees are part of whatever employment site at which they get hired. That is to say, they are actually employees of the business. They also can earn good salaries and receive the same fringe benefits as their nondisabled coworkers, such as health insurance.

The downside to this type of supported employment is that there is often a long waiting list to be placed within the community. That is because there is usually one job coach per one supported employee. So, it takes time to provide services to a lot of people.

Enclaves

Whereas the individual approach to supported employment places one supported employee with one job coach in one job within the community, enclaves involve placing a small group of supported employees in a single place, such as a factory. For example, I worked at an agency that had an enclave at a manufacturer. The owners of the business needed help getting their products packaged and shipped, so they hired a group of my students to come a few times a week to help out.

The nice thing about enclaves is that it enabled me to work with a bunch of students all at the same time. Further, they were able to work alongside nondisabled workers who were doing the same tasks, so there was an opportunity for socialization. Plus, although not as much as in sheltered workshops, enclaves gave my students some structure as well as constant supervision.

The disadvantage to enclaves is that they tend to be temporary. We only were hired to work at the paper plant when they needed the extra help, so my students rarely were hired on permanently. They also didn't get the same pay or fringe benefits that the full-time employees did.

Still, it was a good experience for my students. It gave them a sense of what working in the "real world" was like. It also enabled me to assess their abilities and interests so that I could find better jobs that they would enjoy.

Mobile Work Crews

Mobile work crews are just like enclaves in that they involve groups of supported employees working together under the supervision of a job coach. Unlike with enclaves, where supported employees go to the same place to work, people employed via mobile work crews tend to go from job site to job site.

For instance, one of our mobile work crews involved lawn maintenance. On Mondays, my students would go to one place to cut grass and trim bushes and then they would go to another place on Tuesday, and so forth.

The nice thing about mobile work crews is that they provide employees with opportunities to go to different environments, so they don't get bored going to the same place every day. This, of course, means that people who need consistency probably wouldn't do well with this supported employment option.

Another downside to mobile work crews is that supported employees rarely work alongside their nondisabled coworkers, as with individual placements or enclaves. Consequently, it is difficult to teach social skills. Still, mobile work crews can benefit many individuals.

Entrepreneurial

The entrepreneurial approach to supported employment might sound like a combination of enclaves and sheltered workshops. Basically, with an entrepreneurial model, the adult service program owns a business out in the community. For example, they might own a second-hand clothing store or a bakery or something like that. I once worked at a program that owned a chocolate shop. It was wonderful—although terribly fattening!

Supported employees work at the business alongside employees without disabilities, usually earning at or above minimum wage. And, since the agency owns the business, positions are not temporary, as is often the case with enclaves. Further, employees are not segregated from workers without disabilities, as with sheltered workshops

Work Adjustment Programs

Work adjustment programs focus on giving students the skills that they are lacking so that they can become competitively employed within the community. For instance, suppose that a student with mental retardation is able to work and do employable tasks, but he is socially inappropriate. Work adjustment programs provide him with opportunities to learn how to behave on a worksite and then, once the target behavior has been acquired, he would get a job in the community. Think of this as a kind of vocational "finishing school."

Competitive Employment

Finally, there is competitive employment. Competitive employment programs are often funded or run by Departments of Vocational Rehabilitation. They are like placement agencies specifically for people with disabilities in that they help people with disabilities find a good job. But they don't provide intensive training or support, as with supported employment. Once the person is placed, he is usually on his own.

HOME LIFE

One of my primary roles as a teacher was to get parents to think about their child's future. I frequently sat down with families and asked, "Where do you see your child living after he graduates from high school?" The answer that I usually get is, "At home with us."

When I ask where parents see their child living when they are older and retired, there is usually a long, uneasy hesitation. Most parents don't think that far ahead. They are too busy living day-to-day to worry about twenty years down the road. However, if you have a child with mental retardation, you have to be proactive. You can't just wait for the future to arrive on your doorstep.

Why? Well, as we have discussed before, there are usually tremendously long waiting lists for residential programs. For instance, in my state, there is an eleven-year waiting list for group homes. Eleven years! Further, it takes kids with mental retardation longer to learn the skills required for independent living. So, no matter what options you would like to see your child have, you have to start planning early!

You might be thinking, like so many parents have told me in the past, "My child is going to live with me and then with his brothers or sisters once I am no longer able to take care of him."

That is fine, if that is what you, your family, and your child want to do. I know a lot of older adults living with their siblings who have disabilities. And, for the most part, everything works out fine. But I also know of several family members who feel like they have missed out on life because they feel "tied" to their brother or sister with mental retardation. They feel like they are their sibling's "keeper."

Again, the decision is up to you, your family, and your child. Still, please keep in mind that most people seem to like to get out of the nest and start their own families. I mean, I love my family; but I wouldn't want to live with my brothers for the rest of my life! It would just be too stressful.

With this in mind, I want to use this section of the chapter to talk about some of the residential options that are available for people with mental retardation, just in case your child might want to live some place other than with family forever. I then want to discuss some of the skills that your child will need to live as independently as possible.

There are five broad categories of residential options that are typically available for people with mental retardation. They include

- Transitional independent living programs (TILPS)
- Long-term residential programs (LTRPS)
- Group homes
- Semi-independent living programs (SILPS)
- Independent living programs

They might be called something different in your community but, generally speaking, they provide the following services to people with disabilities.

Transitional Independent Living Programs (TILPs)

Transitional independent living programs, also called TILPs, are temporary housing options for people with disabilities. Usually, people referred to these programs have certain issues that they need to work on before they can be live successfully in the community by themselves. For instance, a person might need to be taught safety skills or how to cook or what have you. They are placed in a TILP until their need has been satisfied. Then they move on to more a permanent placement.

TILPs are often used as "trial runs" where people live with some support for two or three months. During this time, they are evaluated to see what kind of residential program might best suit their needs. Traditionally, such evaluations only last for ninety days.

Long-Term Residential Programs (LTRPs)

Unlike TILPs, LTRPs (long-term residential programs) are permanent placements in which people can live for their entire lives. Also, unlike TILPs, people who live in LTRPs receive constant and intensive support from residential care providers who live on the site. Consequently, these programs usually serve people with multiple or profound disabilities.

Group Homes

Like long-term residential placements, people can live in group homes for as long as they like. The main differences between LTRPs and group homes are the number of people living in each and the degree of services typically provided. Specifically, whereas LTRPs can be very large and serve a hundred people or more, only a handful of people tend to live in group homes, usually a dozen or so. Further, while group homes might have a live-in residential care provider, the services that are provided are often less structured. People who live in group homes can come and go as they please. Residents of LTRPs may not have this option.

Semi-Independent Living Programs (SILPs)

The phrase "semi-independent living programs" (SILPs) means different things to different people. In most communities, SILPs are programs that allow people with disabilities to live in their own homes and get whatever support that they need to live as independently as possible. For example, maybe somebody comes to your child's apartment once a month to help with cleaning or shopping or paying the bills. The idea is that the person lives in his or her own home, but gets whatever services he or she needs to stay there. Usually, these supports are intermittent and can gradually be faded away.

Independent Living Programs

Of course, the final residential option available to people with mental retardation is simply living independently in the community, much like you and I do. I know that you are probably thinking that this probably wouldn't work for your child, and maybe you are correct. But before you write off the idea of your child living independently, realize that it isn't as uncommon as you think. Several of my former students live completely on their own. One even owns her own house.

Independent living programs often help people find affordable housing and low-interest rate mortgages. Some will even serve as an advocate for when a person with a disability is negotiating a lease or offer to buy. They might also help modify the homes so they suit the person's needs, such as widening doorways and bathrooms for wheelchair access. However, once a home is acquired, these programs don't usually provide any additional support.

I think what tends to prevent parents from picturing their child from living on his or her own is that they envision all of the things that their child can't do, not realizing that most people can't do those things either. For example, one of my student's parents didn't want her daughter living on her own. The mother kept saying, "But what if the roof were to cave in!? She wouldn't know what to do!"

So, I asked my student that very question. "What would you do if the roof caved in?" Do you know what she said? "Get out of that house!" She then added, "Then I'd call somebody to fix it before it started raining!"

The point is, this mother seemed to think that her daughter didn't have any common sense. Again, it is the same old story . . . people think that mental retardation means "stupid"—which it doesn't. Her daughter knew exactly what to do. And, although my student certainly couldn't fix a broken roof by herself, neither could her mother . . . and neither could I, for that matter!

Just because your child has mental retardation, that doesn't mean that he can't live in his own apartment or house or trailer or wherever. If you give him the skills that he will need, he should be able to live wherever he wants. But what skills will he need? Good question! That is what we are going to talk about next.

IMPROVING YOUR CHILD'S RESIDENTIAL SKILLS

Okay, now we come to the question of, "What can I do to improve my child's residential skills?" This is an excellent question to ask, whether your child is a newborn or twenty-one years old or fifty-one years old, for that matter. Again, as with all other skills, it is important that you begin teaching residential abilities early in life. Further, because people with mental retardation need frequent exposure in order to learn new skills, you must really overteach each lesson. So keep hitting the main points over and over again.

What should you teach your child so that he or she can live as independently as possible? The first, and probably the most important thing, is that you have to engrain in your child from a very young age that some day she will be expected to move out of the nest and build her own somewhere. We discussed this when we talked about vocational options, but it bears repeating. The worst thing that anybody can do is to teach his or her child that he can't do something because he has a disability. Many of my students developed that learned helplessness from an early age. By the time I get them in high school, it is very difficult to "reprogram" them. They simply don't try because they don't think that they can succeed.

Secondly, you should emphasize safety skills. For example, go over and over with them that they should not touch a hot stove or stick things into electric outlets, that kind of thing. Also, they need to know who should be in their home and who shouldn't be. Generally speaking, we always taught our students that if the person is a stranger, don't let them in unless they are a police officer and have a badge.

Along the same lines, you will need to teach your child how to use a phone and when to call you and when to call 911. This is going to be harder than it sounds. For instance, one of my students got an apartment with one of his friends. We really impressed upon him to call 911 if there is an emergency. Unfortunately, what he considered an "emergency" was completely different from what the 911 operators considered an emergency. He would call them if the refrigerator was leaking or if the toilet overflowed. Needless to say, the operators were not happy.

In the end, we developed a little flowchart that we posted by the phone. It basically had some quick questions that the student asked himself before calling 911. For example, he was only supposed to call if there was smoke, a fire, a stranger in the apartment, or if somebody was hurt. If the situation did not apply to any of those circumstances, then he was told not to call 911. He was supposed to call either me or his parents. When he called one of us, we would walk him though what to do. Eventually, he started to learn how to handle the inevitable surprises that occur when living away from your parents.

In addition to knowing how and when to contact 911, teach your child how to utilize community services. For example, your child should know how to use taxis or public transportation, such as buses. Once he can get around in the community, he can go to shopping malls and buy clothes, or groceries at grocery stores, or go to the doctor's office. The world really opens up when you can get around the community by yourself.

There are several ways that you can teach people with mental retardation how to use public transportation. You can certainly keep riding the bus or the subway with them until they get the hang of it. Or, you can keep quizzing them over how to use the maps. However, one strategy that I used, which I found really effective, involved making a kind of photo album of all the main bus stops that my students used.

With my trusty Polaroid, I took pictures of the bus stop closest to my students' homes. I would then take pictures of the bus stops where the grocery stores and shopping malls were. I took pictures of all of the stops that they might need to use. I also noted the specific buses that they needed to take as well as the times they came by each stop.

In other words, if my students wanted to go to a friend's house, she would go to the bus stop by her house and look at the corresponding picture of the bus stop near her friend's house. On the back of the picture, I wrote the number and color of the bus that they had to take (e.g., red number 2) as well as the times that the bus would be there. When she got to the bus stop, she would match the bus number and color written on the back of the picture with the front of the bus. She would then stay on the bus until she saw the stop on the picture. It was really very easy to use and make. I highly recommend using something like it if your child needs to learn how to use public transportation.

I think that another very critical skill needed for kids to live successfully in the community is how to use money. After all, if somebody doesn't know how to pay bills or budget his or her income, it becomes very easy to get in over your head very quickly. Unfortunately, for whatever reason, these are often difficult skills for even people of average intelligence to master.

For example, I was once engaged to a woman named Rebecca. Rebecca had several credit cards that were all charged to their max. She must have owed $40,000 to $50,000! And she had no plan to pay them off. She would simply pay off the minimum balance every month and then charge more on her accounts.

Now, for all of her many faults (and she had *a lot* of them), Rebecca wasn't stupid. But she couldn't seem to understand that if she only paid a little off each month and then charged that amount, if not more, she would never be debt-free. Eventually, the interest alone would be more than she would be able to pay and she would have to go bankrupt, which she ended up doing.

So, this kind of thing doesn't just involve people with mental retardation, yet it is something that needs to be addressed if people with mental retardation are to live successfully in the community. I have several recommendations that might help.

The first is to have all of your child's bills automatically deducted from his or her bank account. It is a simple and effective way to make sure that everything gets paid on time. Actually, I have all of my bills paid this way, including my mortgage, utilities, and even credit cards.

I would also recommend that any paychecks or Social Security payments be directly deposited into your child's account. If your child is the impulsive type who might take all of his money out and buy something that he doesn't need, you can arrange so that only a certain amount can be withdrawn each week. In fact, one of my college students has her account set up so that she can only withdraw $20 every week. Apparently, she is a bit of a "shopaholic."

Secondly, if your child has difficulty budgeting, I suggest that you use a method that involves placing money in specially marked envelopes. For instance, we would have envelopes for various types of expenses, such as grocery money, rent, heat bill, movies, and so forth. We even had an envelope for "just in case," which was for emergencies. Each envelope had the type of expense that it was for and also a picture. So, the grocery envelope would say "for groceries" on it and it would also have a picture of a shopping bag full of food. That way our students who had difficulty reading would know which envelope was for which expense.

In each envelope, we placed photocopies of dollar bills equaling the amount that we thought that our students would need for that month. If they needed $250 for rent, we would put the equivalent of $250 of photocopied money in the envelope. So, when they got paid, our students would take their real money and put it each envelope, using the fake money as a way to tell how much they needed to enclose. If they had any left over, they could spend it on whatever they liked, which was very motivating for most of our students. Many of them liked to work more just to fill up their "fun" envelope.

At any rate, when the time came, our students would take the real money out of the envelope and pay their bills. For the first few months, we helped them do this. We reminded them and even made sure that they paid the correct people. But, after a while, they were able to do this independently.

Using money in the community was a bit harder. Many of my students were taken advantage of by unethical cashiers and con artists. For example, a group of kids would meet one of my students outside of the bank right after one of my students cashed his paycheck from work. They would then offer him two $1 bills for one $10 bill. They would say things like, "Hey that's a good deal! Two is more than one, right? So you are actually getting more money!" Of course, my student didn't understand the value of the different denominations and would often fall for the trick.

That particular student always insisted on cashing his entire check. So having it directly deposited and giving him an "allowance" for casual spending was out of the question for him. In the end, what we did was create a kind of "cheat sheet" that was laminated and put in his wallet.

The student could count things, and he understood that two was bigger than one and three was bigger than two, and so forth. But he couldn't read numerals. He didn't really understand that "1" equaled one of something and "5" equaled five of something, or that a "1" and a "0" put next to each other was ten. So, comprehending that a $1 bill was somehow different than a $10 bill was very difficult for him.

The cheat sheet translated the numbers into something that he could understand. We put little pictures of the $1, $5, $10, and $20 bills on a piece of paper. We then put the number of smiley faces that corresponded with the number on each bill. For instance, next to the $1 bill, there was one smiley face, which he could count. Next to the picture of the $5 bill, we put five smiley faces, and so on.

He was then able to see that one bill had more smiley faces, and therefore was "worth" more, than other bills. Further, when given multiple denominations, such as three $1s, two $5s, and a $20, he was able to count the total number of smiley faces that he had. It was a very successful strategy that we ended up using for most of our students.

In case you are wondering, we caught the group of teenagers who kept conning my student out of his money. As it turns out, they were doing the same thing to several other individuals who had cognitive problems. They were eventually prosecuted by the state and charged with several crimes. If I recall correctly, two of the teenagers pled guilty to lesser charges and did community service. Three others went to trial, were found guilty, and had to pay some fines.

Another problem that this and other students had when living in the community was shopping. Again, he knew how to count, but he didn't comprehend relative value. To him, an expensive sports car might cost $100. A cookie might also cost $100. He simply had no idea what was a good deal or what he could buy for the amount of money that he had.

Many times, a student of mine would go to the grocery store, load up a shopping cart full of everything that they wanted, push the overflowing cart to the checkout aisle only to find out that they didn't have nearly enough money to pay for it all. I can just imagine how furious the other customers who had to wait behind them in line would get! Or, how annoyed the store clerks would be when they realized that they would have to put away *everything* that my students wanted to buy! So, what did we do?

We implemented a strategy called "next dollar estimating." Basically, what we did was have our students round up when estimating how much money they needed to buy something. For instance, if they wanted to buy something that was $3.15, they would need at least $4.00. And so forth.

So, when they were pushing their cart around the store, and they found something that they wanted to buy, they would look at the dollar amount, add one dollar to it, and then take that much money out of their wallet and place it into an envelope. Once all of the money was gone from their wallet, they couldn't buy any more.

Sometimes we had students use calculators to do the same thing, but not all of my students were able to do this. In that case, the above strategy with envelopes was found to be very effective.

A couple more brief comments about shopping in the community, and then I want to move on to other issues. It was really important for us to find good stores with understanding clerks. We also identified times when the stores weren't very busy, so that our students could get help when they needed it.

Generally speaking, the stores that we approached were very accommodating. After all, they are in business to make money, and my student's money was just as good as anybody else's! In fact, one grocery store developed a program for our students and other people who might require help shopping, such as the elderly. They arranged to have a special clerk be on duty at a certain time every week. My students, as well as other shoppers who needed help finding and paying for things, would come to the store at that time, meet the clerk at the customer service counter, and the clerk would help them get and pay for their groceries.

The problem was, the clerk was often too helpful. Many of my students could shop just as well as anybody else. But they would pretend to need help just so that they could socialize with the clerk. Again, as we have discussed before, people with mental retardation become dependent pretty quickly.

In addition to being able to shop and budget their money, individuals with mental retardation also need to know how to cook nutritious meals. Many of my students were extremely overweight, to the point of living very short and unhealthy lives. If they had their own way, they would eat Twinkies or cupcakes for every meal of the day! Consequently, I began to focus a lot of attention on how to cook.

The nice thing about teaching kids to cook is that it is very motivating. Whenever food is involved, my students just seemed to perk up and pay attention—especially when I told them that they couldn't eat what we made unless they did a good job! Plus, I was able to introduce a whole bunch of other concepts into the cooking lessons. For example, I taught them math skills (e.g., how to count eggs, multiply ingredients for double batches, etc.), measuring skills, safety skills (especially how to operate an stove and sharp knives), how to follow directions (both written and oral), as well as how to clean up and put things away.

Thanks to microwave dinners, even kids with profound mental retardation can learn how to cook meals for themselves. Now, I know what you are thinking. "Microwave dinners" probably sound really unappetizing and unhealthy, right? Some are! But if you go to the health food section of your local grocery market, there are all kinds of healthy meals that require adding only hot water or being microwaved or otherwise very simple preparation. You will still have to teach your child how to use the appliances safely or how to measure things out, but nowadays it is very possible to eat healthy, frozen food every day of the week.

If you want to teach your child how to cook actual meals from scratch, I highly recommend making them a cookbook of ten to fifteen meals that they actually like. Keep the directions very short and simple. Take pictures of every little step. Also, get a good set of measuring cups and spoons that are clearly marked. You can even draw lines on the measuring cups so that it is easier to see where each denotation is.

The trick to teaching kids about proper nutrition is to not be too technical. Don't focus on the difference between whole grains and how many servings of what should be eaten when. Make a list of food that the child likes to eat. Put all of the fruits in one column and all the vegetables in another column and so on. Even create a column for snacks and junk food. Then assign how many selections that the child can have from each specific food group. For instance, they have to eat two things a day from the fruits and vegetables column and two things from the dairy column, and so on.

Moreover, put the columns in order from left to right so that the junk food is to the far end of the list. Then make it so that your child can only eat stuff from the last column (the junk food list) if they eat the proper amount from each of the other columns first. If you are unsure about how much of each food group a child should eat, consult any number of cookbooks or books on healthy living. They can be found in any library or bookstores.

Another strategy to teach nutrition is to map out your local grocery store. Then have your child buy so many items from each section. For instance, they have to buy five things from the produce section, two items from the bread aisle, and one thing from the candy aisle. The idea is to give them guidelines that are general enough so that they can follow them when you aren't there, but strict enough so that they get good food.

Okay, so we have talked about several ways that you can help improve your child's ability to live away from you. We have talked about how you have to promote the desire to live on their own and how you have to teach them basic safety skills. We also talked about how your child will need to access supports that are found within the community, such as being able to call 911 appropriately, as well as utilize public transportation.

There are, of course, many other skills that would be beneficial for anybody to know in order for him to live on his own. I personally would want my child to know how to fix a flat tire or how to change a hose on his car. My mother was adamant about making sure that each of us knew how to swim well enough to save our lives, should we fall into a pool or a pond. You probably have similar priorities.

What you should do is get a pen and a piece of paper, sit down right now, and make a list of the ten most important skills that your child needs to know in order to live successfully as an adult. Then, focus on those ten things. Keep teaching and reteaching those skills until you are confident that your child has mastered them. When he has, teach him the next ten important skills, and so on.

I have generated a list of things that you might want to address below. Your list might be completely different. If you have difficulty teaching your child a skill, ask his or her special education teacher to suggest strategies or techniques. Or better yet, have those skills added to their IEP!

- Desire to live independently
- Personal safety
- How and when to call 911
- Following spoken and written directions
- Basic cooking and cleaning
- Making healthy meals
- Using public transportation
- Accessing community supports
- Using money
- Shopping

Again, the main point here is for you to think about your child's life when he or she will become an adult. Think about what she needs to know for her to have a good life. Then spend a lot of time early on preparing her for her future. It is *never* too soon to start teaching!

SOCIAL AND RECREATIONAL LIVES

We already talked about strategies for developing your child's social skills in chapter 5; however, I think that it is important enough to touch upon it again. I mean, what kind of life would it be if you didn't have any friends? So, in this section, I want to summarize some of the strategies that can help your child develop a rich and rewarding social life.

In chapter 5, we mentioned that children with mental retardation often emulate other people's behaviors. For that reason, it is important for them to have good role models. I suggested having your child play with older, responsible children. I also suggested that you get him involved in as many social activities as possible. This will not only enable him to practice his interactions with people, but he can also make friends and develop interests.

Developing interests is critical! So many of my students had absolutely no interests in anything. All they did was sit at home and watch television. Or, they had interests, but they were age-inappropriate. For example, I would have nineteen-year-old girls who would talk about nothing but "the Powder Puff Girls," which is a cartoon popular with elementary schoolers.

Without having a lot of different interests, life can become boring pretty fast! Plus, without age-appropriate interests, it will be difficult for your child to interact with same-aged peers. After all, if they have nothing in common, what are they going to talk about or do together?

From what I understand, interests are much like taste in food. Young children who do not eat a variety of foods will grow up to be adults who don't eat a variety of foods. The same is true with kids who don't try new things. They tend to grow up into adults who don't have many interests.

So, in order to have a well-rounded adult who has a satisfying social and recreational life, you have to get your child to do new things. The more things that she experiences, the more interests she is likely to have, and the more friends she will likely meet! So, how do encourage your child to try new things?

Well, first of all, put a limit on how much television he is allowed to watch. Having him sit in front of the TV all day isn't going to help him make new interests or meet new friends. Further, it will probably adversely affect his health. It is hard to get a good workout when your butt is permanently adhered to the sofa!

Now, I am not saying that you should throw out all of your televisions or that you should ban TV all together. You shouldn't. Watching television can be very relaxing and, at times, educational. I am just saying that if you restrict how much time your child spends in front of a television, the more time he will spend doing other things.

The same is true for computer and video games. However, some video games can be played by multiple people; these can actually help foster friendships. One of my student's parents came up with the brilliant idea of only allowing her son to play video games that require two or more players. So, if her son wanted to play, he had to go out and find a neighbor kid to play with. She also made sure that he had all of the new and trendy games. He was the envy of the neighborhood. Kids from blocks around would come over and play with him for hours!

In addition to limiting television and solitary game-playing time, you also should promote new experiences. Another one of my student's parents used to have "adventure day" where, one day a week, they would do something that they had never done before. It became a challenge to find new activities, but they always managed to find something fun. She recommends that you check out arts and crafts books from the library or go to a hobby shop. There are tons of ideas for games and activities there.

In addition to going to the library and hobby shops, I highly recommend getting your child signed up for various clubs and sports. If you visit your local park district or YMCA, they should be able to provide you with a list of what is available. You also might want to look into organizations specifically for kids with disabilities, such as Best Friends and Special Olympics. Both can be very helpful in developing new interests and facilitating lifelong friendships.

Special Olympics

Since we are on the topic anyway, I want to spend at least a couple paragraphs talking about Special Olympics. If you don't already know, Special Olympics is an international organization that provides opportunities for people with mental retardation, eight years old and older, to train for and participate in various sports, including:

alpine skiing	figure skating	snowshoeing
badminton	floor hockey	soccer
basketball	golf	softball
bocce	gymnastics	speed skating
bowling	powerlifting	table tennis
cross country skiing	sailing	tennis
cycling	snowboarding	volleyball

Proponents of Special Olympics indicate that these activities enable individuals with mental retardation to have fun, meet friends, and get in better shape. Critics note that Special Olympics is a segregated program where people with mental retardation are only allowed to participate with other people with mental retardation, rather than with their nondisabled peers. In the end, you will have to decide what to believe. For more information about Special Olympics as an organization or upcoming events, go to www.specialolympics.org or call (202) 628-3630.

HEALTHY LIVES

Finally, if you are like most parents, you want your child to be a happy, healthy adult! Right? So how do we make that happen?

Well, you need to teach your child to eat well and exercise often. Easier said than done? Not really. As we said before, such behavior tends to be learned at a very young age. Kids who are exposed to a wide variety of healthy foods early on will most likely grow up to be adults who eat healthy meals. That is why pediatricians are now telling parents to diversify the foods given to infants. The better eaters kids are, the better eaters they will be when they get older!

So, try to limit the trips to the fast-food places. And give fruit, such as grapes, raisins, or dried pineapple wedges, instead of candy. The habits you begin now may be the habits that your child will have throughout the rest of his or her life.

Similarly, you will need to encourage your child to be active. As we mentioned earlier, that might mean cutting back on the television watching and computer game playing. It is hard to be in good physical shape if you sit down and stare at a screen all day.

It also means getting your child involved with activities that will have him running around expelling all of that pent up energy. There are tons of sports and activities from which your child can choose. Just look in the newspaper or call your local park district or YMCA. Keep in mind that just because your child has mental retardation doesn't mean that he or she can't play Little League baseball or join a swim team or do whatever typical kids do. Participating in such activities might also help your child's social life, too.

Again, the idea is to promote behaviors that improve your child's future. Some of these behaviors will enhance multiple areas of his life. For example, participating in team sports or group activities might not only improve your child's overall health, but it might help him develop new interests and friendships!

OTHER IMPORTANT ISSUES

Well, our time together is almost over. But before you go, there are several other very important topics that you should consider. These include:

- Guardianships
- Powers of attorney
- Trust funds and long-term financial planning
- Supplemental Security Income (SSI) and other governmental programs

Guardianship

One of the things that seems to surprise the parents of my older students is that they are not the legal guardians of their children. If your child is over eighteen years old, she is her own legal guardian, no matter what her IQ is or how many disabilities she has. This means that she can make her own legal decisions.

Some parents feel that their adult child should have a guardian to look after them. In such cases, the parents have to go to court and have a hearing. During the hearing, the judge will make a determination of whether a guardian is necessary or in the best interests of the person with mental retardation.

Even if the judge determines that a guardian is warranted, that doesn't mean that the parents will be given control. Often, judges will appoint an independent third party to be guardians over adults with disabilities just to make sure that decisions are made in the best interests of the individual. Moreover, there are several different types of guardianships that the judge could appoint. These include regular guardianships, limited guardianships, and temporary guardianships.

Before considering any of these types of guardianships, please contact an attorney for more detailed information. You should also consider other options that might also suit your child's needs.

Regular guardianships. Of the three types, regular (or "full") guardianships furnish the guardian with the most control over the individual's life. In these situations, the guardian is required to "care for" and "maintain" the ward. This means making sure that the individual is fed, clothed, and housed properly, that he or she is receiving the proper medical attention, and that his or her finances are tended to.

With a regular guardianship, the guardian has complete control over nearly every aspect of the ward's life. The guardian can make medical decisions and invest money for them. They can even determine where and how the individual lives.

There are some checks and balances to make sure that the ward isn't being taken advantage of. For instance, every two years, the guardian must file an accounting of the ward's financial assets. The guardian must also receive court approval before any extraordinary expenditures are made on the ward's behalf.

Limited guardianships. In the cases of a limited guardianship, the judge sets limits as to what the guardian can and can't do for the ward. For example, the judge might allow the guardian to make financial or medical decisions, but that is it. In all other circumstances, the adult with mental retardation can do as he or she pleases.

Temporary guardianships. With temporary guardianship, the judge appoints a guardian, with either full or limited powers, for up to sixty days. Usually, temporary guardians are only appointed if there is an emergency or if the judge is trying to determine whether the individual is in danger.

I have had three students who have been appointed temporary guardians. In each case, they were appointed a temporary guardian because their parents were either abusing them or stealing their money. Further, in all three cases, the guardian was an officer of the court and not a family member.

Powers of Attorney

Powers of attorney are legal documents in which the individual turns over control to an appointed person. They are similar to guardianships, with a few important exceptions. For instance, guardians are appointed by the court—sometimes against the will of the ward. Powers of attorney are appointed by the person. Further, a person can withdraw his or her consent from a power of attorney at any time, while guardians can only be removed by a judge.

As with guardianships, powers of attorney come in many different forms. There can be powers of attorney that have complete control over the person and can make all decisions. There are also powers of attorney that look after certain aspects of the person's life, such their finances or their property.

Trust Funds and Long-Term Financial Planning

Most of my students' parents were concerned about the financial well-being of their children after the parents died. In several of these cases, parents established trust funds for their child.

A trust is a legal entity that holds the ownership of assets for a beneficiary. As with guardianships and powers of attorney, there are many different types of trusts. Further, there are many legal ramifications of setting up one. So, before you do, please consult a lawyer who specializes in such matters.

With that said, trusts are often used as a way of making sure that people have money over an extended period of time. For instance, several of my students had trust funds that would begin paying them a monthly "allowance" once they reached a certain age, such as twenty-two or fifty. The trustee, which could be a person or an institution, is responsible for tending to and allocating the funds as prescribed in the trust agreement. In the cases of my students, the most of the money was preallocated for certain expenditures, such as housing, medical care, and daily living expenses.

Now, you are probably thinking that you have to be wealthy to have a trust for your child. That isn't the case at all. You can put as little or as much as you want into a trust fund. It is up to you.

Of course, saving for your child's future is much like saving for your own retirement. The earlier you start, the more money you will have. Consider two families for a moment. Family A had a child with a disability and started putting money into an interest-bearing account (e.g., 5 percent) right when the child was born. Family B had a child with a disability and started putting money into the same account when the child turned twenty-one. If both families put in $100 a month, every month, for twenty years, Family A will have nearly three times the amount saved by the time their child reaches age sixty-five than Family B will (i.e., $355,220 versus $138,237). See table 8.2.

Remember, both families put the exact same amount into the same kind of savings account, so it isn't like one family was wealthier or saved for a longer period of time. It is just that, by starting early, Family A was able to let

Table 8.2. The Effects of Long-Term Financial Planning

	Cumulative Savings for:	
Age of Child	*Family A*	*Family B*
1 year old	$1,200.00	—
5 years old	$6,561.30	—
10 years old	$15,004.82	—
15 years old	$25,781.14	—
20 years old	$39,534.75	—
25 years old	$50,457.47	$6,630.76
30 years old	$64,397.94	$15,093.47
35 years old	$82,189.90	$25,894.28
40 years old	$104,897.46	$39,679.14
45 years old	$133,878.69	$52,100.37
50 years old	$170,866.90	$66,494.74
55 years old	$218,074.28	$84,866.01
60 years old	$278,324.18	$108,312.92
65 years old	$355,220.02	$138,237.79

their money generate far more interest than Family B, who didn't start saving until their child turned twenty-one. The morale of the story? If you need money, talk to Family A!

Supplemental Security Income (SSI) and Other Governmental Programs

Finally, I think that we should talk about various governmental funding programs for which your child might be eligible. Specifically, I want to talk about Supplemental Security Income (SSI), Medicaid, and Medicare. These programs vary greatly from state to state and from year to year, so it will be difficult to discuss them other than in very general terms. If you think that your child might be eligible for these programs, please contact your local Social Security office, go to www.socialsecurity.gov, or call 800-772-1213.

In simple terms, SSI is a federal program that pays monthly benefits to, among others, individuals with various disabilities who demonstrate an economic need. Both children and adults are eligible, although the eligibility of children is affected by the income of their parents. Determination for eligibility often takes up to six months; however, the applications of people with mental retardation, Down syndrome, and cerebral palsy are often expedited.

Medicaid is a health care program for people who have low incomes. Most of the time, children who qualify for SSI also qualify for Medicaid. However, since Medicaid is heavily influenced by state regulations, you should check with your local Social Security office to see if your child is eligible.

Medicare is a federal health program for people who are sixty-five or older and for people who have been receiving Social Security disability benefits for more than two years. Because people with mental retardation are not eligible for Social Security disability benefits until they turn eighteen, children with mental retardation are not eligible for Medicare until they turn twenty.

The state Children Health Insurance Program (CHIP) is a program that provides health insurance for children. To be eligible, children must come from working families who earn too much money to qualify for Medicaid, but cannot afford to purchase private health insurance. The program covers prescription drugs, vision, hearing, and mental health services.

To find out more about these and other governmental programs, please contact your local Social Security and state health agencies. Also consult the resources in the back of this book.

FINAL THOUGHTS

Well, here we are at the end of the book! I hope that you have learned something useful in our time together. But, before you go, I want to reiterate several key points that we have been discussing since we began this journey.

First of all, mental retardation doesn't mean "stupid!" It doesn't mean that a person will be a child forever, or that she can't learn, or that he'll stop learning and reach his "potential" earlier than do other people. Mental retardation doesn't mean any of these things.

Mental retardation is simply a term used to describe people with poor adaptive skills and who don't learn as fast as do the rest of the general population. They *can* learn. They *can* love. They *can* work. They *can* live by themselves. They *can* vote. They *can* drive. They *can* go to bars or coffee shops or wherever and have a good time with their friends. They *can* get married, have sex, and have their own families. They *can* even write books and become rich and famous. In short, they can have lives much like you or I have had.

The main problem is getting people with mental retardation prepared for life. This means that you have to teach many of the same skills that you would teach a child without mental retardation. However, because children with mental retardation require more time to assimilate new knowledge, you will have to start teaching them early. Further, you might have to use different teaching strategies, such as providing hands-on experiences.

Finally, the most important theme of this book is that you should not make mental retardation into a disability! As a teacher, most of my students were more "disabled" by how they were treated than by what their actual abilities were. I had students who wouldn't even try to learn new things because people constantly told them that they couldn't learn or that they didn't need to because somebody would always "take care" of them.

If there is anything, anything at all that I can give to you and your child it is this: Don't undervalue your child just because he or she is different. Try to give your child the future that you would want for anybody, regardless of intelligence or adaptive abilities. Empower your child to make good choices. Expect him or her to be an active and contributing member of society. Prepare your child for life when you are no longer around. And, above all, teach your child how to have a long, happy, healthy, and meaningful life.

I hope that this book has been helpful and that I have made a positive difference in your life and the life of your child. If you have any questions or comments, please feel free to contact me at robertcimera@yahoo.com. Good luck and remember—*mental retardation doesn't mean "stupid"!*

RESOURCES

The following are some resources that I thought might be of interest to parents and teachers of children with mental retardation. It is by no means an extensive list, but it should help answer any questions that you may have. Or, at least, it should get you pointed in the right direction.

Summaries from all books were provided by, and with permission from, www.amazon.com. Mission statements from organizations come directly from the organization's websites.

Just because something is included within this section doesn't mean that I vouch for its content, philosophy, or quality. You will have to do that for yourself. All information was current at the time that this book was published.

BOOKS OVERVIEWING MENTAL RETARDATION

Title:	*Mental Retardation* (6th edition)
Author(s):	Mary Beirne-Smith, Richard F. Ittenbach, James R. Patton
Publisher (Date):	Prentice Hall (June 5, 2001)

Summary: This introductory textbook features key words and learning objectives. It concentrates on basic concepts; biology, psychology, and sociology of mental retardation; intervention issues; and family considerations.

Title: *Handbook of Mental Retardation and Development*
Author(s): Jacob A. Burack, Robert M. Hodapp, Edward F. Zigler
Publisher (Date): Cambridge University Press (February 28, 1998)
Summary: This book reviews theoretical and empirical work in the developmental approach to mental retardation. Armed with methods derived from the study of typically developing children, developmentalists have recently learned about the mentally retarded child's own development in a variety of areas. These areas now encompass many aspects of cognition, language, social and adaptive functioning, as well as of maladaptive behavior and psychopathology. In addition to a focus on individuals with mental retardation themselves, familial and other "ecological" factors have influenced developmental approaches to mental retardation. Comprised of twenty-seven chapters on various aspects of development, this handbook provides a timely, comprehensive guide to understanding mental retardation and development.

Title: *Mental Retardation: A Lifespan Approach to People with Intellectual Disabilities* (8th edition)
Author(s): Clifford J. Drew, Michael L. Hardman
Publisher (Date): Prentice Hall (April 7, 2003)
Summary: Provides an introduction to mental retardation that is readable and comprehensive, and which reflects the broad array of stories associated with this disability. The authors combine a developmental approach—discussing their subject as it evolves from birth to the elder years—with a multidisciplinary perspective that

acknowledges the need for collaboration in regard to diagnosis and intervention in order to effectively assist people with mental retardation and their families. Coverage pays particular attention to multicultural issues and incorporates the latest research in the field. For future special education teachers, or those in the psychology and social work field.

Title: *Teaching Students with Mental Retardation: A Life Goal Curriculum Planning Approach*
Author(s): Glen E. Thomas
Publisher (Date): Prentice Hall (February 5, 1996)
Summary: This book emphasizes and identifies (1) a prioritized life goal curriculum planning approach to identify the functional skills and concepts needed by a student with mental retardation or severe disabilities to become as successful as possible in adult life, and (2) a diagnostic/prescriptive teaching approach to assess each student's abilities and progress toward those individual life goals.

Title: *Understanding Mental Retardation (Understanding Health and Sickness Series)*
Author(s): Patricia Ainsworth, Pamela C. Baker
Publisher (Date): University Press of Mississippi; (July 1, 2004)
Summary: *Understanding Mental Retardation* explores a diverse group of disorders from their biological roots to the everyday challenges faced by this special population and their families. With parents and those who care for people who have mental retardation in mind, Patricia Ainsworth and Pamela C. Baker write in a style that is at once accessible, informative, and sympathetic to the concerns of those affected.

Title: *Mental Retardation: A LifeSpan Approach to People with Intellectual Disabilities* (8th edition)

Author(s): Clifford J. Drew, Michael L. Hardman
Publisher (Date): Prentice Hall (April 7, 2003)
Summary: Provides an introduction to mental retardation that is readable and comprehensive, and which reflects the broad array of stories associated with this disability. The authors combine a developmental approach—discussing their subject as it evolves from birth to the elder years—with a multidisciplinary perspective that acknowledges the need for collaboration in regard to diagnosis and intervention in order to effectively assist people with mental retardation and their families. Coverage pays particular attention to multicultural issues and incorporates the latest research in the field. For future special education teachers, or those in the psychology and social work field.

BOOKS ON SPECIAL EDUCATION

Title: *The Truth about Special Education: A Guide for Parents and Teachers*
Author(s): Robert E. Cimera
Publisher (Date): Scarecrow Education (March 2003)
Summary: Few parents and educators understand special education and its terms, philosophies, and processes. This easy-to-read book contains a step-by-step discussion of the special education process and had hundreds of additional resources for parents, including professional organizations, support groups, and useful websites. *The Truth about Special Education* will help parents and students minimize the inevitable anxiety associated with enrolling in a special education program. Readers will also gain insight into the legal rights and responsibilities associated with having a child in special education, learn how to develop effective educational plans and strategies for building suc-

cessful teams, and gather basic information regarding common disabilities. Primarily written for family members of children with disabilities, this book will also be useful for educators who are unfamiliar with special education, as well as special educators who are new to the field.

Title: *Negotiating the Special Education Maze: A Guide for Parents & Teachers* (3rd edition)
Author(s): Winifred Anderson, Stephen Chitwood, Deidre Hayden
Publisher (Date): Woodbine House (May 1, 1997)
Summary: *Negotiating the Special Education Maze* assists parents and teachers in the development of effective education program for their child or student. Every step is explained, from eligibility and evaluation to the Individualized Education Program (IEP) and beyond. This edition covers changes in disability laws, including the Americans with Disabilities Act (ADA) and Individuals with Disabilities Education Act (IDEA). It reviews early intervention services for children from birth to age three, and for those who have young adults with special needs, it also covers transitioning out of school.

Title: *Special Education in Contemporary Society: An Introduction to Exceptionality*
Author(s): Richard M. Gargiulo
Publisher (Date): Wadsworth Publishing (March 29, 2002)
Summary: This engaging text, designed for students of special and general education, provides comprehensive coverage of human exceptionalities across the life span. It employs a traditional organization beginning with four foundations chapters covering such important topics as the history of special education, key litigation and legislation, including up-to-date coverage of

the reauthorization of the IDEA, service delivery models, cultural and linguistic diversity, and a full chapter on parents and families. Nine "categorical" chapters, each of which follows a common format, follow these chapters. The book features a strong emphasis on inclusion with coverage of inclusion in each of the categorical chapters. Each categorical chapter also features sections on transition, multicultural consideration, and use of technology.

Title: *Birth to Eight: Early Childhood Special Education*
Author(s): Frank Bowe
Publisher (Date): Delmar Thomson Learning (September 1, 2003)
Summary: Text offers a comprehensive look at the early childhood special education field. Revised to expand coverage through age eight.

Title: *Exceptional Children: An Introduction to Special Education* (6th Edition)
Author(s): William Heward
Publisher (Date): Prentice Hall (July 28, 1999)
Summary: Grounded in scholarship, yet written with the human experience in mind, this best-selling book effectively conveys the stories of teachers and children in special education. This latest edition adds a focus on master teachers and integrates professional standards from CEC and PRAXIS™ to make this the best book to help you train effective special educators and to introduce pre- and in-service general education teachers to exceptional children. This book provides some of the most comprehensive coverage of the characteristics of learners with special needs, as well as some of the latest assistive technologies like hand-held PDAs, the AAMR's new 2002 definition and classification system for mental retardation. For teaching professionals in the field of special education.

BOOKS ON LEGAL ISSUES

Title: *Wrightslaw: Special Education Law*
Author(s): Peter W. D. Wright, Pamela Darr Wright
Publisher (Date): Harbor House Law Press (November 1, 1999)
Summary: Special education law is more than a legal specialty niche. Special education laws govern eligibility, IEPs, evaluations, placement, educational progress, transition plans, discipline, and educational records—and are vitally important to parents of disabled children, educators, child advocates, school psychologists, health care providers, and school administrators.

Title: *Getting Comfortable with Special Education Law: A Framework for Working with Children with Disabilities*
Author(s): Dixie Snow Huefner
Publisher (Date): Christopher-Gordon Pub. (December 1, 2000)
Summary: A complete guide to understanding the needs of children with disabilities . . . the complex legal relationship between federal and state governments . . . the contributions being made by legislation, regulations, and court decisions . . . and the ultimate responsibilities of parents and teachers to make appropriate education a reality for all children with disabilities. Part One gives you an outstanding overview of the issues and laws. In Part Two you get an update on Section 504 and see what it does and does not do. Part Three shows what you need to know about the major issues that have arisen under IDEA. Endorsed by CASE, the Council of Administrators of Special Education.

Title: *Special Education Law* (1st edition)
Author(s): Nikki L. Murdick, Barbara C. Gartin, Terry Lee Crabtree
Publisher (Date): Prentice Hall (May 1, 2001)

Summary: With IDEA and its regulations as the foundation, this readable book provides the most current information on special education law and regulation today. The authors' approach allows readers to go to the original legislation and to examine current legislation from a historical perspective. It also gives readers the opportunity to understand the evolving nature of legislation and how it is interpreted by case law. Topics include: Overview of Special Education Services; A New Foundation for Special Education Services; Free Appropriate Public Education; Nondiscriminatory Evaluation; Individualized Education Program (IEP); Least Restrictive Environment (LRE); Procedural Due Process; Parental Participation; Enforcement of Special Education Law; Mediation and Impartial Due Process Healing; Ethics and the Special Education Professional.

Title: *The Law and Special Education* (1st edition)
Author(s): Mitchell L. Yell
Publisher (Date): Prentice Hall (November 10, 1997)
Summary: This book presents the necessary information for educators to understand the history and development of special education laws and the requirements of these laws. This book provides the reader with the necessary skills to locate pertinent information in law libraries, on the Internet, and other sources to keep abreast of the constant changes and developments in the special education field. Appropriate for people interested in special education and the Law.

BOOKS ON CONDITIONS RELATED TO MENTAL RETARDATION

Title: *Babies with Down Syndrome: A New Parent's Guide (The Special-Needs Collection)*(2nd edition)

Author(s):	Karen Stray-Gundersen
Publisher (Date):	Woodbine House (October 1, 1995)
Summary:	The book that thousands of new parents and professionals have turned to as their first source of information on Down syndrome. This classic guide provides new parents with straightforward and compassionate advice and insight. It helps families become more confident in their ability to cope, to learn about their child's development, to know where to seek help, and to advocate for their child. This second edition, written by the same knowledgeable parents and professionals who contributed to the first edition, covers these important areas: diagnosis; medical concerns and treatment; coping with your emotions; daily care; family life; early intervention; special education; and legal rights. The satisfying blend of practical information and emotional support make *Babies with Down Syndrome* the guide new families will want to refer to first.

Title:	*Early Communication Skills for Children with Down Syndrome: A Guide for Parents and Professionals* (2nd edition)
Author(s):	Libby Kumin
Publisher (Date):	Woodbine House (July 1, 2003)
Summary:	For children with Down syndrome, communicating is just as urgent and essential as it is for anyone else. In the newly updated and expanded edition of *Communication Skills in Children with Down Syndrome*, Libby Kumin offers comprehensive, authoritative, and practical advice based on her nearly twenty-five years of firsthand experience with kids with Down syndrome. She explains the role of a SLP, the stages of communication development, and how certain characteristics of Down syndrome, such as low muscle tone, hearing loss, and cognitive delays, can slow

progression of those skills. Delays can lead to frustration and other problems for children who do not have intelligible speech until age two or later.

Title: *A Parent's Guide to Down Syndrome: Toward a Brighter Future* (Revised 2nd edition)
Author(s): Segfried M. Pueschel
Publisher (Date): Paul H Brookes Pub. Co. (October 1, 2000)
Summary: For over ten years, parents and professionals have trusted Dr. Pueschel's best-selling book—and now they can get the latest information in his new edition. Crossing the lifespan, this thorough volume highlights developmental stages and shows recent advances that can improve a child's quality of life. New topics covered include the Individuals with Disabilities Education Act (IDEA) of 1997; innovative services, programs, and support groups; the latest prenatal genetic testing methods; the impact of play on gross motor development; and the association of Down syndrome with other disorders. Written by leading experts, many of whom are parents of children with Down syndrome, this book offers readers the advice and insight they need.

Title: *Thinking in Pictures: And Other Reports from My Life with Autism*
Author(s): Temple Grandin
Publisher (Date): Vintage Books (November 1, 1996)
Summary: Temple Grandin, Ph.D., is a gifted animal scientist who has designed one third of all the livestock-handling facilities in the United States. She also lectures widely on autism because she is autistic, a woman who thinks, feels, and experiences the world in ways that are incomprehensible to the rest of us. In this unprecedented book, Grandin writes from the dual perspectives of a scientist and an autistic person.

She tells us how she managed to breach the boundaries of autism to function in the outside world. What emerges is the document of an extraordinary human being, one who gracefully bridges the gulf between her condition and our own while shedding light on our common identity.

Title: *Let Me Hear Your Voice: A Family's Triumph over Autism* (reprint edition)
Author(s): Catherine Maurice
Publisher (Date): Ballantine Books (August 1, 1994)
Summary: *Let Me Hear Your Voice* is a mother's illuminating account of how one family triumphed over autism. It is an absolutely unforgettable book, as beautifully written as it is informative.

Title: *Facing Autism: Giving Parents Reasons for Hope and Guidance for Help*
Author(s): Lynn M. Hamilton
Publisher (Date): Waterbrook Press (March 1, 2000)
Summary: Now parents of autistic children can find the hope and practical guidance they need. Perhaps one of the most devastating things parents can learn is that their child has been diagnosed with autism. A multifaceted disorder, autism has long baffled parents and professionals alike. At one time, doctors gave parents virtually no hope for combating the disorder. But in recent years, new treatments and therapies have demonstrated that improvement is possible. With intensive, early intervention, some children have recovered from autism and have been integrated into school, indistinguishable from their peers. In this greatly needed new book, author Lynn M. Hamilton draws upon her own experience of successfully parenting an autistic child to give overwhelmed moms and dads guidance, practical information, and—best of all—hope for battling

this disorder in their children's lives. In *Facing Autism*, parents will learn ten things they can do to begin battling autism right away, investigate cutting-edge biomedical treatments and other therapies, explore the benefits of dietary intervention, and much more as they learn how to begin the fight for their child's future.

Title: *Activity Schedules for Children with Autism: Teaching Independent Behavior (Topics in Autism)*
Author(s): Lynn E. McClannahan, Patricia J. Krantz
Publisher (Date): Woodbine House (March 1, 1999)
Summary: Based on a decade of research conducted at the Princeton Child Development Institute, Activity Schedules for Children with Autism offers a proven teaching tool to help children with autism make effective use of unstructured time, handle changes in routine with more ease, and choose among an established set of activities independently. It can be used successfully with young children, adolescents, and adults, rewarding them with more control over their lives.

Title: *Children with Cerebral Palsy: A Parents' Guide* (2nd edition)
Author(s): Elaine Geralis
Publisher (Date): Woodbine House (August 1, 1998)
Summary: A revised and updated edition of this classic primer for parents provides a complete spectrum of information and compassionate advice about cerebral palsy and its effect on their child's development and education.

Title: *Fetal Alcohol Syndrome: A Guide for Families and Communities*
Author(s): Ann Pytkowicz Striessguth
Publisher (Date): Brookes Publishing Company (January 15, 1997)

Summary: Compelling and easy to understand, this book explains the medical and social issues surrounding fetal alcohol syndrome (FAS) and fetal alcohol effects (FAE). Compassionately written by the expert psychologist who conducted some of the earliest examinations of children with FAS and FAE more than twenty years ago, this guidebook explains how to identify and work with children and adults who have the disorder and how to educate prospective mothers and society at large. Photographs, illustrations, and case studies reveal the physical and behavioral manifestations of FAS and FAE, particularly in children. For parents, educators, pediatricians, psychologists, adoption workers, social workers, nurses, and child care providers, this timely book speaks to everyone seeking an understanding of the challenges faced by children who have these entirely preventable disabilities.

Title: *The Best I Can Be: Living with Fetal Alcohol Syndrome-Effects*
Author(s): Liz Kulp, Jodee Kulp
Publisher (Date): Better Endings New Beginnings (April 1, 2000)
Summary: A young teen with Fetal Alcohol Effects challenges the world to peer inside her life and brain. Through her own writings the reader is taken on a life changing journey that will impact their thinking about how to help and understand children with brain damage due to fetal alcohol.

Title: *Alcohol, Pregnancy and the Developing Child: Fetal Alcohol Syndrome*
Author(s): Hans-Ludwig Spohr, Hans-Christoph Steinhausen (Editors)
Publisher (Date): Cambridge University Press (August 22, 1996)
Summary: This authoritative new publication comprehensively reviews the important relationship between maternal

alcohol abuse during pregnancy and the resulting in utero damage to the child, as well as the results of this damage during the child's development. The first part of the book discusses clinical issues of alcohol-related fetal malformation, the clinical picture of Fetal Alcohol Syndrome, the epidemiology of maternal alcohol abuse, and the developmental outcome of the affected children. The second part addresses pathogenesis and neuropathology. Part Three reviews developmental issues of the growing affected child. The final part evaluates approaches to rehabilitation and intervention while reviewing social and public health issues.

Title: *Seizures and Epilepsy in Childhood: A Guide* (3rd edition)
Author(s): John M. Freeman, Eileen P. G. Vining, Diana J. Pillas
Publisher (Date): Johns Hopkins University Press (December 1, 2002)
Summary: The award-winning *Seizures and Epilepsy in Childhood* is the standard resource for parents in need of comprehensive medical information about their child with epilepsy. Now in its third edition, this highly praised book has been thoroughly revised and updated to reflect the latest approaches to the diagnosis and treatment of epilepsy in childhood, including the use of the ketogenic diet as a treatment for children who either do not respond to traditional drug therapy or who suffer intolerable side effects from medications.

Title: *Growing Up with Epilepsy: A Practical Guide for Parents*
Author(s): Lynn Bennett Blackburn
Publisher (Date): Demos Medical Publishing (August 1, 2003)
Summary: St. Louis Children's Hospital, MO. Consumer text is designed to help parents of epileptic children.

Demonstrates how to discipline the child, support social development, and negotiate the educational system. Provides advice regarding various medications and how to manage potential side effects.

Title: *Silenced Angels: The Medical, Legal, and Social Aspects of Shaken Baby Syndrome*
Author(s): James R. Peinkofer
Publisher (Date): Auburn House; (January 2002)
Summary: *Silenced Angels: The Medical, Legal and Social Aspects of Shaken Baby Syndrome* delves into the realms of child abuse that has never been explored before in such detail. The book examines how the physical assault of violent shaking on a young body can lead to a lifetime of despair or even death. Every important detail of this tragic form of child abuse is analyzed, providing the reader a more definitive understanding of the condition known as SBS. This is the first book written exclusively about SBS, which is 100 percent preventable. SBS cases can be frequently misdiagnosed and are more frequently underinvestigated and poorly prosecuted, leading to a sense of injustice among families and child abuse prevention advocates.

Title: *Noonan Syndrome: A Medical Dictionary, Bibliography, and Annotated Research Guide to Internet*
Author(s): Not Listed
Publisher (Date): Icon Health Publications (April 2004)
Summary: This is a 3-in-1 reference book. It gives a complete medical dictionary covering hundreds of terms and expressions relating to Noonan syndrome. It also gives extensive lists of bibliographic citations. Finally, it provides information to users on how to update their knowledge using various Internet resources. The book is designed for physicians, medical students preparing for board examinations, medical

researchers, and patients who want to become familiar with research dedicated to Noonan syndrome.

Title: *Prader-Willi Syndrome: A Practical Guide (Resource Materials for Teachers Series)*
Author(s): Jackie Waters
Publisher (Date): Taylor & Francis Group (July 1, 1999)
Summary: An examination of the cognitive, medical and psychological aspects of educating a child with Prader-Willi Syndrome. Practical advice is given for every part of the schooling process, from classroom management to helping the child with difficult lessons such as math. The section on further education discusses the ethical issues concerned with learning skills for independent living and the potential for future employment.

Title: *Management of Prader-Willi Syndrome* (2nd edition)
Author(s): Louise R. Greenswag, Randell C. Alexander
Publisher (Date): Springer-Verlag (March 1, 1995)
Summary: *Management of Prader-Willi Syndrome* brings together the contributions of professionals with considerable expertise in diagnosis and management. Clinical, social, family, and community issues are explored and management strategies are identified. The text presents historical, medical and genetic information to orient the reader. The major portion deals with pragmatic guidelines, rather than research and diagnosis, and is directed to health educational specialists in academic, clinical and community settings. This manual is endorsed by the Prader-Willi Syndrome Association, which is recognized worldwide.

Title: *Prader-Willi Syndrome: A Medical Dictionary, Bibliography, and Annotated Research Guide to Internet*
Author(s): Not Listed

Publisher (Date): Icon Health Publications (April 2004)

Summary: This is a 3-in-1 reference book. It gives a complete medical dictionary covering hundreds of terms and expressions relating to Prader-Willi syndrome. It also gives extensive lists of bibliographic citations. Finally, it provides information to users on how to update their knowledge using various Internet resources. The book is designed for physicians, medical students preparing for board examinations, medical researchers, and patients who want to become familiar with research dedicated to Prader-Willi syndrome.

Title: *Children with Fragile X Syndrome: A Parents' Guide*

Author(s): Jayne Dixon Weber

Publisher (Date): Woodbine House (July 15, 2000)

Summary: A comprehensive book for parents on fragile X syndrome, a condition caused by a mutation on the X chromosome. Helps families adjust and understand the child's strengths and weaknesses, and know where to seek further help and expertise. Topics include diagnosis, parental emotions, daily care, family life, education, and more

Title: *Fragile X Syndrome: Diagnosis, Treatment, and Research* (3rd edition)

Author(s): Randi Jenssen Hagerman, Paul J. Hagerman

Publisher (Date): Johns Hopkins University Press (April 15, 2002)

Summary: Fragile X syndrome is the most common inherited form of mental retardation. Now substantially revised and updated, this acclaimed book discusses the clinical approach to diagnosing the disorder, supported by the latest research in epidemiology, molecular biology and genetics, and neuropsychology. It also presents information on treatment: genetic counseling, pharmacotherapy, intervention, and gene therapy.

Title: *Understanding Williams Syndrome: Behavioral Patterns and Interventions*
Author(s): Eleanor Semel, Sue R. Rosner
Publisher (Date): Lea (January 1, 2003)
Summary: Text presents the basic medical condition, paradoxical profile, and neurobiological mechanisms associated with Williams syndrome. Offers discussions on the typical aptitudes and behavioral problems common in those with Williams syndrome. Also included are methods for treatment and intervention.

BOOKS ON BEHAVIOR MODIFICATION AND DISCIPLINE

Title: *Enhancing Your Child's Behavior: A Step-By-Step Guide for Parents and Teachers*
Author(s): Robert Evert Cimera
Publisher (Date): Scarecrow Education (August, 2003)
Summary: Robert Cimera uses an applied approach in this user-friendly book to explain how to improve the behavior of children with and without disabilities. Parents and teachers can follow a step-by-step process to determine the cause of the behaviors they want to change and select strategies that might help. *Enhancing Your Child's Behavior* also provides places for readers to record their thoughts and develop a behavioral modification plan.

Title: *A Treasure Chest of Behavioral Strategies for Individuals with Autism*
Author(s): Beth Fouse, Maria Wheeler
Publisher (Date): Future Horizons (August 1, 1997)
Summary: A resource manual that provides theory and the best practices in behavior management with individuals with autism. It is an easy reference for using behavioral interventions.

Title: *Your Child: Emotional, Behavioral, and Cognitive Development from Birth through Preadolescence*
Author(s): David Pruitt
Publisher (Date): HarperResource (April 1, 2000)
Summary: *Your Child* takes you step-by-step through the developmental milestones of childhood, discussing specific questions and concerns and examining more troublesome problems. From choosing your baby's doctor to dealing with sleep problems, from helping a child develop self-esteem to discerning when certain behaviors call for professional help—and how to find it—this book offers comprehensive and accessible information for parents on the emotional, behavioral, and cognitive development of children from infancy through the preadolescent years. Expertly and definitively offering practical advice and invaluable information, *Your Child* will guide you through every stage of your child's growth and help you meet the daily challenges of parenting.

Title: *Designing Teaching Strategies: An Applied Behavior Analysis Systems Approach*
Author(s): R. Douglas Greer
Publisher (Date): Academic Press (July 17, 2002)
Summary: Discusses how best to teach, how to design functional curricula, and how to support teachers in using state of the art science instruction materials. Discusses how to determine the effectiveness of curricular initiatives toward meeting mandated standards in national assessments.

BOOKS ON VOCATIONAL, RESIDENTIAL, AND OTHER TRANSITION ISSUES

Title: *Preparing Children with Disabilities for Life*
Author(s): Robert Evert Cimera

Publisher (Date): Scarecrow Education (February 1, 2003)
Summary: This book explains in lay terms what special education is and how to make the special education process more successful for everyone involved. Written for families of children with disabilities and for educators, the book covers the history and legalities of helping children with disabilities, preparation for employment, residential living, interpersonal relationships, and educational plans. Many professional organizations, web sites, and support groups are listed.

Title: *Helping Adults with Mental Retardation Grieve a Death Loss*
Author(s): Charlene Luchterhand, Nancy Murphy
Publisher (Date): Accelerated Development (May 1, 1998)
Summary: Adults with mental retardation often grieve the loss of their loved ones. However, many times this grief goes unnoticed, without tears, and individuals are never given the chance to express their grief and recover from the death of those close to them. This special guide designed for professionals will help give these adults that chance. Luchterhand and Murphy's text will be essential reading for all helping professionals, including therapists, clergy, nurses, psychologists, hospice professionals, and specialists in developmental disabilities.

Title: *Supported Employment in Business: Expanding the Capacity of Workers with Disabilities*
Author(s): Paul Wehman
Publisher (Date): Training Resource Network Inc (July 1, 2001)
Summary: *Supported Employment in Business: Expanding the Capacity of Workers with Disabilities* is a definitive reference book that covers all the cutting edge issues of supported employment. The book's practical yet comprehensive approach provides a resource for

practitioners and academics alike. In 322 pages, it addresses topics ranging from funding to job development to intervention techniques.

Title: *Transition and Change in the Lives of People with Intellectual Disabilities (Research Highlights in Social Work, 38)*
Author(s): David May
Publisher (Date): Jessica Kingsley Publishers (December 1, 2000)
Summary: One claim made for the policy of care in the community was that it would rescue people with intellectual disabilities from social marginality. To what extent has this promise been fulfilled and their lives transformed? David May presents the lives of people from this group as a series of transitions and offers us a view of the world that is as complex and changeable as any other. Each section covers a different aspect of choice, opportunity and transition on the life path, for example, moving from home to school leaving school employment living independently and growing old The contributors have extensive research experience in the field of intellectual disabilities and provide a comprehensive review of this research, drawing out the implications for policy and practice. This book will be an invaluable resource for professionals in careers working with those with intellectual disabilities, as well as their families.

Title: *The Road Ahead: Transition to Adult Life for Persons with Disabilities*
Author(s): Keith Storey, Paul Bates, Dawn Hunter
Publisher (Date): Training Resource Network (March 1, 2002)
Summary: *The Road Ahead* is for people with disabilities and their families and those who help them transition to a quality adult life. Covering key areas in the transition from school to adult life, it is edited by Keith Storey,

Paul Bates and Dawn Hunter, nationally recognized transition experts. The book is a must resource, featuring twenty experts in ten broad-ranging chapters. It explores transition planning, assessment, instructional strategies, career development and support, social life, quality of life, supported living, and post-secondary education. Each chapter begins with a group of key questions that are addressed in the text and the index gives you quick access to important topics. When you want cutting edge ideas to help students have a meaningful life after school, turn to *The Road Ahead*—it provides strategies for improving the lives of people with disabilities now and tomorrow.

Title: *Beyond High School: Transition from School to Work*
Author(s): Frank R. Rusch, Janis Chadsey
Publisher (Date): Wadsworth Publishing; (December 15, 1997)
Summary: This edited text contains eighteen articles concerning the preparation of special education students for the transition from school to adulthood. The course focuses on practical ways to make special needs students functional in community and employment situations.

SUPPORT GROUPS AND ORGANIZATIONS

Organization: National Down Syndrome Society
Mission Statement: The mission of the National Down Syndrome Society is to benefit people with Down syndrome and their families through national leadership in education, research and advocacy.
Website: http://www.ndss.org
Contact Information: 666 Broadway
New York, NY 10012
(800) 221-4602

Organization: United Cerebral Palsy
Mission Statement: United Cerebral Palsy's mission is to advance the independence, productivity and full citizenship of people with disabilities through an affiliate network.
Website: http://www.ucp.org
Contact Information: 1660 L Street, NW, Suite 700
Washington, DC 20036
(800) 872-5827

Organization: National Down Syndrome Congress
Mission Statement: It is the mission of the National Down Syndrome Congress to be the national advocacy organization for Down syndrome and to provide leadership in all areas of concern related to persons with Down syndrome. In that capacity, NDSC will function as a major source of support and empowerment to persons with Down syndrome and their families.
Website: http://www.ndsccenter.org
Contact Information: 1370 Center Drive, Suite 102
Atlanta, GA 30338
(800) 232-NDSC

Organization: United Leukodystrophy Foundation
Mission Statement: The United Leukodystrophy Foundation (ULF), incorporated in 1982, is a nonprofit, voluntary health organization dedicated to providing patients and their families with information about their disease and assistance in identifying sources of medical care, social services, and genetic counseling; establishing a communication network among families; increasing public awareness and acting as an information source for health care providers; and promoting and supporting research into causes, treatments, and prevention of the leukodystrophies. Leukodystrophies are a

	group of genetic nervous system disorders affecting the myelin sheath, which insulates the axon through which nerve impulses are conducted. The ULF is supported solely by donations.
Website:	www.ulf.org
Contact Information:	2304 Highland Drive Sycamore, IL 60178 (800) 728-5483

Organization:	Huntington's Disease Society of America
Mission Statement:	The Huntington's Disease Society of America (HDSA) is dedicated to finding a cure for Huntington's Disease (HD) while providing support and services for those living with HD and their families. HDSA promotes and supports both clinical and basic HD research, aids families in coping with the multifaceted problems presented by HD and educates the families, the public and health care professionals about Huntington's Disease. Our HD families give a face to Huntington's Disease. HDSA is its voice.
Website:	http://www.hdsa.org
Contact Information:	158 West 29th Street, 7th Floor New York, NY 10001-5300 (800) 345-HDSA

Organization:	The Turner Syndrome Society of the United States
Mission Statement:	The Turner Syndrome Society of the United States creates awareness, promotes research, and provides support for all persons touched by Turner Syndrome.
Website:	http://www.turner-syndrome-us.org
Contact Information:	14450 TC Jester, Suite 260, Houston TX 77014 (800) 365-9944

Organization:	Five P- Society
Mission Statement:	To encourage and facilitate communication among families having a child with 5p- syndrome and to spread awareness and education of the syndrome to these families and their service providers.
Website:	http://www.fivepminus.org
Contact Information:	none listed

Organization:	The MAGIC Foundation
Mission Statement:	The MAGIC Foundation is a national nonprofit organization created to provide support services for the families of children afflicted with a wide variety of chronic and/or critical disorders, syndromes and diseases that affect a child's growth. Some of the diagnoses are quite common while others are very rare.
Website:	http://www.magicfoundation.org
Contact Information:	6645 W. North Ave. Oak Park, IL 60302 (708) 383-0808

Organization:	Angelman Syndrome Foundation, Inc.
Mission Statement:	ASF's mission is to advance the awareness and treatment of Angelman Syndrome through education, information exchange, and research.
Website:	http://www.angelman.org
Contact Information:	3015 E. New York Street, Suite A2265 Aurora, IL 60504 (800) 432-6435

Organization:	The ARC of the United States
Mission Statement:	The ARC of the United States works to include all children and adults with cognitive, intellectual, and developmental disabilities in every community.

Website:	http://www.thearc.org
Contact Information:	1010 Wayne Avenue, Suite 650 Silver Spring, MD 20910 (301) 565-3842

Organization:	Aicardi Syndrome Foundation
Mission Statement:	The Aicardi Syndrome Foundation, Inc. is a not-for-profit organization incorporated in August 1991. The foundation is funded by private donations and various fundraising events. The ASF provides funds for the purchase of medical and adaptive equipment for affected daughters, publication and distribution of the Aicardi Syndrome Newsletter, and contributes to ongoing research into the causes of Aicardi syndrome.
Website:	http://www.aicardisyndrome.org
Contact Information:	P.O. Box 3202 St. Charles, IL 60174 800) 374-8518

Organization:	National Coalition for PKU and Allied Disorders
Mission Statement:	The National Coalition for PKU and Allied Disorders is a nonprofit organization comprised of individuals, metabolic support groups, and professionals directly involved with issues related to errors of metabolism requiring low-protein diet, including PKU, MSUD, HCU, the OAs, UCDs, and tyrosenemia.
Website:	http://www.pku-allieddisorders.org
Contact Information:	None listed

Organization:	Autism Society of America
Mission Statement:	The mission of the Autism Society of America is to promote lifelong access and opportunity for all individuals within the autism spectrum, and their families, to be fully participating, included mem-

bers of their community. Education, advocacy at state and federal levels, active public awareness and the promotion of research form the cornerstones of ASA's efforts to carry forth its mission.

Website: http://www.autism-society.org

Contact Information: 7910 Woodmont Avenue, Suite 300
Bethesda, MD 20814-3067
800-3AUTISM

Organization: National Autism Association

Mission Statement: The mission of the National Autism Association is to advocate, educate, and empower. We will advocate on behalf of those who cannot fight for their own rights. We will raise public and professional awareness of autism spectrum disorders. We will empower those in the autism community to never give up in their search to help their loved ones reach their full potential.

Website: http://www.nationalautismassociation.org/

Contact Information: P.O. Box 1547
Marion, SC 29571
877-NAA-AUTISM.

Organization: The Williams Syndrome Foundation

Mission Statement: The Williams Syndrome Foundation (WSF) seeks to create or enhance opportunities in education, housing, employment and recreation for people who have Williams Syndrome and other related or similar conditions. The WSF identifies, initiates, funds and provides strategic guidance for major, long-range development projects, either by itself, or by cooperating with other organizations.

Website: http://www.wsf.org

Contact Information: University of California
Irvine, CA 92697-2300
(949) 824-7259

Organization: Support Organization for Trisomy 18, 13, and Related Disorders (SOFT)

Mission Statement: SOFT is a network of families and professionals dedicated to providing support and understanding to families involved in the issues and decisions surrounding the diagnosis and care in Trisomy 18, 13 and related chromosomal disorders. Support is provided during prenatal diagnosis, the child's life and after the child's passing. SOFT is committed to respect a family's personal decision—in alliance with a parent/professional partnership.

Website: http://www.trisomy.org

Contact Information: 2982 South Union Street
Rochester, NY 14624
(800) 716-SOFT

Organization: National Tay-Sachs & Allied Diseases Association (NTSAD)

Mission Statement: National Tay-Sachs and Allied Diseases Association (NTSAD) was founded in 1956 by a small group of concerned parents with children affected by Tay-Sachs disease or a related genetic disorder. Dedicated to the defeat of Tay-Sachs and several allied diseases.

Website: http://www.ntsad.org

Contact Information: 2001 Beacon Street, Suite 204
Brighton, MA 02135

Organization: National MPS Society, Inc.

Mission Statement: The National MPS Society's goal is to ultimately find a cure for MPS and ML disorders. The National MPS Society will achieve this goal by supporting research, providing support to individuals and their families affected by an MPS or ML disease, promoting public and professional

	awareness, and significantly increasing participation by regions.
Website:	http://www.mpssociety.org
Contact Information:	P.O. Box 736 Bangor, ME 04402-0736 (207) 947-1445
Organization:	Rett Syndrome Association
Mission Statement:	We are a national organization giving help, advice and support to parents, caregivers, siblings and professionals, in fact anybody involved with a child or adult who has Rett syndrome.
Website:	http://www.rettsyndrome.org.uk
Contact Information:	113 Friern Barnet Road London N11 3EU U.K.
Organization:	National Gaucher Foundation
Mission Statement:	The National Gaucher Foundation (NGF) was established in 1984 as a nonprofit, tax exempt organization dedicated to supporting and promoting research into the causes of, and a cure for Gaucher Disease.
Website:	http://www.gaucherdisease.org
Contact Information:	5410 Edson Lane, Suite 260 Rockville, MD 20852-3130 (800) 428-2437
Organization:	International Birth Defects Information System
Mission Statement:	Amelioration and Prevention of Birth Defects and Genetic Disorders
Website:	http://ibis-birthdefects.org
Contact Information:	None listed
Organization:	National Fragile X-Foundation
Mission Statement:	The National Fragile X Foundation unites the fragile X community to enrich lives through

	educational and emotional support, promote public and professional awareness, and advance research toward improved treatments and a cure for fragile X syndrome.
Website:	http://www.nfxf.org
Contact Information:	P.O. Box 190488 San Francisco, CA 94119 (800) 688-8765
Organization:	National Organization for Rare Disorders (NORD)
Mission Statement:	The National Organization for Rare Disorders (NORD), a 501(c)3 organization, is a unique federation of voluntary health organizations dedicated to helping people with rare "orphan" diseases and assisting the organizations that serve them. NORD is committed to the identification, treatment, and cure of rare disorders through programs of education, advocacy, research, and service.
Website:	http://www.rarediseases.org
Contact Information:	55 Kenosia Avenue P.O. Box 1968 Danbury, CT 06813-1968 (800) 999-6673
Organization:	Prader-Willi Syndrome Association
Mission Statement:	Prader-Willi Syndrome Association (USA) is dedicated to serving individuals affected by Prader-Willi Syndrome (PWS), their families, and interested professionals.
Website:	http://www.pwsausa.org
Contact Information:	5700 Midnight Pass Rd. Sarasota, FL 34242 (800) 926-4797

Organization:	The Noonan Syndrome Support Group
Mission Statement:	The Noonan Syndrome Support Group, Inc. is committed to providing support, current information, and understanding to those affected by Noonan syndrome and its associated anomalies.
Website:	http://www.noonansyndrome.org
Contact Information:	P.O. Box 145 Upperco, MD 21155 (888) 686-2224

Organization:	Council for Exceptional Children
Mission Statement:	The worldwide mission of The Council for Exceptional Children is to improve educational outcomes for individuals with exceptionalities.
Website:	http://www.cec.sped.org
Contact Information:	1110 North Glebe Road, Suite 300 Arlington, VA 22201-5704 888 CEC-SPED

Organization:	American Association on Mental Retardation
Mission Statement:	AAMR promotes progressive policies, sound research, effective practices, and universal human rights for people with intellectual disabilities.
Website:	http://www.aamr.org
Contact Information:	444 North Capitol Street, NW, Suite 846 Washington, DC 20001-1512 800 424-3688

Organization:	TASH (formerly The Association for Persons with Severe Handicaps)
Mission Statement:	TASH is an international association of people with disabilities, their family members, other advocates, and professionals fighting for a society in which inclusion of all people in all aspects of society is the norm.

Website:	http://www.tash.org
Contact Information:	29 W. Susquehanna Avenue, Suite 210 Baltimore, MD 21204 410-828-8274

E-GROUPS

E-Groups are online communities where people with similar interests e-mail each other back and forth, sharing resources and experiences. Please keep in mind that the content offered via these groups is often unmonitored, so accuracy cannot be guaranteed. However, they are can be a great source of support.

All of the following groups are from www.Yahoo.com. Other groups exist from other Internet service providers.

Name of Group: ABA4ALL

Web Address: http://groups.yahoo.com/group/ABA4ALL/

Description: ABA (Applied Behavioral Analysis) is a teaching methodology that can be effective for a variety of children with special needs at varying levels of functioning and development. Children with mental retardation, complex multiple disabilities, and other syndromes/disorders, as well as children with social skills issues, ADD/ADHD, and others who are "high functioning" may benefit from the type of individualized, direct instruction that ABA offers. ABA programs are designed to meet the individual needs of each child; this may or may not include DTT (discrete trial training).

ABA is best known for being the chosen teaching method for children on the Autism Spectrum, unfortunately this often means that many parents of children with other disability labels never come across ABA in their research; this is disheartening as ABA could very well turn out to be successful for these children and families.

ABA4ALL is a place to share ABA information, strategies, and experiences. Most of all, this group should give hope to parents who have watched their child struggle for years yet make little to no progress in their current educational programs.

Name of Group: Autism Adolescence
Web Address: http://groups.yahoo.com/group/Autism_Adolescence/
Description: There is not a whole lot of research on the net about Autism Spectrum Disorders and adolescence. I am the mother of two sons. My oldest son has Aspergers syndrome, and is 12. My youngest son is 10 and is classified as Autistic. I am hoping to connect with parents who have pre-teen, or teenaged children. Though all are welcome here. Please free to share your stories, advice, woes, rants, tears, and especially laughter here with us. We are all in this ship together. I think I can speak for all of us when I say we are in it for the long haul.

Name of Group: Autism Awareness Action
Web Address: http://health.groups.yahoo.com/group/autism-awareness-action/
Description: This list is an autism informational list to share and receive information and support on autism. Members on this list are from all across the United States and worldwide.

All issues of autism are explored—from diet, supplements, interventions, legislation, treatments, and educational and vocational strategies, and even some off topic humor. The purpose of this list is to be a well-rounded resource for autism and all it encompasses.

Name of Group: Autism Comorbidity
Web Address: http://health.groups.yahoo.com/group/autism-comorbidity/
Description: This list is meant for people who have, or are related to someone who has, an Autistic Spectrum Disorder (autism, Asperger's, PDD, Rett's or CDD) along with one or more comorbid disorders. Common comorbid disorders of ASDs include ADD/ADHD, Tourette's syndrome and epilepsy/seizures, but people who are related to ASDs with additional physical impairments, blindness, deafness, other neurological disorders, learning disabilities, mental retardation, Down syndrome or other developmental disabilities, psychiatric conditions (depression, bipolar, OCD etc.), chronic illnesses or any other health problem are also welcome, as well as people who have one or more health conditions and assume they may have an additional ASD.

Here, we can discuss how being autistic affects handling the comorbid disorder(s) and how the comorbid disorder(s) influence an autistic person and his/her needs. Come to share your frustrations, sadness, hope and success, exchange information, and support each other.

This list—created by a legally blind adolescent who suspects an additional ASD—is meant for Autistics themselves as well as parents, family members, friends, relatives, teachers, professionals and others interested in or related to ASDs and comorbidity.

Name of Group: Autism Aspergers
Web Address: http://health.groups.yahoo.com/group/autism-aspergers/
Description: This list is for parents and caregivers of kids with autism and Asperger's, and any other disability. I am the mother of four special-needs boys, and I created

this list to share stories, ideas, treatments, therapies, advice and support. It's a list where we can all make friends and have fun.

Name of Group: Autism Downs MR
Web Address: http://groups.yahoo.com/group/autism_downs_mr/
Description: This list is for people who are teachers or caregivers (group home workers, etc.) and are interested in learning more about disabilities. This list will allow you to explore all of these disorders (autism, Down syndrome, mental retardation, ADD, ADHD and many more). This list is for any person who would like to share theory's, opinions, thoughts, and stories about the unique and interesting people they have encountered. I have been working with students and adults for eight years and I can tell you AWARENESS is the KEY. If you feel like this is a list you would like to join please do so. I can't wait to hear your stories and thoughts.

Name of Group: Autism in Girls
Web Address: http://health.groups.yahoo.com/group/Autism_in_Girls/
Description: Restricted membership! This list is for all parents and professionals who wish to exchange information regarding treatment of autism in girls, how autism effect females in the family, and any other issues dealing with autism and females and/or the comparison of males and females with autism. Other than the restricted membership, the list will not be censored in any way so as to promote the free flow of information between its members.

Name of Group: Birth to Three Support
Web Address: http://groups.yahoo.com/group/BirthtoThreeSupport/

Description: Support for all parents and professionals in Birth to Three Programs or Early Intervention or ECI programs. We each struggle with the same early issues. We welcome parents of children with any disability or at risk for a disability and professionals who work with these families.

Name of Group: Cerebral Palsy
Web Address: http://groups.yahoo.com/group/cerebral_palsy/
Description: This is an International Rare Disease Support Network eGroup (IRDSN) open to anyone interested in making friends, sharing information and providing support for persons affected by Cerebral Palsy.

Name of Group: Children with Autism
Web Address: http://groups.yahoo.com/group/children_with_autism/
Description: My 6-year-old son is autistic. We found out when he was 4. I have created this group to help us parents find out more about this disorder. If anyone has info please feel free to post. We are here to help each other and be there so we are not alone in this! You will find a lot of useful information under our group links. You will find topics such as, SSI, sensory issues, laws for children's education rights, info on autism, and much more.

Name of Group: Colpocephaly
Web Address: http://health.groups.yahoo.com/group/colpocephaly/
Description: Colpocephaly is a disorder in which there is an abnormal enlargement of the occipital horns—the posterior or rear portion of the lateral ventricles (cavities or chambers) of the brain. This enlargement occurs when there is an underdevelopment or lack of thickening of the white matter in the posterior cerebrum. Colpocephaly is characterized by microcephaly (ab-

normally small head) and mental retardation. Other features may include motor abnormalities, muscle spasms, and seizures. Although the cause is unknown, researchers believe that the disorder results from an intrauterine disturbance that occurs between the second and sixth months of pregnancy. Colpocephaly may be diagnosed late in pregnancy, although it is often misdiagnosed as hydrocephalus (excessive accumulation of cerebrospinal fluid in the brain). It may be more accurately diagnosed after birth when signs of mental retardation, microcephaly, and seizures are present. There is no definitive treatment for colpocephaly. Anticonvulsant medications can be given to prevent seizures, and doctors try to prevent contractures (shrinkage or shortening of muscles). Come join other parents that have children with this diagnosis.

Name of Group: Downs Heart
Web Address: http://groups.yahoo.com/group/Downs-Heart/
Description: A contact point for families who have a member with Down syndrome and associated congenital heart disease. Support and information for those whose child is facing heart surgery, who has had surgery, those whose condition is inoperable, and those families who are bereaved.

Name of Group: FASForum
Web Address: http://health.groups.yahoo.com/group/FASForum/
Description: This list is for professionals and families living with and working with individuals who were prenatally exposed to alcohol. The purpose of the list is to exchange information and support. All members are welcome to freely discuss any issues pertaining to their involvement with Fetal Alcohol Syndrome or Fetal Alcohol Effects.

Name of Group: FASResource
Web Address: http://health.groups.yahoo.com/group/FASResource/
Description: FASResource was created to give families who live with Fetal Alcohol Syndrome/Effects a place to learn more about the disability and exchange information with families just like themselves. As people living with children disabled by prenatal alcohol exposure we are often subject to burn-out—this list will help us express our feelings on that subject as well!

Name of Group: High Functioning Autism
Web Address: http://groups.yahoo.com/group/HighFunctioningAutism/
Description: This is a place where people who have an interest in the life of a child with the diagnosis of high functioning or mild autism, PDD, PDD-NOS, or semantic pragmatic disorder or have no official diagnosis but have autistic-like traits can come together to: 1. Exchange stories, ideas, and information. 2. Vent the inevitable frustrations and heartaches of the everyday life experiences involved with a special needs child.

Name of Group: Home School Special Needs Kidz
Web Address: http://groups.yahoo.com/group/Homeschool_SpecialNeedsKidz/
Description: There is hope! This is a support group for those who live mainly in the USA who are home schooling a "special needs" child, ages preschool to 19. Whether your child has ADHD, a learning disability (LD), dyslexia, emotional or neurological disorder, bipolar, Tourette syndrome, deafness, autism, anxiety disorder, oppositional defiance disorder, blindness, any type of emotional or physical handicap, etc., then this group is for you.

Name of Group: Megalencephaly
Web Address: http://health.groups.yahoo.com/group/megalencephaly/
Description: Megalencephaly, also called macrocephaly, is a condition in which there is an abnormally large, heavy, and usually malfunctioning brain. By definition, the brain weight is greater than average for the age and gender of the infant or child. Head enlargement may be evident at birth or the head may become abnormally large in the early years of life. Megalencephaly is thought to be related to a disturbance in the regulation of cell reproduction or proliferation. In normal development, neuron proliferation—the process in which nerve cells divide to form new generations of cells—is regulated so that the correct number of cells if formed in the proper place at the appropriate time. Symptons of megalencephaly may include delayed development, convulsive disorders, corticospinal (brain cortex and spinal cord) dysfunction, and seizures. Megalencephaly affects males more often than females. Unilateral megalencephaly or hemimegalencephaly is a rare condition characterized by enlargment of one-half of the brain. Children with this disorder may have a large, sometimes asymmetrical head. Often they suffer from intractable seizures and mental retardation. Come join other parents that have children with this diagnosis.

Name of Group: Mild MR Group
Web Address: http://groups.yahoo.com/group/mildmrgroup/
Description: For parents of children with mild mental retardation/challenges, high functioning mentally retarded/challenged, "slow" learners, to pool our minds and experiences in any and all areas of life, allowing us to better help our children, and not feel so all alone while we're at it.

Name of Group:	Moms Of Spec Needs Kids
Web Address:	http://groups.yahoo.com/group/momsofspecneedskids/
Description:	This list was created for mothers of special needs children to have a place to vent about the trials of their every day lives, and talk to other moms in similar situations.
Name of Group:	Parent2Parent
Web Address:	http://health.groups.yahoo.com/group/parent2parent/
Description:	Quick description is that we are all parents, teachers, or caregivers of special kids—that is our common bond. Our kids are in special education or will be, are on the spectrum or have other developmental delays. On this group we support each other as people, listening, offering advice in all aspects of life for ourselves as well as on how to help our kids.
Name of Group:	Polymicrogyria
Web Address:	http://health.groups.yahoo.com/group/polymicrogyria/
Description:	This listserv was established as a place to share medical information and emotional support. We are parents and relatives of children with PMG, not medical professionals. If you have a child or a relative diagnosed with polymicrogyria (or a similar neuronal migration disorder) and are looking for information and support, please feel free to join this community.
Name of Group:	Porencephaly
Web Address:	http://health.groups.yahoo.com/group/porencephaly/
Description:	Porencephaly is an extremely rare disorder of the central nervous system involving a cyst or cavity in a cerebral hemisphere. The cysts or cavities are usually the remnants of destructive lesions, but are sometimes the

result of abnormal development. The disorder can occur before or after birth. Porencephaly most likely has a number of different, often unknown causes, including absence of brain development and destruction of brain tissue. The presence of porencephalic cysts can sometimes be detected by transillumination of the skull in infancy. The diagnosis may be confirmed by CT, MRI, or ultrasonography. More severely affected infants show symptoms of the disorder shortly after birth, and the diagnosis is usually made before age 1. Signs may include delayed growth and development, spastic paresis (slight or incomplete paralysis), hypotonia (decreased muscle tone), seizures (often infantile spasms), and macrocephaly or microcephaly. Individuals with porencephaly may have poor or absent speech development, epilepsy, hydrocephalus, spastic contractures (shrinkage or shortening of muscles), and mental retardation. The prognosis for individuals with porencephaly varies according to the location and extent of the lesion. Some patients with this disorder may develop only minor neurological problems and have normal intelligence, while others may be severely disabled. Come join other parents that have children with this diagnosis.

Name of Group: Smith-Magenis Syndrome
Web Address: http://health.groups.yahoo.com/group/sms-list/
Description: The SMS Mailing list is designed to promote the exchange of information and communication about Smith-Magenis syndrome among parents, professionals and researchers working with this condition. Members of the SMS mailing list will include parents and/or relatives of persons with SMS, as well as special educators, health professionals, and researchers working specifically with this rare condition.

Name of Group: SpecialEDontheWeb
Web Address: http://groups.yahoo.com/group/specialedontheweb/
Description: This is your place to go when you want to find information about any topic in Special Education. Need to find some web resources on a Special Education topic? Just leave a message and others will try to help you out!

Name of Group: Special Educators
Web Address: http://groups.yahoo.com/group/Special_Educators/
Description: In this list you can ask questions and get advice about lesson plans, teaching styles and about the Special Education population. This is also a place to let off some steam after a long day or to share accomplishments of students and even of yourself. If you love teaching or are a teacher, then this is the place for you!

Name of Group: The Ultimate Advocate
Web Address: http://health.groups.yahoo.com/group/TheUltimateAdvocate/
Description: The focus of The Ultimate Advocate is on those who have a child with an Autistic Spectrum Disorder but EVERYONE is welcome. If you have a question, someone here either has the answer, or can lead you to someone who has.

The Ultimate Advocate has been formed to help parents learn to navigate the Special Education "maze" and to learn how to effectively advocate for their child(ren). Parents need to understand their Rights and Responsibilities under special education laws, as well as what the educators are required by law to provide our children. We can help answer questions about IDEA, IEPs, letter writing, complaints, and much more. We are here to share information, both locally and globally, and most importantly, to support each other.

GLOSSARY

AAMR: American Association on Mental Retardation

AAMR's classification system: A classification system for mental retardation based on the amount of support an individual requires rather than on intelligence.

Aarskog syndrome: A condition often associated with mental retardation. See chapter 4.

absence seizure: Seizures that often cause a person to stare off into space as if they were daydreaming; also called petit mal seizures.

acrodysostosis: A condition often associated with mental retardation. See chapter 4.

Aicardi syndrome: A condition often associated with mental retardation. See chapter 4.

Angelman syndrome : A condition often associated with mental retardation. See chapter 4.

annual goal: Section of the IEP that denotes what general areas (e.g., math skills, appropriate behavior, etc.) will be addressed during the school year

APA: American Psychiatric Association

atonic seizure: Seizure characterized by the sudden loss of muscle tone.

autism: A condition often associated with mental retardation. See chapter 4.

backward chaining: A teaching technique where students are taught each step of a task in the reverse order in which they are normally performed.

Bourneville-Pringle syndrome: A condition often associated with mental retardation. See chapter 4.

cat cry syndrome: A condition often associated with mental retardation. See chapter 4.

CDD: Childhood Disintegrative Disorder

cerebral palsy: A condition often associated with mental retardation. See chapter 4.

chaining: A teaching technique where students are taught each step of a task in either forward or reverse order.

childhood disintegrative disorder: A condition often associated with mental retardation. See chapter 4.

classic punishment: Decreasing the performance of an inappropriate behavior by giving the student something that is not desired; also called presentation punishment.

competitive employment: An employment option through which adults with disabilities get jobs within the community. Unlike supported employment, support is usually not provided once a job is obtained.

CP: Cerebral palsy

developmental period: The period up until the eighteenth birthday.

dignity of risk: Allowing people to risk failure so that they can learn from their mistakes.

direct instruction: A teaching technique where students are provided frequent practice and immediate feedback.

Down syndrome: A condition often associated with mental retardation. See chapter 4.

DSM-IV-TR: Diagnostic and Statistical Manual of Mental Disorders, 4th edition, text revision

D-Team: Diagnosis team; often the term used for the group of people who diagnose mental retardation for special education programs.

educable mentally retarded: A classification of mental retardation that usually includes people with IQs between 70 and 50. Considered by many people to be inappropriate terminology.

EMR: Educable mentally retarded. Considered by many people to be inappropriate terminology.

enclaves: An approach to supported employment where groups of supported employees work together, usually temporarily in some sort of factor.

entrepreneurial supported employment: An approach to supported employment in which supported employees work in a business owned by the supported employment agency.

E-Team: Evaluation team; often the term used for the group of people who diagnose mental retardation for special education programs.

external locus of control: Believing that things are generally out of your control.

FAE: Fetal alcohol effects

FAPE: Free and appropriate public education

FAS: Fetal alcohol syndrome

fetal alcohol effects: A condition often associated with mental retardation. See chapter 4.

fetal alcohol syndrome: A condition often associated with mental retardation. See chapter 4.

forward chaining: A teaching technique where students are taught each step of a task in the order in which they are normally performed.

fragile X syndrome: A condition often associated with mental retardation. See chapter 4.

free and appropriate public education: The component of IDEA that guarantees special education students an "appropriate" education in a public school without additional costs to their parents. Note that "appropriate" does *not* mean the "best" education possible.

frontal lobe seizure: Seizure characterized by twitching or odd feelings in hands, legs, or face.

full-scale IQ: Statistical measure of somebody's overall intelligence based upon the results of a standardized test.

galactosemia: A condition often associated with mental retardation. See chapter 4.

Gorlin syndrome: A condition often associated with mental retardation. See chapter 4.

grand mal seizure: Seizures characterized by stiff muscles and convulsions. Also called tonic-clonic seizure.

group homes: Residential programs where people with disabilities live in small groups.

guardianship: A situation where a person (i.e., the guardian) can make all decisions for another person (i.e., the ward). After the age of eighteen, guardianship is appointed by a judge.

Hunter syndrome: A condition often associated with mental retardation. See chapter 4.

Hurler syndrome: A condition often associated with mental retardation. See chapter 4.

hydrocephaly: A condition often associated with mental retardation. See chapter 4.

IDEA: Individuals with Disabilities Education Act

IEP : Individualized education plan

IFSP: Individualized family service plan

IHCP: Individualized health care plan

independent living programs: Residential programs where people with disabilities are given assistance finding a home, but little other support is provided once a home is found.

individual supported employment: An approach to supported employment in which a supported employee works in the community with the aid of a job coach.

individualized written rehabilitation plan: A formal, nonlegally binding, plan of services provided by vocational rehabilitation counselors.

individualized education plan: A formal and legally binding agreement between the parents of a special education student and school officials outlining what services are going to be provided and when.

individualized family service: A formal plan outlining services for children in birth to three programs.

individualized health care plan: A formal plan outlining health-related services provided to a student.

individualized program plan: A formal, nonlegally binding, plan often utilized in adult service programs, such as sheltered workshops.

intelligence: A concept used to describe how efficiently people learn.

internal locus of control: Believing that you are in control of most things.

IPP: Individualized program plan

IWRP: Individualize written rehabilitation plan

learned helplessness: Learned belief that you are going to fail before you even start.

least restrictive environment: The component of IDEA that requires that special education students be educated along side of their nondisabled peers as much as appropriate. Note that this does *not* mean that all special education students need to be taught in general education classrooms.

Lesch-Nyhan syndrome: A condition often associated with mental retardation. See chapter 4.

long-term residential programs: Residential programs where people with disabilities live in large, highly structured, groups.

LRE: Least restrictive environment

LTRPs: Long-term residential programs

mental retardation: A condition consisting of subaverage intelligence, poor adaptive skills, and an age of onset within the developmental

microcephaly: A condition often associated with mental retardation. See chapter 4.

mild mental retardation: A classification of mental retardation that usually includes persons with IQs between 70 and 55.

MMR: Mild mental retardation

mobile work crews: An approach to supported employment where groups of supported employees work together in several different locations, such as mowing lawns.

moderate mental retardation: A classification of mental retardation that usually includes persons with IQs between 55 and 40

MoMR: Moderate mental retardation

M-Team: Multidisciplinary team; often the term used for the group of people who diagnose mental retardation for special education programs

multisensory teaching: A teaching technique that utilizes as many of the student's senses as possible

myoclonic seizure: Seizure characterized by sudden jerking motions.

natural consequences: Allowing people to experiences the potentially negative consequences that naturally arise from their actions.

negative reinforcement: Increasing the performance of an appropriate behavior by taking away something that the student doesn't desire.

nondiscriminatory identification and evaluation: The component of IDEA that requires students be assessed in a fair manner. It also requires that all students in special education be evaluated at least every three years to see if they still qualify for services.

Noonan syndrome: A condition often associated with mental retardation. See chapter 4.

occipital lobe seizure: Seizure characterized by temporary loss of their vision.

parental and student participation: The component of IDEA that mandates that parents must be allowed to participate in the development of their child's education plan and that the plan must be based upon the student's unique needs and interests.

parietal lobe seizure: Seizure characterized by a tingling, choking, or sinking feeling.

people-first language: Using terms that put the person before the disability, such as "a child with mental retardation" rather than "a mentally retarded child"

performance IQ: Statistical measure of somebody's nonverbal skills based upon the results of a standardized test.

performance subtests: Portions of standardized tests that measure nonverbal skills, such as fine motor control and visual discrimination.

petit mal seizure: Seizures that often cause a person to stare off into space as if they were daydreaming; also called absence seizures.

phenylketonuria: A condition often associated with mental retardation. See chapter 4.

PKU: Phenylketonuria

PLEP: Present level of educational performance

PLOP: Present level of performance

PMR: Profound mental retardation

positive reinforcement: Increasing the performance of an appropriate behavior by giving the student something that is desired.

power of attorney: A situation where a person willingly gives some or all of their decision-making abilities to another person.

PPT: Pupil personnel team; often the term used for the group of people who diagnose mental retardation for special education programs.

Prader-Willi syndrome: A condition often associated with mental retardation. See chapter 4.

present level of educational performance: Section of the IEP that summarizes the student's current strengths and weaknesses; also called present level of performance

present level of performance: Portion of the IEP that summarizes the student's current strengths and weaknesses; also called present level of educational performance

presentation punishment: Decreasing the performance of an inappropriate behavior by giving the student something that is not desired; also called classic punishment

procedural due process: The component of IDEA that allows parents and school officials to mediate disputes.

profound mental retardation: A classification of mental retardation that usually includes persons with IQs below 25.

punisher: Something that decreases the performance of inappropriate behaviors.

reinforcer: Something that increases the performance of appropriate behaviors.

reliability: A statistical term used to indicate whether a test measures things consistently.

response cost punishment: Decreasing performance of an inappropriate behavior by taking away something that the student likes every time the inappropriate behavior is performed.

Rett syndrome: A condition often associated with mental retardation. See chapter 4.

Rubinstein syndrome: A condition often associated with mental retardation. See chapter 4.

Sanfilippo syndrome: A condition often associated with mental retardation. See chapter 4.

self-fulfilling prophecy: Performing behavior that results in a preconceived notion of how things will turn out.

self-regulatory skills: Being able to control your actions.

semi-independent living programs : Residential programs where people with disabilities live in their own apartments or houses with minimal support.

severe mental retardation: A classification of mental retardation that usually includes persons with IQs between 40 and 25.

sheltered workshops: An "employment" option through which adults with disabilities work in environments segregated from people without disabilities. Critics often point out that the activities that sheltered employees do is often just "busy work."

short-term objective: Section of the IEP that breaks annual goals into more manageable steps.

SILPs: Semi-independent living programs

SMR: Severe mental retardation

special education: A federally mandated entitlement program that gives qualifying students an appropriate education.

special education and related services: Section of the IEP that indicates what services are going to be provided by who, where, and for how long.

Special Olympics: An international program that enables individuals with disabilities the opportunity to play various sports against other athletes with disabilities.

STO: Short-term objective

subaverage intelligence: Traditionally thought of as having an IQ at least two standard deviations below the mean (usually, IQs below 70–75 depending upon the intelligence test).

supported employment: An employment option through which adults with disabilities can get jobs within the community and are given as much support as is needed.

system of least restrictive prompts: A teaching technique whereby support is gradually faded so that the student can perform the action independently.

task analysis: A breakdown of a task into smaller, more manageable steps.

Tay-Sachs disease: A condition often associated with mental retardation. See chapter 4.

TBI : Traumatic brain injury

TILPs: Transitional independent living programs

TMR : Trainable mentally retarded; considered by many people to be inappropriate terminology.

tonic seizure: Seizure characterized by a sudden stiffness of muscles.

tonic-clonic seizure: Seizures characterized by stiff muscles and convulsions; also called grand mal seizure.

trainable mentally retarded: A classification of mental retardation that usually includes people with IQs below 50; considered by many people to be inappropriate terminology.

transitional independent living programs: Residential programs where people with disabilities live temporarily and learn skills needed to live in more independent environments.

Trisomy 18: A condition often associated with mental retardation. See chapter 4.

Trisomy 13: A condition often associated with mental retardation. See chapter 4.

trust funds: A financial arrangement where money is set aside for a person until a predetermined date.

Turners syndrome: A condition often associated with mental retardation. See chapter 4

validity: A statistical term used to indicate whether a test measures what it claims to measure.

verbal IQ: Statistical measure of somebody's verbal skills based upon the results of a standardized test.

verbal subtests: Portions of standardized tests that measure language skills, such as verbal expression and comprehension.

vocational career plan: A formal, nonlegally binding, plan often utilized in vocational programs.

vocational rehabilitation: A program that helps people with disabilities find and maintain employment.

Williams syndrome: A condition often associated with mental retardation. See chapter 4.

work adjustment: An employment program that teaches individuals with disabilities skills that they need to get and maintain jobs within the community.

zero reject: The component of IDEA that prevents qualified students from being denied or kicked out of special education.

INDEX

ABOUT THE AUTHOR

Robert Evert Cimera is an associate professor at a university in Wisconsin. Prior to earning his Ph.D. in special education from the University of Illinois, he taught students with severe mental retardation, learning disabilities, and behavioral disorders. In addition to this book, he has also written *Making ADHD a Gift: Teaching Superman How to Fly*, *Enhancing Your Child's Behavior: A Guide for Parents and Teachers*, *Preparing Children with Disabilities for Life*, and *The Truth about Special Education*. Dr. Cimera can be reached at robertcimera@yahoo.com.